Sandra Dodd's

Big Book of Unschooling

Also on unschooling by Sandra Dodd:
Moving a Puddle, and other essays (2006)

Sandra Dodd's Big Book of Unschooling

By Sandra Dodd

Foreword by Pam Sorooshian

Copyright © 2009 by Sandra Dodd

ISBN: 978-0-557-18155-1

Third batch, with a few corrections, late November 2009
First edition with ISBN number, early November 2009
Initial Conference Edition, September 2009, Sandra Dodd, Albuquerque

For Hema A. Bharadwaj, who said she wanted my whole unschooling website in a book. I said it wasn't possible, but the thought stayed, and here's an artistic impression of my website in a book, for Hema.

Contents

Foreword xv
Author's Introduction xvii
Expressions of Gratitude xviii

Part One 1
   Unschooling 3
   Cautions 8
   Why Rush to Get It? 9
   Principles and Priorities 10
   Comforts 12
   Schooling 13
   Deschooling 14
   Who can Unschool? 18
      Help 19
      Do It 20
      Teachers 21
   What Teaching Can Never Be 22
   Dads 25
   Who Cannot Unschool? 26
      Negativity 27
      Divorce 28
      Control 29
      Reluctance 30
      Stress 31
   Terminology 32
      John Holt 33
      Why "Radical" Unschooling? 34
      Any Jargon? 35
   Beginning to Unschool 36
      Stages of Unschooling 37
   Where is the edge of unschooling? 38
      Learn Nothing Day 39
      Comments on Learn Nothing Day 40

Other kinds of unschooling 41
Principles instead of Rules **42**
    "Just say No" 45
    Proof or Research 47
    What about situations with rules? 48
    Exchanging one set of rules for another 49
Choices **51**
    "Have To" 53
    Self-regulation 55
    Self-control and other control 56
Infants **57**
    "Partners and not adversaries" 58
    Saying Yes to Infants 59
    Communicating with Babies 60
    Co-sleeping 62
Toddlers and Young Children **63**
    Guests in your home, and in your life 64
    Attentive Parenting 65
    Saying Yes to Toddlers 66
Special Education **68**
    School's special needs 69
    Seeing your child, rather than a label 70
    Giftedness 71
Howard Gardner **74**
Abraham Maslow **76**
Piaget **77**
Subjects **79**
    History 80
    Geography 81
    Science 82
    Music 83
    Art 84
    Reading 86
    Phonics and Whole Language 93
    Writing 94
    Language Arts 98
    Shakespeare 102

  Mathematics 105
"Methods" **109**
  Curriculum 110
  Learning, not Teaching 112
  Connections 113
  Substance 117
  Strewing 120
  Experiences 123
  Building an Unschooling Nest 125
Playing **126**
  Games 127
  Humor 128
Typical Days **129**
TV **136**
  Economics of Restricting TV 137
  Gilligan's Island and *Star Trek* 140
  Learning from Cartoons 141
Movies for Unschoolers **144**
Books **148**
  Book Worship 149
  Reading equated with "Wisdom" 149
Video Games **151**
  Educational Benefits 152
  Family Benefits 154
  Courtesy and Responsibility 155
Sleeping **156**
  Opportunities 157
  Future jobs 158
  Peace 160
  The Purpose of Sleep 161
Food **162**
  The Clock isn't Hungry 163
  Not forcing 163
  Not Limiting 164
  How Does it Balance Out? 165
  Advantages of Eating in Peace 166
  The Purpose of Family Dinner 167

Social Obligations, and oddities 168
Longterm Problems with Controlling Food 169
Health Food / Diets 171
Research 171
The Purpose of Eating 172
Holidays and Sugar 173
Monkey Platters 174
Chores **175**
Serving Others as a Gift 176
"Necessary?" No… 178
Relationships 178
"It Seems Unfair." "It's CRAZY." 179
Modeling Joy 180
True Tales of Children Helping 181
Service 182
Gratitude 185
Focus, Obsessions, Hobbies **186**
Barbie 187
Feed Passions 188
Judging Interests 189
Priorities **190**
Personal Change **192**
Happiness 193
Becoming the Parent you Want to Be 194
Abundance 195
Phrases to avoid 196
Words 197
No more bad days 198
Mindfulness **199**
Being 201
Breathing 204
Flow 206
Tone 208
Parenting Peacefully **209**
Noisy peace 210
Boredom 216
Bribery 217

Coercion	218
Freedom	219
Respect	220
Myths too many Parents Believe	221
Empowerment	223
Online Safety	225
When Siblings Fight	226
Guns	229
Violence	230
Spanking	232
The Effects of Spanking	233
Other punishments?	234
Clarity	**235**
If I let him...	236
Truth/Honesty/Lies	242
Fact/Fallacy/Opinion	243
Regrets	245
Sex Education	**250**
Teenagers	**251**
Saying Yes to Teens	252
Driver's education	253
Rebellion	255
How are they as people?	257
Jobs	259
College	261
Interesting Alternatives to College	263
Young Adults	**264**
Partners	265
Saying Yes to Grown Children	267
Changes in the Parents	**268**
Unexpected Outcomes	**269**
Spouses	270
Healing	271
Patience	272
Joy	275
Values	276
Pets	277

Trees and Plants	278
Wonder	279
Honoring Other Voices	**280**
Joyce Fetteroll	280
Pam Sorooshian	280
Schuyler Waynforth	281
Deb Lewis	281
Ren Allen	282
Robyn Coburn	282
Jenny Cyphers	282
Kelly Lovejoy	283
Mary Gold	283
Danielle Conger	283
Criticisms of Unschooling	**284**
Humanism	285
Anarchy	286
"It's hedonism gone berserk!!"	287
Arrogance	288
Karma	291
Part Two	**293**
Essays	**295**
Precisely How to Unschool	295
To Get More Jokes	298
To Be Fascinating at Cocktail Parties	301
A Mom's-Eye View of Driver's Ed	303
Magic Window	307
Quotes	**310**
Other Resources	**326**
Thinking Sticks	327
Chats	329
Sound Files	330
Video	330
Blogs	331
Conferences	332
Justifications for Being Online	333
Always Learning	334

Websites 336
About the Dodd Family's Unschooling 337
Always Learning: Sandra Dodd's Interview 346

About the Author

Art Credits

Front cover:
Lettering and concept by Sandra Dodd
Photoshop artistry by Holly Dodd
Images clockwise from the upper right:
- Sheepherder's wagon, Shakespeare, New Mexico, by Sandra Dodd, on the ghost-town trip with Marty
- A robin's skull, found in the yard and photographed by Sandra Dodd
- Mimosa blossoms, by Sandra Dodd for a blog post
- Sandra typing, by Holly Dodd (photo of wedding ring)
- Pattern blocks, Sandra Dodd
- Petroglyphs behind the McNeills' house, by Sandra Dodd
- Kirby and Marty in bumper boats at the New Mexico state fair, photographed by Sandra Dodd the mom
- Albuquerque from the trail to the rock house, Sandia Crest, by Sandra Dodd
- "The Bus," in the orchard below my cousin Nada's house in Dixon, New Mexico. My dad made a camper of an old school bus in the 1960's, and later my Aunt Doris lived in it.
- Pansies at the grocery store near our house, 2009, by Holly Dodd
- Steve's harmonicas, by Holly Dodd
- Quiche, fountain, baby spider plants rooting by Sandra Dodd

Back cover:
"Learn Nothing Day" logo by Holly Dodd (also inside)
Logos for Chatroom and Symposium by Sandra Dodd
Trees by Bo King

Details on Learn Nothing Day art:
SandraDodd.com/learnnothingday/artguide

Foreword

"Think dangerous thoughts." I heard Sandra Dodd say those words, and I felt a thrill go through me. She went on to tell us, the audience at a California homeschool conference, that if we were afraid, maybe we could duct-tape ourselves to a chair and get a spotter to stand by and watch us while we let ourselves really think about the possibility of simply NOT schooling our children at all. She pointed out that just thinking about it wasn't doing it, that it was actually perfectly safe to think about it, and that we could, afterward, go right back to whatever we were previously doing.

My family's life was forever changed right then and there. I was energized and emboldened and inspired and—I did it—I thought dangerous thoughts. I thought about everything Sandra said that day about the nature of human beings and their innate desire to learn, and I thought about how that love of learning was so very apparent in young children and so often snuffed out by the time they'd been in school for a few years. I thought about my own school experiences and made myself really think, honestly and bravely, about my own childhood and what had been done to me in the name of education. I thought about what I wanted for our then young children, and I thought about how their eyes always sparkled with curiosity and the joy of discovery. I thought about them sitting in dull and stultifying classrooms, and I let myself feel the heartache of sending them away to that, each day, knowing that, every time I did so, a little of their openhearted joy and boundless enthusiasm might be snuffed out. And then I thought about what I, myself, might do to them if I became their teacher, and how horrible it would be if I was the one who was slowly, systematically, crushing their sense of confidence in their own ability to learn what they needed to learn, when and how and where they needed to learn it.

I was stunned. I was hooked. I couldn't get enough of Sandra's words. I read everything Sandra wrote, which, in those days, was mostly on the America Online message boards, and I went to conferences where she was speaking. Her words went straight to my heart. They shook me up. Sometimes I gasped aloud, and I was occasionally reduced to tears when something she said struck very close to my own childhood experiences.

Fifteen years later, in this book, Sandra is still speaking those words that so affected me and many others. Although it is a big book, there is no "filler"—every page is chock-full of valuable and to-the-point content. Sandra always gets right to the heart of an issue and offers analysis and ideas and amazing insight in her own remarkably clear and honest voice.

I can't promise that reading this book is perfectly safe. You will probably find that some of your own deeply held beliefs are examined, questioned and rejected. I guarantee it will make you think differently about children and learning and parenting. So, as you read this book, be brave and let yourself be shaken up. If that scares you, maybe you could duct tape yourself to your chair and get someone to stand by and spot you while you think some dangerous thoughts.

—Pam Sorooshian

Author's Introduction

This is a summary of an extensive website on unschooling. The site includes writings that go back over twenty years, and it still expands as gems of writing are created by unschoolers discovering and honing their unschooling skills. You will find a collection of some of the good parts of writings on unschooling and mindful parenting produced by parents and their unschooled offspring in various unschooling discussions over the past decade and some. This book is a little figurine of that larger sculpture.

Similarly, the world of unschooling is a small part of the larger world. We use the big, whole, real world for learning, but that world includes people who have never heard of unschooling, and people who never will.

On some of these pages, I wrote what I might have said if someone called me on the phone and said "What about science?" or some such. If you think, as you read, "But she totally left out [something]," then it's no problem that I left it out, because you had it in your mind already. What I wrote triggered your own thoughts. That's how learning works. You tie what you perceive to what you already know, and what you know becomes greater.

The greatest difficulty here was deciding the order of topics. On web pages, any one page can link to three or ten others, and so it's easy to follow a path in a "choose your own adventure" way. It's a good model for life. It's not a good model for a linear list. I've moved some pages within the book more than once, but at some point I had to stop moving them around and send it to the printer.

My son Marty says this might need to be one of those books people leave in the bathroom and flip to just any old page. I don't think Marty knows that not all houses have a little library in the bathroom.

There will be a test, but I will neither create it nor proctor it. The test will be when something you learned from this book could make your life better. The bonus points come from your using something you learned in this book to make someone else's life better.

Expressions of Gratitude

For many years people have said "Of course; I'd be flattered," or "Please do!" when I've asked if I could quote their writing on my unschooling pages. Some are quoted dozens of times there, some only once, but those words have changed lives and will continue to do so. Some of the sweet quotes inside this book don't have a name attached, but if you go to the webpage listed below it, the names will show there. Some of the quotes that were not so positive are saved without citation even on the website, because it was the idea, and not the person, that I kept.

My own unschooling has been honed and grown through discussion and examination of large and small ideas and their implementation and practice. There is no better way to learn these things than to associate and communicate with other unschoolers. The internet makes this international.

Flo Gascon requested to give people the opportunity to buy *Moving a Puddle* as part of their conference registration when she was first planning the 2009 Good Vibrations Unschooling Conference, in San Diego. Figuring most of her attendees would already own that book, I said I'd write a new one.

Hema Bharadwaj told me I should put my website in a book. The website would print out to two thousand pages or more, though, and half or more is not my own writing. Even this book is only a summary of some of those pages, not all. Without Hema's suggestion and Flo's request, though, you would not be holding this book.

There would be more befuddlement and typographical glitches if not for the manuscript-reading assistance of Keith and Holly Dodd, Robin Bentley, Jenny Cyphers, Jill Parmer, Chris Sanders and Roxana Sorooshian. My next wave of helpers were Dina Pugliese, Beth Moore and Julie Daniel.

I'm always grateful to my husband, Keith, for having provided me with computers and paper and a place to write for most of my life. When I'm deep in deadlines, he brings me food. We have had a good life with our children, all of whom are grown up and out of childhood. I hope those of you who haven't met them will get a chance to know at least one of them someday.

Unread books are nothing but paper. Readers bring the ideas back to life. Thank you for reading.

Part One

Unschooling is arranging for
natural learning to take place.

Unschooling

What is unschooling?

Unschooling would be difficult to understand even if it were easy to define. From the point of view of the parent, it is creating and maintaining an environment in which natural learning flourishes.

"The Open Classroom" was big with school reformers in the late 1960's and early 70's. It involved learning from experience and experiment with things in the real world. If a child could just read for hours, or just play with a puzzle until he was done, or watch the lizard or the hamster for hours (because every school should have some live animals, they figured, and some pets), then that's how he should learn. If he wanted to read for one minute and look at the lizard on the way outside to climb, fine. A school would not divide the children into small rooms, but divide the materials up, with a science center, a math center with physical "manipulative" tools and toys, many kinds of paper and pens and paints for writing and drawing, art supplies, history in books and pictures and objects and stories. Although children would be tracked as to what they had done, it would be the teachers following them and recording it, not the teachers telling them what to do.

Each school would have many different cubby holes and soft places for readers to be where they could read in relative peace, whether leaning in a corner, or lying down, or near a window.

When I studied education, this was the ideal. For me, unschooling is "the open classroom" without any classroom at all—learning in various ways in the real world, as large and as accessible as the parents can make it.

Later I'll talk about why that didn't always work in real schools, when I address ways in which parents can cause unschooling to fail. For now, though, please do the best you can to survive the bumps and unexpected turns of the trails through the unschooling world, which will necessarily cross back over and through themselves, which is how learning works–a little now, a little more later to connect to what you've learned since, and detours that end up being short cuts.

Is it neglect?

Neglect is not unschooling. Unschooling involves being with children more, not less.

Is it lazy?

Is it lazier to do an original painting than to buy a paint-by-numbers kit? Is it lazier to explore your neighborhood and map it yourself than to buy a map? Is it lazy to figure things out instead of memorizing answers?

Is it "child-led learning"?

This definition is probably the most common quick description, and one of the most harmful to the success of unschooling. It suggests that parents wait for children to decide what to learn. We have learning all the time; no waiting. Neither parents nor children need to "lead" learning, if the environment is flowing and rich.

Is it "unparenting"?

No, though detractors like to say so. Unschoolers are unlikely to be grounding their children or spanking or forcing them to eat or to do schoolwork. Some parents do all that and more, and call it good parenting. They like to insult parents who are kinder and gentler and more involved with their children.

Is it passive?

If one sees school at home as "active," then they might see unschooling as passive, but that would be because they're used to saying "It's either *this* or *that*," as though everything in the world had an absolute opposite. Unschooling is not the opposite of schooling. It is living a life of learning.

School at home might be active for the teaching parent, but the children are waiting to be told what they have to do, and one lesson inherent in any lesson is that it's possible to waste time doing or learning too much.

As to learning, unschooling is nothing but action.

Does the name seem negative?

Many people new to unschooling have wanted to change its name. Considerations end up coming back around after a while, because other designations divide the world in even less desireable ways. The original name was based on a 7-Up commercial popular when John Holt was starting to think maybe schools couldn't be reformed, and starting to encourage people to keep their children home if they wanted to. "7-Up: The *Un*-cola," the commercial went. You can watch it at one of the links below.

In response to "the word is so negative," Suzanne Carter, who used to write on the AOL forum as "Matreshka," wrote something in the 1980's that has inspired people ever since:

> Lots of people make this point, but I never see the negation as negative in a value-judgment sense when I use the word—to me unschooling is as positive as unchaining, unbinding, unleashing, unfolding, unfurling, unlimiting....
>
> All mean freedom and growth and vast possibilities to me.
>
> —Suzanne Carter

SandraDodd.com/unschool/definition
SandraDodd.com/unschool/theterm

How much time does it take?

It depends how you look at it. If you're looking for moments of one-on-one instruction or school work, it takes none of that. If you're looking for hours of mindful living with the hope and expectation of learning, then it will take all your time.

If you come to see and understand unschooling, then the question about how much time it takes will seem like asking "How many hours a day are you alive?"

Once someone was asking how many hours she should spend with her child, or something, and I said at least as many hours as she would've been in school, counting transportation, and there was shock and surprise. The best answer might be that it should be *twice* as much time as she would've spent in school. Because honestly, a child shouldn't lose the mom-time she would've had at night and on weekends, should she?

The shock probably came from thinking that those hours would be teacher-style hours, of being stuck in one place doing something not too fun. That vision can only come from someone who hasn't looked into unschooling enough to know that the best unschooling hours are fun, natural, real activities. The shock can turn to excitement and joy, as a parent learns more about learning.

During proof-reading, my husband Keith wrote:

> I would propose that the shock probably came from the emotional knee-jerk reaction to thinking that the person would have to go through school AGAIN and that brought up all the trauma and time-wasting she had already suffered through.

Good point. I liked school myself, and for someone who didn't, it must be doubly stressful.

SandraDodd.com/howto

How much does unschooling cost?

Unschooling is priceless. It cannot be bought. And "cost" is a difficult concept, so if you have an easy answer floating to mind, try to scatter it and look from many different angles.

If a child is in a private school, unschooling won't "cost that much," meaning no one will send you a tuition bill and a steady stream of fundraising requests and tell you what clothes and shoes you have to buy.

If both parents are working and decide one should quit work and stay at home with the children, will it "cost" a full-time income? In one way of looking at it, perhaps. But counting potential is a trap.

If a family values love and relationships, unschooling can pay off in a jackpot of closeness and joy that could hardly be possible with school in the equation, and could never be bought back with a thousand hours of expensive therapy down the road. (Maybe factor in the time savings of not spending a thousand hours sitting and talking about what you could've done differently, in addition to the cost of it.)

Unschooling doesn't need to be expensive, but anyone choosing unschooling simply to save money is making a mistake. If parents don't want to spend *any* money on games, toys, museums, out-of-town trips, books, or whatever it is the kids might be interested in, then unschooling will not work at their house.

One doesn't need to be rich to unschool, but it takes dedication and focus, creativity and resourcefulness.

SandraDodd.com/nest

Cautions

Don't do what you don't understand. Although faith in others' stories and experiences might get you started, what will bring growth and confidence is seeing the changes in your children, and seeing them relax into the world of learning. Other unschoolers can help you move toward better relationships with your children, but it's only a start.

Some families emulate the behaviors of other unschoolers without understanding what's being done or why.

Don't change your whole life suddenly. Making hundreds of deliberate, small changes is better than one big declaration that says, basically, "Everything we told you before is hereby replaced with something I don't quite understand." That's no way to build trusting relationships.

If an idea in this book piques your interest, keep reading and keep thinking. Think about your own childhood or those you've seen or contributed to. Think about arguments that seemed pointless in retrospect, and the damage done by them. Picture and remember the difference between going to sleep content and crying yourself to sleep. Remember moments in your childhood when the world seemed bright and big and happy. Then the next time you have a decision to make with or for your child, lean a bit toward the happy contentment answer.

Gradual change is more comfortable for children and other family members as well. Doing what you understand while seeking to understand even more will make you a confident unschooler, while jumping in before you really get it will be unsettling for all involved.

Having made my case for slow being good, though, I'm going to explain why you need to hurry up and get with it.

SandraDodd.com/gradualchange

Why Rush to Get It?

There is the possibility that a family can run out of time.

Young children who are unschooled have their whole lives to memorize 7x8 if they want to, and so time seems to stretch out beyond the mental horizon.

The mother of a twelve-year-old has *very* little time if she wants to help him recover from school and spend a few unschooling years with him before he's grown and gone. She doesn't have time to ease into it gradually. If she does, he'll be fifteen or sixteen and it just won't happen.

If the mother of a five-year-old is trying to decide how much reading instruction and math drill to continue with before she switches to unschooling, I want to press her to decide it's "NONE," because "some" is damaging to the child's potential to learn it joyfully and discover it on his own. And "lots" will just hurt that much more. "None" can still be turned to "some" if the parent can't get unschooling. But if she doesn't even try unschooling, she misses forever the opportunity to see that child learn to read gradually and naturally. It will be gone forever. *Forever.*

So I don't say "Gosh, I'm sure whatever you're doing is fine, and if you want to unschool you can come to it gradually at your own rate."

Until a person stops doing the things that keep unschooling from working, unschooling can't begin to work.

It seems simple to me. If you're trying to listen for a sound, you have to stop talking and be still.

Some people want to see unschooling while they're still teaching and assigning and requiring.

They have to stop that first. And then they have to be still. And then they have to look at their child with new eyes.

If they don't, unschooling will not happen.

SandraDodd.com/doit

Principles and Priorities

Although much of this book and even more of the website is about specific things you can do with your children, and how you might do them, unschooling parents need to change from rules to principles, meaning that instead of saying "This is what you do, because I said so," considering the purpose of the requested action, and the accompanying emotional or relationship damage, if any.

Rulesdiscourage thought. Principles require thought.

When you're trying to make a decision, nothing helps more than to know what your principles and priorities are.

Joyce Fetteroll once wrote, "If the reasons behind rules make sense, then there isn't a reason to make a rule....If the reasons behind rules are nonsense, then people memorize nonsense..."

Some principles my husband and I shared even before we had children are:

- Houses are for living in.
- It's good to help other people.
- Learning is preferable to doing the same old thing.
- Saving things is okay. (At our house, we're packrats who use that habit to help others.)

When Kirby came along, we added things we learned from La Leche League and our friends there, and some things I had learned from three years in Adult Children of Alcoholics, and knowledge we had from ten years in the Society for Creative Anachronism. As our children came along and got bigger, the list of everyday principles grew.

- People shouldn't eat if they're not hungry; if they are hungry, they should eat.
- If someone's asleep, you don't necessarily need to wake them up to go to bed.
- Comfort is important.
- It's good to take care of our things.

- Breathing and thinking is better than anger; find ways to be calm.
- Children should feel safe in their own homes (even, or especially, safe from siblings and parents).
- Sharing space and time and attention makes more of it for everyone.
- Being nice to guests is good. (And we treated our children as guests, in many ways, as they were new to the world and we invited them into our home by having children in the first place.)
- If something is safe and isn't hurting anyone else, if the kids want to try it, help them.
- Being gentle and honest and compassionate is as much for the doer as for the object. Being nice to the dog makes one a nicer person (regardless of the dog's opinion, I mean).

There are other things, but this might be enough to give one the idea that principles are beliefs and attitudes that change the way people live.

If a family lives in such a way that learning is more important than a clean house, the relationships and results will be different than a family that thinks nothing is more important than a clean house, and learning should take place during school hours, somewhere else.

Occasionally someone will come to a discussion on unschooling and say she respects all ideas equally, or that two things in her life are of equal priority. That belief is paralyzing.

If you know where you want to go, other people can help you get there. If you have no idea where you want to go, you probably won't get very far.

SandraDodd.com/principles

Comforts

There are benefits to unschooling that go far beyond "subject matter." Having close family relationships is nearly a lost concept in modern culture when children belong to the school and parents belong to their jobs.

Not everyone can unschool; not everyone will want to. But those who choose this way of family life will discover that much of what is considered "normal" in our culture is the direct effect of schooling and the negative messages traditionally passed from father to son and mother to daughter.

If you decide not to repeat the voices in your head that have put children down for generations, then you simultaneously benefit your child and yourself. If I decide not to say "I'm ashamed of you" to my son, I also acknowledge that it would have been possible for my mother not to have said it to me. It might have been possible for her mother not to have said it to her.

There are realities in some families that make "possible" impossible. In my own family history, The Great Depression. The dust bowl. WWII. None of those need to affect my own children as directly as they affected me. Though I didn't live through any of them, every adult who dealt with me had.

Life can be based on comforting others, on finding ways to be comfortable ourselves. I don't mean "comfortably wealthy," I mean being at peace—not making other people *un*comfortable.

There are emotional and mental and physical comforts most people never knew existed, but unschoolers have learned to get used to them!

There is a song from the 1950's that is sometimes sung in churches and at meetings, and the first line is "Let there be peace on earth, and let it begin with me." Every bit of peace makes the world more peaceful. If you can engineer one peaceful moment, you can have two or ten.

SandraDodd.com/peace

Schooling

"You got schooled!" is a phrase used by kids, and it's never a compliment.

While school can be a good place for some people and for some things, "to be schooled" isn't the sweetest of thoughts.

The belief that school is necessary blinds one to other possibilities. The idea that being a student is a full-time job suggests that any learning after school hours would be overtime, and worthy of resentment.

At the most basic level, though, of assembly line insertion of the material on a curriculum, schooling has its own measures of efficiency which have to do with classroom management and proof that salaries were justified, rather than with the nurturance of any individual student.

When assembly line, curricular considerations come before people, children have unlimited opportunities to fail. When grades are overlaid on that, at least a third of them are predestined to fail, because there can be no value in an A or a B without some counterbalancing D and F. And all those kids in the middle, branded "average"? They will go to school for years to get a paper that says "Here. You're average."

School can be better than home. School as a small part of a rich, healthy family life can be bearable and maybe even fun. School as a guarantee of learning or of success is a fantasy school; it's a myth.

When parents want to bring school home in the form of buying a curriculum and "doing school," they bring many of the problems of school home, too. If those methods worked, they would be working for every student in school.

There is very little on my site about school, but it's here:
SandraDodd.com/school

Deschooling

Deschooling is akin to detoxing, and for a good reason. Part of getting away from a soul-destroying situation is to learn new ways and reasons to be.

When someone goes from school to school at home without a big break between, it's likely the kids will decide they preferred school.

When someone goes from structured learning (whether it was at school or at home) to unschooling, that's not one side step. That's quite a turnaround, and for the parents more than for anyone else. You don't need to leave your house nor even to rearrange it, but you will need to rearrange your mind extensively.

It's easier for young children. They play and watch movies and run around and go some cool places, they learn a new answer to "What grade are you in?" and they're ready to learn.

When our oldest was four and I started reading all I could find about unschooling and homeschooling, the gauge used on deschooling was "one month for each year of school." What unschoolers added to that as time went on was "and for the parents, one month for each year they were in school, or taught, or homeschooled with a curriculum." So while the children might be rarin' to go at four or five months, the parents might not really understand it until after a year or two.

I myself was in public school for 11 years, college for four and some parts of more (but not full-time school), and taught for six. That's 21 "units" of deschooling for me.

Luckily for my family, I was in my 30's when my children were born, and my own high school, college and teaching were on the school-reform end of the '60's and '70's spectrum. It probably only took me half the prescribed time.

I've seen many others recover from the damage their schooling did to their ability to learn naturally. I've never seen it take more than one-month-per year if they really did relax into deschooling. I have seen it take more than two years if the person kept relapsing into buying a curriculum or pressuring their children. I have seen it take less time when the parent immersed him- or herself in the philosophy and possibilities of unschooling.

Those who take the longest seem to be those who are sure they don't need it.

Ren Allen wrote, "I wonder about the process of re-discovering the joy of discovery. We talk about deschooling a lot at the lists, and how it usually takes about a month per year of school for healing. I know a lot of adults who seem to have lost all curiosity, so for some, the damage seems to be permanent."

So what should deschooling look like? I liked to think of it as a long vacation of nothing but the finest Saturdays I could remember. Someone who had bad memories of Saturdays objected to that. So if it helps you to think of it as a long, leisurely summer that lasts more than three months, or a vacation where there are no pesky tourist attractions, that might help.

Or you could think of yourselves as tourists in your own town. What museum or historical site or interesting natural feature have you not gone to see, or maybe haven't taken your children to lately? Pretend you're only in town for two weeks and do some cool things. Or if that seems awkward to you, import a tourist. Maybe an unschooling family could be persuaded to come and visit you, and you could take them sightseeing and also discuss unschooling. Just let the kids play, though, and play with them or watch them. Look at what they're drawn to. Look at how they examine things or what they ask about. Don't be teacherly in your responses. Answer them as you would a tourist friend who was visiting town. Tell the good parts in an inspiring way. You don't need to put it in historical or political context. Give one cool fact and if they want to know more they'll ask. That's how conversations work. Have conversations.

What else can help with school recovery? While you're watching your children, also quietly watch your own thoughts and emotional responses. Here are some I have felt or seen in other people or had reported to me that you might look out for:

Jealousy. It's easy for a parent to be jealous of a child's opportunities and freedom if the parent was limited and heard "no" a lot. Think of it as an investment in the joy of your grandchildren, then. Give your children what you would like to have had as a child, and you can heal your own inner child in the process. Adults carry many hurts from families, schools and random problems beyond their childhood control.

Think of the child you were when you help your offspring be the people they can be.

The urge to haze. Hazing of new sports team members or club members, fraternity brothers or military recruits has a long and sadistic history. There are parallels in the practical jokes played on children, and in minor mistreatments so common we might not even see them. Should your child have to suffer because you had to suffer? If you have *any* memories of fear, shame, humiliation or "initiation," avoid passing those on.

The overlay of school. Each time you feel you're looking at the world through school-colored glasses, you'll know you need to deschool some more.

Plain old Fear: Some of the fears people have felt and reported are fear of "the truant officer," the principal, the police, social services, the neighbors, their own parents and other relatives. Another set of fears are that the children will never leave home, that they will never get a job, that they couldn't get into college if they wanted to. The way to overcome the first set is to be circumspect and polite and helpful. Stay out of trouble. The way to deal with the second set is to meet some unschoolers, or at least find a place where you can read about them as they're growing up, those who are older than your own children. If possible, find locals to hang out with, or attend a conference or two.

New unschoolers are often afraid. If you feel fear, that's natural. If you've taken a child out of school, there is still a school there you could put him back into, so if your fear is that it's a once and forever decision, it's not. Schools are right there, still.

If you feel that you're turning your back on your entire culture, take a deep breath and note that when you turn your back on school, all that's behind you is a school. What's *not* school is infinite. What is school is small.

Fear of rejection by all your relatives can be frightening. Think of worst case scenarios. If these people have been controlling you with threats and shame for twenty or thirty years, do you owe them another thirty years?

I've been accused of encouraging parents to separate children from their grandparents. I know why some grandparents would have said that. And the tone with which I was approached was very familiar to me, too. It was along the lines of "Who do you think you are, little missy?"

Yeah. It wasn't even my mom, mother-in-law or grandmother! But it was someone's.

I don't want children separated from their parents or grandparents. I want the parents and grandparents to be kind and generous to the children. I want parents to be kind and gentle with their children even if the children are 25 or 45 years old. I'm old enough now that any parent of any age who wants to explain to me *how it is in the real world* can back down and hush. I'm not theorizing and I'm not being reactionary. I'm making conscious choices and helping others see the possibility of doing so as well, for the sake of their relationships with their children and partners, friends and parents. Choices, though; not just choosing to continue to be told what to do.

School has become so much a part of life in the past few decades that it seems to some that taking their children out of school is like leaving the planet altogether. You will be relieved, then, to discover that school takes kids out of the world but unschooling gives it back. I know it can sound wrong and crazy. Keep reading. Keep watching your kids. Listen to your memories of childhood.

SandraDodd.com/deschooling

Who can Unschool?

At this point you might have noticed that in order for parents to unschool, they need to become unschooling parents. Read that as many times as you need to. It will involve them recovering from being school kids or the parents of school kids, or both.

Someone who cannot change cannot unschool.

Unschooling needs parents to be

- available
- curious
- playful
- thoughtful
- attentive
- resourceful
- eager to make children's lives happy
- passionate and *com*passionate
- generous
- calm (sometimes, not always)
- lively (even calm people can be lively)
- positive
- kind
- gentle

These qualities, steeped in some unschooling success, can produce

- joy
- improved relationships
- trust
- confidence

SandraDodd.com/unschooling

Help

What unschoolers do to help other unschoolers is to share how they came to unschooling, and the effect it has had on their children and their home lives.

It helps for new unschoolers to read some, then try some, maybe meet some people if they can, read more, try more, maybe listen to something or watch something, try more, and shuffle it up that way.

I have seen people read for two years without actually trying any of the ideas. Those participating on lists or message boards with them assumed they were unschooling, but it turned out they were just reading and talking about it.

I've seen people kind of barely hear of unschooling, think they understand it, and go off and make a big confused mess of their home and children that can take months or years to straighten out.

I've seen people who went to several conferences, chatted and partied, laughed and had bumper stickers on their cars, but didn't seem to understand much about the principles of unschooling. I've heard people brag that they went to conferences, but never went to hear the speakers.

Those new to unschooling need most or all of the same things others needed when they were new: local information, access to laws and policies, reassurance, suggestions for deschooling, answers to questions (although the answers are ever more easily available as people collect up the best answers of the past). They need inspiration and ideas.

If you're new: read, change a little; read more, change more; repeat.

SandraDodd.com/help

Do It

If you're going to unschool, do it now and do it well.

Part of doing it "well" is moving into it deliberately and with clarity, and going gradually, but by "gradually" I don't mean over five or ten years. Childhood lives in weeks, days and hours, not in months, years and decades.

If you decide you want to unschool, free help is available. A few people are offering to help others for money by the hour, but I don't recommend that if the free help will suffice.

If your family is happy and your children are happy in school, if they go to sleep happy and wake up happy, then you don't need unschooling at all. If you're doing school at home and the kids spontaneously hug and kiss you and they enjoy textbooks and worksheets, then you don't need unschooling at all. Then *don't* do it.

But this book is really for those who think unschooling will make their lives richer and more peaceful. In those cases, waiting is counter-productive.

The second link below is a page of regrets, poignantly expressed by parents who can't go back and be kinder sooner. There are many there, but here are some snippets, and I'm leaving out the sad parts.

> I feel overwhelmed with grief when I think of the ten years I have been parenting my son from a place of judgment.
>
> I'm happy I found unschooling, but I wish I would have found it many, many years ago.
>
> [A curriculum] was an expensive ($500) lesson on stuff we don't need. Money we now spend on trips and museums and stuff the kids want or are interested in.
>
> I could just kick myself for not pursuing it any earlier.
>
> I wish I had pulled them out sooner, but I can't change that now.

SandraDodd.com/doit
SandraDodd.com/ifonly

Teachers

Many unschoolers are teachers or former teachers. Some find it easy to unschool because of what they know about school and schooling. Others have said "It's hard for me, because I was a teacher."

Partly, it seems, that has to do with personality and temperament. People become teachers for different reasons, and see the profession in different ways.

Those whose interest is in children and learning easily see the benefits in "one-on-one," and in answering a child's real questions, right where he is. Those who loved the idea of teaching as a profession, of being organized and beloved and respected, resist the idea of being where there's no spotlight or cubby in the office with one's name, no teacher's lounge, no summers off.

What is certain in any case is that those who were teachers are less criticized by those around them for homeschooling or unschooling. And in a family in which one parent is a professor, other people rarely say a word beyond "Ooooh...teaches at a university!"

Ironically, then, those who think homeschooling is wrong think it's less wrong when a "professional educator" does it. It seems different to them. Those who think homeschooling school-style is okay, but unschooling is bad are also hesitant to criticize "a real teacher."

What can be difficult, then, is for "real teachers" to stop teaching and start creating a learning environment with all learning and no teaching.

Help is available, though, and many others have successfully overcome the desire to manage another person's learning entirely.

The success comes when the parents are as happy learning all the time as the children are. When home and the world become the fabric and the substance of learning, it's not just the children who are learning all the time.

SandraDodd.com/learning

What Teaching Can Never Be

For years I have recommended that new unschoolers stop using the word "teach" and replace all statements and thoughts with phrases using the word "learn" instead. I've gotten much flak back from people saying it doesn't matter, or that's "just semantics." What started as a theory with me became belief and then conviction. Unschoolers who cling to the idea of teaching will handicap their own understanding of how learning works.

The boldface lines below are quotes from someone in a discussion once who was sure she could change my mind:

So if teaching "really" means competently and compassionately facilitating learning, then teaching *does* exist, no?

> The word exists.
> The idea exists.
> In English we expect words to have meanings. We expect a thing to be a THING. And a verb to be ACTION! Wham! Pow!
>
> The action of "teaching" isn't simple and clear.
>
> When there are pairs of words like "pitcher and cup" or "pitcher and catcher" or "ball and socket," we assume the two things are complementary parts of a whole.
>
> So we have (and have had for many languages back up the line, I'm guessing, maybe) "teacher and student."
>
> Now that I'm thinking about it, though, maybe this is, in part, an English language problem, because in Romance languages (Latin-based, Italian, French, Spanish...) they use "maestro" or forms thereof. "Master" or "Mistress" of an art or body of knowledge. Someone can be a maestro with no followers or students. One can't very well be a teacher without the presence of a student.
>
> But anyway, we do have in modern English the pair "teach and learn."
>
> If I want to teach someone how to use quotation marks, I can talk, show them, make jokes, draw stick figures with speech-balloons, and I could maybe sing songs about it. So *if* the person who's in the room "being taught" is thinking about how to file down that one piece of a machine gun that can turn a legal semi-automatic into an

illegal automatic, and how to hide that part really well, disguised as something altogether different, what am I doing?

I'm talking, writing, drawing, dancing, and singing. But I'm not teaching. I'm reviewing for myself something I already know. I'm just performing a play of sorts, without any audience. I'm playing with myself. I'm ...well, you know.

So if I'm reading a magazine about machine guns and someone comes and says, "How do I punctuate a quote within a quote?" I can show them. If they don't totally understand, I can draw pictures or give other examples. When I perceive that they have learned the thing they wanted to learn, I should shush up and go back to my magazine, because the action is completed.

They learned. I helped them learn. I was "the teacher" but I didn't do the work that resulted in learning. The learner did that in his own head. I could put ideas in the air, but only he could hear and process and ask more questions. Without his active work, no teaching can possibly take place.

So if teaching *really* means competently and compassionately facilitating learning, then teaching does exist, no?

There's that Buddhist talk about being the water, being the ocean. Think of it as kneading bread, maybe. Here's a truth: teaching has no action to show for itself that is "teaching." You can't really pour useful information into anyone else's ears or eyes against their will. They can learn like crazy, but you can't make them.

Fold and push. People learn from other people.

Fold and push. There are people paid to teach. Some are aware that there are limitations to what they can do. Others are not philosophical and believe that, if they "taught" (presented information), only the lazy and uncooperative could possibly fail to "learn."

Fold and push really hard.

"Teaching" is an idea that most people understand on a quick, simple level. It's an idea that the best teachers and the best homeschoolers (i.e. we unschoolers) think about more carefully and examine more closely.

I feel that I've taught my kids to be kind and patient. If they reject that "teaching" though, they're not taught at all. I would have modeled and discussed and totally failed miserably to teach. But somehow I persuaded them to believe that what I believe was important. Sometimes, somehow, I persuade people to believe unschooling will work and is important. Some people fail to learn it, but I keep singing and dancing anyway.

I don't much like jazz, but philosophy, ideas, and teaching are kind of like jazz. Early in playing an instrument you're told the One Right Way to hold it, to blow/strike/pluck, to use the keys so you don't damage them, to stand or to sit just so, making it easier for you and safer for the instrument. Those are The Rules.

If you get so good at your instrument that you can play it in the dark, quickly, while carrying on a conversation with someone else at the same time (not wind players, but you know what I mean...), the rules no longer apply to you.

At that point you cannot be a beginner who accidentally broke an instrument out of ignorance or carelessness. You will love that instrument and know it really well and maybe be able to repair it. At first the instrument was the sacred goal, but once your musicianship is greater than the instrument, you are beyond and above the simple rules.

Here's a rule: You have to stand to sing. Otherwise your diaphragm is cramped up and it won't be able to support your notes and control your pitches. HAVE to stand up.

Professionals in musicals and operas? They sing sitting, they sing lying in beds, they sing dancing, they sing in all kinds of positions. Folksingers and traditional musicians of various kinds sing sitting in various situations.

I can teach like they can sing. So why am I saying teaching doesn't exist? Beginners need to know that teaching isn't a thing you do to someone else. Rather, learning is something that you *might*, if you're lucky, get to assist with.

In beginning stages, like student teachers and beginning home-schooling parents and assistant karate teachers (which my son is) and games teachers (Marty and Holly have both "taught a game" in the past couple of days, or rather recited rules in the presence of other people) need to look for and see learning as a separate process from their own song and dance. In advanced stages there is teaching, but it is compassionately and competently facilitating another's learning.

SandraDodd.com/teaching

Dads

Most of us have had and known fathers and grandfathers. Some readers will have been fathers and grandfathers. When I talk about dads and unschooling, I'm not talking about biological fathers, necessarily. I'm not talking about authoritarian fathers who use the phrase, "Because I'm your father, that's why."

When a representative of a family peeks into the unschooling world to see if it might be something they'd like to know more about, the scout is usually the mom. Sometimes it's a teenager. Very occasionally it's the dad.

Statistically speaking, the dads are at work and the moms are home with the children, or the parents both work but the moms do the reading about educational options. Either way, dads are sometimes the last to understand and accept unschooling. In worst cases, the dads have no interest in learning more about it at all, and unschooling fails in those families.

I would rather see unschooling fail and a family stay together than to see a rift over learning, but what is truly beautiful to see is when both parents understand that they can be partners with their children in a way of living that benefits all of them in unexpected ways. Half of this book is about those surprising benefits.

Dads can be swayed by seeing older unschoolers in comparison to other teens they know who were in school. Sometimes dads make the mistake of comparing their children to idealized school children from their own imaginations. Dads can benefit from seeing children other than their own, and from watching for what they want or don't want to emulate, in other families.

To dads: If you don't know where you're going, it's hard to begin to get there. If where you want to go is a fantasy, then it's impossible to get there. No matter how hard you work, you won't become Ozzie Nelson nor any other classic fantasy dad. You will be you, and your children will be the humans they were born to be, and you can, if you want, find ways to nurture a relationship with them that will improve generations of your family to come.

To read the words of unschooling dads, go here:
SandraDodd.com/dads

Who Cannot Unschool?

For many years people have told me "You can't tell me I can't unschool." I seem to be the only person out there saying "Well, then you can't unschool..." when people say, "I can't be with my child every day," or "I can't put any time or money into this," or "I don't mind unschooling if my child will figure out everything on his own, and he's not going to be playing on the computer or watching TV, either."

Some people coo and say, "Ooooh, *any*one can unschool." I never have said that.

Other people have said, "You can't tell me I'm not an unschooler." Usually it's right after they have told me and a hundred others that they're not really clear on what unschooling is, or that they unschool after school or in the summer, or that they unschool history but not math and English.

Those who can't see and don't want to see the connection between music and history, or art and mathematics, and who don't want to try to see such things cannot unschool.

Someone who wants to teach for a few hours, five days a week, and not be involved with learning the rest of the time cannot unschool.

Someone who wants a kid to get a high school diploma and go to college as soon as possible with no sidetracking and no unnecessary chit-chat cannot unschool.

It is possible, though, to change, if the goal is important enough, or if the current emotional state is unproductive or painful.

Those who cannot change cannot unschool.

SandraDodd.com/change

Negativity

Those who are negative, pessimistic, and hateful will find it difficult to even want to unschool. Those who are cynical and critical can unschool but their progress will be slow, until they learn to see the sunshine and clouds and trees instead of the dirty cracks in the stupid sidewalk. People who care more about furniture than about children probably shouldn't have had children in the first place, and so will not want them to be home all day every day, endangering expensive couches.

One who says "that is stupid" any more than once a month or so will need to learn to stop seeing the world through "stupid"-glasses, or leave the children in school where the teachers might be more hopeful and open to the world.

If joy and optimism seem stupid, don't even try to unschool until after you've gotten some therapy or made direct strides toward recovering from the sooty veil of negativity. Children won't benefit from a life guide who is sure he or she is smarter than all the rest of the world. Arrogant certitude prevents learning.

In a discussion of cartoons, I wrote:

> I know my opinions won't match other people's and that's fine. What I can defend isn't what other people can defend.
>
> When there's someone who can defend *nothing*, though, who is so cynical or shut down that all movies seem lame and all cartoons seem mindless and all music is boring and all museums are irritating, I think there's a problem with that person's attitude and perceptions, rather than their stated opinion being damning evidence against movies, cartoons, music and museums.

SandraDodd.com/negativity

Divorce

When I first started sharing with others about how unschooling can work, "divorce" wasn't something that even crossed my mind. In the seventeen years since we started unschooling, I have seen many families come apart. Most were not unschoolers. I think that's important from both directions.

If you want to unschool, keep your marriage strong. Children are crushed by divorce even if they buck up to make the moms and dads feel better. All other things being equal, marriage and school are better than divorce and unschooling.

Marriage and school together are common. Divorce and school together are common. Divorce and unschooling together are very rare for reasons of income, facilities, the opinions of relatives on whom one might come to depend for shelter and food, and the intractable opinions of judges and social workers who could end up with more say than you have in what your kids do and where they live.

Children need an intact family more than they need to unschool. If you can have both, great! If you can't have both, maybe you can't have either. Tread softly and think. If your children's peace and learning are important, don't risk their chance for as whole and peaceful a life as they can have.

People are delusional sometimes about divorce. They get fantasy ideas about never dealing with their problems again! There are new and worse problems potentially to come in any divorce situation. Remarriage or new partners are high on the "I didn't think of that" list.

There is a marriage-counseling program at Retrouvaille.org. The Catholic church sponsors it, but the program is not religious in nature. I know people personally who are happily married because of that program. If you love your children enough to think about unschooling, you love them enough to keep your marriage strong.

SandraDodd.com/divorce

Control

Use of the word "control" implies one *knows* the right answer and if he's not "out of control" or "lacking self control," there will be no choice; he will control himself.

Some people, whether they have "self control" or not, love the idea of controlling others—spouses, friends, children, co-workers, neighbors, strangers. They want to control what their children see and eat and do and think.

They will fail.

If you want to make the sun come up, first see what time it's expected to rise, and command it right at that moment.

If you want to make children do what you want, find out what they want to do and would enjoy doing, and make it seem like you've provided that thing or opportunity, if you want, at first, if it makes you feel like you made the sun come up. But those who insist that they should and can and will control another person often end up alone, emotionally if not physically.

To have a life of learning and joy, spontaneity is more important than control. Acceptance is more valuable than resistance.

If the "control force" is great with you, maybe use it to control your own clutter or organize your papers or rearrange your books or clothing. File your photos and negatives. Scan some stuff. Don't turn that awful control beam on people you love.

(Control is not what makes marriages strong.)

SandraDodd.com/control

Reluctance

If a parent doesn't want to unschool, no words from me or anyone else can change that. If a parent is sure what he's doing is better than any alternatives, then there will be no unschooling. It's not worth outsiders even talking to them.

What if one parent wants to and the other one doesn't? A parent can no more force a spouse or partner to unschool than she can force a child to read, or to do math. And that's a realization that might make more of unschooling clear.

If a parent is enthusiastic and excited about unschooling, then it could work! If *both* parents are enthusiastic and excited, it can hardly fail.

If the reluctant spouse has a good relationship with the other, perhaps unschooling could be given a shot to work, but it can no more work with someone standing by quizzing and criticizing than Alcoholics Anonymous can work if everyone had a bottle and a glass in front of him, open, pouring drinks. Chugging down.

It won't work unless people want it to work, and make the changes necessary for it to work.

Unschooling can prove itself if it's not thwarted.

SandraDodd.com/reluctance

Stress

Stress can be mentally and physically debilitating. Stress is bad for a single adult living alone.

Stress can destroy a marriage. Stress is harmful for a childless couple.

Stress affects children. Stress is disastrous for a family with children.

Some people seem to be addicted to stress, drama, adversity, feelings of persecution. Some of them will take a paragraph like this personally, and stress further, thoughts spinning like wheels in the mud, spattering, splattering, going nowhere.

Those people cannot unschool.

If you lived with debilitating stress but you were single and childless, would you get help?

If you lived with debilitating stress that was affecting your partner in a childless marriage, would you get help?

If you lived with stress that could destroy the family of your children, or worse, would you get help?

Even if you have no interest in unschooling, I hope your answers above were "Maybe, Probably and DEFINITELY."

After getting that help, unschooling will be a possibility. Don't stall. Children are older every moment.

SandraDodd.com/stress

Terminology

I don't always get my way, but I have attempted to keep jargon out of unschooling discussions I'm in. When a new term is proposed, I rush to be the first to say "Use plain English, please." Some people are using "RU" and pronouncing it "ARE YOU" or "RUE" and some people are "Ruing," and I don't like it. It's a bad idea.

When other people ask me I say "We homeschool." (Soon, "We homeschooled," because Holly is nearly eighteen.) When other homeschoolers ask me, I say "We're unschoolers." When other unschoolers ask me, I might say "We're radical unschoolers."

There are a few others you might hear discussed more than once if you're out and about in unschooling discussions: "radical," monkey platter, strewing.... Those and some other terms are defined or discussed in the next few pages, and probably elsewhere in this book as well.

John Holt

In the 1960s, John Holt's writings were popular among school reformers. In the 1970's, he started encouraging people to keep their children at home, with a book called *Teach Your Own*. Many people were already homeschooling on the sly, or legally, and some of them were hippies and some weren't, but from my point of view in New Mexico, John Holt came and learned from some of the reformers in Colorado who created The Rocky Mountain School, and he met with the people who were running the Santa Fe Alternative School and spoke with a meeting of parents and students there.

Most of his work was done in Boston, where he had a newsletter that turned into a magazine and then a bookstore. The magazine was *Growing Without Schooling*. It survived for a few years after John Holt's death in 1985. The bookstore was John Holt's Books and Music, and the stock was bought out by FUN Books, which is also linked from my John Holt pages.

John Holt's writing is different, and inspiring. He involved himself in schools and saw problems and successes from a different perspective than anyone else I've ever read.

John Holt had no children so he himself wasn't an unschooler, but he inspired others to do things differently from school, to avoid testing and rote learning. He encouraged people to respect children and to give them a great range of experiences and opportunities.

John Holt wrote about learning outside of schools, for about ten years. Since then, many families have raised children to adulthood without any school or schooling at all. I wish he could know Roya, Roxana and Rosie Sorooshian. I wish he could spend some time with Kathryn Fetteroll. How cool would it be if he could pop in for the day at a big unschooling conference in San Diego and meet a couple of hundred twenty-first-century unschooled kids all in the same place?

SandraDodd.com/johnholt

Why "Radical" Unschooling?

When people waited two months for a copy of *Growing Without Schooling*, there wasn't much opportunity for discussion. When *Prodigy came along and ordinary people could get to user groups and "BB"s, and soon to AOL chat rooms, homeschoolers finally had the means to get information the same day they needed it!

By then, John Holt wasn't the loudest voice speaking to homeschoolers. Conservative fundamentalist Christians in hordes and droves were creating, selling and buying Christian curriculum packages and teaching to the test and making sure their kids were in local spelling bees and geography contests and such (in the U.S.; this wasn't a problem in the rest of the English-speaking world).

Unschoolers were shocked by those no-nonsense school-at-home standards, and the unschoolers didn't mind the chance to find a corner for a chat or a forum of their own. As more homeschoolers showed up online, it became easier to sort ourselves out by philosophy and interest.

Those unschoolers who came to it from the La Leche League angle were accustomed to letting young children choose foods, and accustomed to co-sleeping. If attachment parenting is extended past weaning, it pretty much becomes unschooling.

Unschoolers who wanted to maintain their rules and discipline but to teach without a curriculum, didn't want the rest of us saying "unschooling involves more choices." So the term "radical unschooling" came to be used to refer to those who went all the way with it, seeing learning in all aspects of life, and not separating academics from everyday life. I think of it as committed, clear, purposeful, whole-life unschooling.

"Radical" means from the roots—radiating from the source. The knowledge that learning is natural to humans can radiate forth from that point in every direction.

SandraDodd.com/unschool/radical

Any Jargon?

Not really "jargon," but some terms unschoolers are generally familiar with are:

Deschooling: recovering from school to the point that natural learning starts to happen again, as it did before a child went to school. The term is used by homeschoolers in general, not just by unschoolers.

The Open Classroom: a school reform concept and practice from the 1960's and 70's, involving children learning individually or in groups as they chose, in short bursts or long sessions, inside a classroom with materials they could get to as they wanted to, or outside the classroom with the assistance of adult facilitators. It stressed choices, flexibility, individuality and comfort.

Strewing: literally, scattering something out, like rose petals or herbs or straw on a medieval floor. Figuratively, leaving interesting things out where they will be discovered.

Monkey platter: a variety tray of finger foods of different kinds.

"Unparenting": a derisive term used to insult unschoolers, as when one says, "Some people go beyond unschooling to un*parent*ing."

Unschooling: the adjective "unschooled" meaning untrained or self-taught or uneducated (depending on the context) is not a new word in English, but the verb "to unschool" is a John Holt term to refer to taking children out of school and letting them learn in natural ways in the world. He got it from a commercial for "7-Up—the *UN*cola."

SandraDodd.com/unschool/theterm

Beginning to Unschool

Go gradually. Read some, do some, read some more, do some more; repeat.

If you find yourself tempted to present a lesson, or to teach, feel that feeling and refrain from it. If your child asks a question, just answer the question. Answer it in an interesting way if you can. Look it up if you need to. Don't turn it into "a lesson."

If a child asks a question he might ask another one. Be prepared for one question to turn into fifteen of them. Be prepared for it not to.

You can't wait until you understand it to begin. Much of your understanding will come from the changes you see in your child and in your own thinking, and in your relationship with and perception of learning itself. You can't read a touch and then go and unschool for a year and then come back and see what you did wrong; you could be a year in the wrong direction.

Read some, do some. Think. Rest. Watch your child directly and as clearly as you can, without the filters and overlays you might be used to. If you think of any terms other than his name as you're looking, shake those off and think his name. Don't think "small, ADHD, rough, shy," or "girly, bright, verbal, musical." You might get back to some of those sometimes, but try to see "Holly, touching a leaf," or "Marty, eating soup." Sometimes the school-colored glasses can keep us from seeing anything but "is doing school work" or "is doing nothing." Unschoolers don't do school work, and "nothing" falls right off the radar.

Gradually incorporate as many of the ideas in this book as you can.

SandraDodd.com/beginning

Stages of Unschooling

The first stage is all the fear and uncertainty and angst.

Then comes deschooling and noticing how much of one's thoughts might be school-based and how easy it is for adults to belittle and discount children. That will take a year or so.

After school starts to recede it will be like the stars showing on a clear dark night in the country. They were always there, but you couldn't see them for the glare of the sun or the city lights. So now you'll start to see that they're not all the same, and there are patterns, and a history, and there's science, mythology, art, and then the moon comes out! And then you hear coyotes and owls and water moving somewhere… what water?

It might be like that, or it might be exactly that. But until you stop doing what you were doing before, you will not see those stars.

After a few years of reveling in natural learning and the richness of the universe, if you or your children decide to take a class it will be an entirely different experience than you would have had when school loomed so large in your vision of the world.

SandraDodd.com/stages

Where is the edge of unschooling?

If a family doing school at home wants to unschool, the radical unschoolers' talk about food and chores and bedtimes could overwhelm and confuse them. Because there *can* be unschooling in a family where kids also have chores and bedtimes and have to clean their plates.

Because it won't have the depth or benefit, ultimately, as a house where the children's preferences and freedoms have high priority, it's not something I will spend time and energy encouraging or assisting with.

There's a very old joke about a man saying "Doctor, doctor, it hurts when I do this," and the doctor replying, "Well don't do that."

When someone comes to a radical unschooling discussion to complain about their children's response to bedtimes or limits or "having to" read, they won't get the help they think they want. They will get advice to stop doing that. People will point out that the parents' actions and expectations are the problem, and the children's responses are rational and maybe inevitable.

One unschooling mom wrote, "Unschooling didn't blossom until I stepped away from traditional parenting."

The edge of unschooling is not a solid line. It will depend on the principles by which a family intends to live, and the philosophy of learning and parenting through which they see the world.

For me, learning has no stopping place, and so there are not days or places or times that are "learning time" (or unschooling time) and others that are "time out" or time off. (Well, there's that one holiday, Learn Nothing Day, July 24.)

SandraDodd.com/option

Learn Nothing Day

Unschoolers need a holiday.

When people ask if they homeschool in the summer, unschoolers say yes. When people ask when they have a break from learning, they say never.

This has gone on for a long time now.

> July 24 is **Learn Nothing Day—**
> a vacation for unschoolers.

Learn Nothing Day was first observed in 2008. With months to prepare and consider how to put a halt to learning, no great successes were reported. Some families gathered in public places with other unschoolers to celebrate together, but those proved to be cascading disasters of learning experiences.

Each year, though, there will be new unschoolers who might find a way around the dilemma of perpetual learning.

Learn Nothing Day is void in Utah, and people in Utah will know why. Special dispensation for Utah unschoolers: Learn Nothing could be celebrated in Utah on July 25.

> SandraDodd.com/learnnothingday
> *The logo in color is really beautiful.*

Comments on Learn Nothing Day

Some people didn't get it. Some said so.

> "I still don't get the idea. If I can't learn nothing what do I do? Just pretend it's not learn nothing day?"

I don't know how to answer a stunning question like that. It made me think of "What if I think a guy said 'Do you still beat your wife?' but I pretend he didn't say it?" And nothing had made me think of that in my whole life!

Is it possible for a person to learn nothing for a whole day? Yes, I think so.

Do I think it's possible for an experienced unschooler to learn nothing? No, I'm certain it is not possible.

Another interesting comment:

> "Why does unschoolers have to have an OFFICIAL DAY to learn nothing Day??? IT seems Like you are showing the world that you are learning nothing all year round. So why have a day of it..."

The spelling and punctuation were that way in the blog comment in which it was deposited by a mother of two. I cut and pasted it without editing.

Learn Nothing Day has inspired some art and commentary and several gatherings of unschoolers.

Flo Gascon wrote, "I just can't learn nothing, it's impossible, even with my old, feeble brain. I turned on the computer and was assaulted with all sorts of information. Imagine how hard it will be for the girls with their sharp, shiny new brains."

This is from documentation by a mom named Tracy:

> 9:37 am - Took a break to remind the kids (who were just getting up) that today was Learn Nothing Day and that they should certainly take advantage of this opportunity to learn nothing.
>
> They looked at me like I was a total moron.

Whether you believe in not learning or not, these might be fun for you:

SandraDodd.com/learnnothingday/2008
SandraDodd.com/learnnothingday/critics

Other kinds of unschooling

I have heard of, read about and communicated with people who referred to themselves as part-time unschoolers, relaxed homeschoolers, eclectic homeschoolers, academic unschoolers and other terms. Some of them had kids in school. Some used a curriculum in a loose way. Some "did math" (had math lessons and tests) but let the children pick up whatever history and science they could on the side. Some taught their children to read and then let them unschool.

I know few such families whose kids went the full twelve or thirteen years without going to school.

I know of no such families in which the relationships between the parents and children are as good as the best and middlest unschoolers I've known. I've known a few unschooling families whose relationships weren't great, but I've always thought they were better than they would have been if the kids had been in school and the parents only saw them occasionally.

Different kinds of schooling will have different benefits.

Limited kinds of unschooling will have limited benefits.

SandraDodd.com/unschool/vsRelaxedHomeschooling
SandraDodd.com/unschool/marginal

Principles instead of Rules

The idea of living by principles has come up before and will come up again. When I first started playing with the idea, in preparation for a conference presentation, I was having a hard time getting even my husband and best friends to understand it. Really bright people local to me, parents, looked at me blankly and said "principles are just another word for rules."

I was determined to figure out how to explain it, but it's still not simple to describe or to accept, and I think it's because our culture is filled with rules, and has little respect for the idea of "principles." It seems moralistic or spiritual to talk about a person's principles, or sometimes people who don't see it that way will still fear it's about to get philosophical and beyond their interest or ability.

Rules are things like "Never hit the dog," and "Don't talk to strangers."

Principles are more like "Being gentle to the dog is good for the dog and good for you too," or "People you don't know could be dangerous." They are not "what to do." They are "how do you decide?" and "why?" in the realm of thought and decision making.

The answer to most questions is "it depends."

What it depends on often has to do with principles.

What the police thought:

When our middle child, Marty, was fourteen years old, he went to an intensive week-long Junior Police Academy sponsored by the Albuquerque Police Department. On June 7, 2003, I wrote this report for some of my unschooling friends:

> The same day I read that we were lazy hedonists, this happened:
>
> The final day, graduation from the Junior Police Academy, they march in like soldiers, doing face drills and filing in and pledging allegiance (we briefed Marty on that this week; he said he knew it from a humorous version in the bathroom, just leave out the joke parts)...
>
> Ceremonial this'n'that, certificates, pins, Marty was awarded a certificate as "Top Gun" (electronic target practice guns, F.A.T.S. and paintball guns) which also came with $15 gift certificate to a sporting goods store. Seven or eight other kids (of 32) got awards

for things like most push-ups, most improved, most physically fit male.

Of Marty, I thought "All that Nintendo Duck Hunt paid off."

Then we ate good local barbecue, served up by their instructors, and as people were taking pictures and saying goodbye, I went up to one of his instructors and sat to thank him. He said Marty was just a joy to work with. Chit chat you'd expect.

Then he said the big thing. (Brace yourselves. And I really like the guy.)

He said, "You can always tell a kid who comes from a family with a lot of discipline and rules."

He said Marty was really well-behaved and enthusiastic and cooperative. (I wish I had the exact quotes there; I wish I had *videotape*.)

I said "We hardly have any rules at our house. We just tell them to always make the best choice, to be helpful and not hurt people." (That's maybe 85% close to exact words; I need my audio back!)

He said they had talked about a lot of things like that over the week. I wanted to make light again, because it was maybe kinda tacky to counter, "You can always tell" with "GOTCHA! Wrong! CAN'T always tell." So I said, "Y'know, Monday was really his first day at school of any sort. It was his first day taking notes or anything like that."

"Oh, right, he's homeschooled, right?"

"Yes."

"Most of the homeschooled kids I've met were not so good at social interactions. Marty's really confident and outgoing."

I told him Marty had gone home and re-written his notes from Monday, and had been really focused on his assignments and getting ready for the next day. He said, "Initiative! Good!"

Probably there was nobody there who was as eager and excited to be there as Marty was. So we made some more sweet chitchat and that was it.

I could hardly wait to get into the van and close the doors so I could tell Keith, Marty and Holly what he had said about discipline and rules. We talked about that most of the way home. Holly can hardly believe that some people think that rules upon rules will make people "good" away from home. It just makes no sense to her.

Marty said one of the kids got in bad trouble this afternoon, threatened with being sent home, for throwing pieces of rubber at other kids, and for throwing paintballs. One broke on the exercise track. NOT at the targets, where the mess was supposed to be.

Marty couldn't fathom why someone would be at such a cool place and act that way.

But Marty had also told me there were two people there who hadn't even wanted to be there. I didn't ask (yet) whether this kid was one of those. Marty was exhausted when he got home and went to bed at 10:00.

This evidence is really important, that someone who works with kids a lot (Police Athletic League volunteer), someone who's in law enforcement, sees an enthusiastic, well-behaved, cooperative kid, and is confident that he came from a house with discipline and rules.

Discipline and rules? All-fired flaming hedonists? (Whatever the accusation was.)

Neither of the above.

SandraDodd.com/rules

"Just say No"

Just say "no" to drugs, and abstain from sex, and "It won't hurt your kids to hear 'no'." Our culture is full of no, no, no, don't, and the assumption that "No" equals health and wealth.

One speaker and conservative parenting columnist refers to "Vitamin N" and says children should hear "no" more than they hear "yes."

I heard about that years after I had been advising people to imagine that when the baby is born the parent is issued a coupon book with 200 "no" tickets. Save some for the big stuff. Some parents say "no" 200 times in the first year. Here was "a professional" saying people should say "no" even more, and for no reason other than it's good for kids to hear no.

I shudder to imagine those poor kids' lives. And maybe they're smart and can get around it as I did when my mom said, "The next time you want to go somewhere the answer is going to be no." (Think of what you might have done to get around such a doom, and I'll tell the answer in a bit.)

Someone came to a discussion and asked what we would do, at a gathering of families, if a young child were running around with a burning stick. I wrote:

> I might pick the stick up! But that would give him something to wrestle about and whimper and fight about.
>
> I'd probably pick the little guy up and say "Drop the stick" if it was a seriously dangerous situation, and because I have LOTS of "No" tickets stored up, if I said "Drop the stick," my kid would drop the stick in a heartbeat.
>
> Parents who say "No" too much have used up all their tickets. I see it all around me. "No" is so devalued it's like dust, covering everything, making it all dull and boring and the kids don't care anymore.
>
> With babies, if a baby has a knife or something dangerous, the best way to get him to drop it is to offer him something pretty. If you just hold it out and he wants it, he'll drop the knife to grab the new thing. It's not until they're older that they figure out they can hold one thing in each hand.

It works with older kids too, though—even teens. You just have to figure out what is more attractive than the thing they're holding (physically or figuratively).

I was very slightly late getting home one night from a date and my mom said the next time I wanted to go out, the answer was going to be no. I wanted to go out on Friday. So on Wednesday I asked if I could go out, and begged a little and explained why I wanted to go, but my mom held fast to her position, and thereby I was punished. I didn't really have anywhere to go, I just wanted to get that "next time 'no'" appointment out of the way. My mom felt like a really good mom, and on Friday I got to go out.

I did it without lying, by the way. I never added any details like where, or that I had been asked out; nothing. I asked if I could go to a movie or something with Joseph. *No.* Please? **No.** Okay. Contrition. Check.

My children have no reason to dodge or manipulate that way, because Keith and I haven't concocted any made-up arbitrary rules and their accompanying punishments. With safety and communication as principles and priorities, we've had safe, communicative kids.

If people want you to be disdainful of your children or to treat them harshly, just say no.

SandraDodd.com/logic

Proof or Research

I saw an online book review for a book concerning the history of public education and homeschooling and the reviewer said most of the books he had read about homeschooling had been belief or opinion.

In my opinion, I believe that's lame. Just because a book gives statistics doesn't make it thorough and true. Information on homeschooling 200 or 100 or 50 or 10 years ago doesn't help someone do it this year.

In my fairly long life I've seen five three-legged dogs. One I knew personally. If I had seen fifty of them, or if I had only seen one, it was still more than belief and opinion that not all dogs have four legs. I don't need to know what percentage of dogs have three legs to refute "all dogs have four legs."

If someone says "Without high school, one is doomed to poverty," that is a false statement. All of us probably know people who didn't graduate from high school (or its English-school-system or other equivalent) who are happy and maybe wealthy. All of us know (or have been) people who went to a university for four or ten years and ended up working side by side with people who *maybe* graduated from high school and maybe didn't.

I don't mind people doing research, as long as they don't want to do a longitudinal study on unschoolers with a bunch of tests and write-ups. That would ruin the unschooling environment for every child involved. Research makes some people relax, or worry, but it doesn't change the simple, clear fact that people can and do learn outside of school, without being taught, when they feel safe and supported and encouraged. It would only take seeing one adult unschooler to know that not all happy, employed, successful people went to school. I've seen dozens.

Most of what passes for research on education has to do with administrators getting masters' degrees or PhDs, or with those who want to sell equipment or programs to the schools justifying the expenses to districts and taxpayers. As with so much of the carts-before-horses school system, research isn't intended to help children, but to justify sales and salaries.

Sandra Dodd.com/research

What about situations with rules?

(This was written in or about 2004; I didn't want to change the present tense to past in the writing.)

I don't mind following rules. The principle that it's best to do what others need you to do in a situation covers that. I obey most of the laws of which I'm aware (though it's been years since I filed a statement of intent to homeschool, and Holly reads speed limit signs to me sometimes in a meaningful way).

My kids don't mind following rules when they join clubs or attend meetings in places with rules. The gaming store where they play (and where Kirby came to work after a while) has a language rule. They can say "crap" but nothing else of its sort or worse. There's a 25¢ fine. If they don't have a quarter, they do push-ups. But because of that rule, families go there that wouldn't go if it had the atmosphere of a sleazy bowling alley. (It has the atmosphere of a geeky gaming store.)

I think one reason they don't mind following rules is that they haven't already "had it up to here" with rules, as kids have who have a whole life of home rules and school rules. They find rules kind of fascinating and charming, honestly. When Holly has had a dress code for a dance class or acting class she is *thrilled.*

Maybe also because they haven't been forced to take classes or go to gaming shops, they know they're there voluntarily. Part of the contract is that they abide by the rules. No problem.

Probably some families make rules so that their kids will learn to follow rules. It's possible. Too much practice can kill the joy, though. Being forced to play an instrument can create an adult who doesn't even bother to own one of the instruments he knows how to play, because now that he's out of school he doesn't "have to." If someone made me practice eating before every meal, I wouldn't be very hungry.

So here I have kids who can sleep as long as they want, who set their alarms and get up; who have all kinds of clothes and no rules, who dress well and appropriately to the situation; who don't have to come home but they DO come home.

Something important is happening.

SandraDodd.com/rules

Exchanging one set of rules for another

People will come to unschooling discussions and ask whether unschoolers can do this, or use that. They ask what they have to do first. They want a new set of rules.

Once when a mom came to a discussion asking us to tell her whether to buy a particular game or not, the responses infuriated her. She wrote:

> The reason this conversation is really bothering me, is because Sandra kept responding with other points that had nothing to do with my one and only question. Her points are GREAT ones, and ones I in fact agree with, but they are points about something other that my one question: Should I give my 4 & 7 year olds that particular game? She never said Yes (and why) or NO (and why). You might ask yourself if you were trying to have a conversation with someone and they were skipping over your particular question, and making lots of other points that had nothing to do with what you were still trying to talk about!!! I'm not wound up and defensive and angry. Although I find myself frustrated, and now on the defense trying to tell you (and Sandra) that I agree with all those points she made, BUT IT'S NOT WHAT I'M TALKING ABOUT. That's all.

I responded:

> A question like "should I buy this, yes or no?" isn't the kind of question others can answer very well. And if we did, we'd need to say WHY we thought so, which would involve explaining a principle. And as with all of the best answers, it needs to start, "It depends."
>
> If we answer questions with "yes" and "no," and give people what they claim to want, or what they think they want, we are chucking fish out instead of providing information on how to fish, how to make one's own custom fishing equipment and when and where the fishing is great. Unschooling can't work as a series of yes/no questions.
>
> Another principle at work: Helping people learn to find their own answers is vastly superior to distributing answers on demand. And those who volunteer their time and experience are not willing to hold others' hands for years or months. They want to empower others. Empowerment is a principle, not a rule. Learning to examine one's own life and needs and beliefs is necessary for

unschooling to work. When priorities and principles are coming clearer, such questions as whether or not to buy a particular game or tool or movie or food are EASY, simple, happy questions. That's why the mom quoted above didn't get the simple straight answer she thought she needed. No one wanted to waste time or energy sending her down the wrong path.

SandraDodd.com/rulebound

Choices

In May, 1987, when Kirby was a baby, I was at an SCA/medievalist campout. A friend was being knighted the next day, and I went to his vigil. He told me that he was worried about his duty, as a knight, to set a good example, and that his camp wasn't very nice, nor very authentic to period. I told him it had taken years for our camp to become more elaborate and more period, and that he could improve his gradually, too.

We talked about replacing dishes, or benches, or lanterns, as better ones were found, and not try to replace everything at once.

I suggested that when he got a new tent, if his choices were nylon or canvas, to get canvas; if the choice was brown or orange, choose brown. "Always make the more medieval choice," I said.

I went back to my own camp and shared this idea with Keith and my friend Jeff (who were in that context Gunwaldt and Artan), and it was passed on to all my husband's squires and my students from then on.

Meanwhile, back in my regular life, I had two more children and as they started making their own choices, the idea of making the better choice was a good tool. I added to that the idea that until one has thought of at least two options, it's impossible to make a choice.

The concept has been helpful with unschooling and with mindful parenting, and first came forth in that area of thought in August 2002, at the HSC conference when Richard Prystowsky and I did a joint talk called "Peaceful Parenting." I recommended that people think of two things to do and make the more peaceful choice.

Although this tool is useful in the moment, its best use is for incremental change. If my best choice used to be to yell or hit, and I yelled, then the next time I thought about it, hitting wasn't even going to begin to be one of my choices. Would I yell or wait? Or yell or speak quietly? Yell or leave the room? Maybe leave out the yelling, and choose between "speak quietly" or "breathe before speaking."

Some critics of this advice say children will never decide if they have unlimited choices. No one has "unlimited choices," but compared to children in traditional culture, a parent has a huge range of choices. More often than not they don't choose, because they don't even stop to think. They just react in familiar ways, thoughtlessly. They do the first thing they think of and say "I had to do that, because..." and they fill in the blank with something justifiable. It's not mindful parenting.

A person can choose to have choices. A person can choose not to choose; still a choice, but they think of it as "no choice" or "have to."

SandraDodd.com/choices

Keith and Kirby in those days (as Gunwaldt and Magnus)

"Have To"

When people are making the change from feeling powerless to seeing the vast range of choices they have, the biggest stumbling block is usually the concept and phrase "have to." People will argue that they "have to" do this or that. They're certain that they "have to" make their children do things.

This was someone's "have to" example:

> I committed to a black belt. No matter how long it took, no matter how many knee surgeries were involved, no matter how many times I had to drag myself out to do kata when I wanted to just go to sleep.

It sounds very painful, that way. Changing nothing but the terminology and thoughts, it can be seen as a choice made anew every morning, every session, before every class. The writer could have chosen to just go to sleep, but the "commitment" took away choice. It was the choice of no choice at that point.

A black belt shouldn't involve powerlessness. It should be something that is chosen over and over again, joyfully. Willingly.

Parents will come to unschooling discussions throwing "have to" around without hearing or reading their own words. Two examples:

- I had to say ... Hey let's do this science experiment to get him off the play station last night. I had to have some one take notes because the directions called for...
- There are days where I might not want to fix breakfast, lunch, or supper, to do laundry, to clean up a child's vomit, the cat's poop mess after getting locked in the van, etc., but it's gotta be done and so I do it."

Parents enslaved by the directions for science experiments, and by cats and dishes? "Have to"? A powerless life of no choices? If the parents are content to live without choices, what will inspire them to give their children choices? If the adults feel trapped and weak, freedom in the children will be the cause of resentment and the parents won't even know why they're tense and irritable.

As to a science experiment with directions, and "having to" take a child away from a game involving experimentation and logic to do an exercise about experimentation and logic... it's not a giant step toward unschooling. The materials for the experiment could be kept ready somewhere for a time when nothing else is happening, and then do it! It's done. Or don't do it. If it's a freely chosen project, more will be learned than if it was done for some "have to" reason.

As to a cat being locked in the van and a baby puking and laundry, there are options there too. Paying a neighbor to clean the van, or to clean up after the baby maybe, or throw a wet towel on the baby puke and get it later. Why do three meals a day and laundry "gotta be done"? What about two or four meals a day, and wearing togas made of extra bed sheets for a day? What about a picnic near a laundromat? You could do one load of laundry for the next day without committing to washing all the clothes you own at once.

There are choices. There's more about these ideas in the section on chores, too.

The ideal change is for the parents to find reasons to want to do laundry, and to want to clean up cats, and to do it willingly and cheerfully. Lots of new unschoolers roll their eyes at that and say it's stupid. It's not. It's the path to happiness, even though it involves poo and puke.

What's dangerous nonsense is knowing there's a choice, and still thinking of deciding to live the rest of your child's life in frustrated resentment, feeling helpless about your own life and all-powerful about your child's. You don't have to do that.

SandraDodd.com/haveto

Self-regulation

"Regulation" is about rules, and controls. Regulation isn't a word that's used in the presence of options and choices.

"Children have to be taught to self-regulate." That "rule" is parroted by non-thinking parents with great regularity. It can be replaced with "I would like to help my child make thoughtful choices."

If you think of controlling yourself, and of your children controlling themselves, it's still about control. If people live by principles their choices come easily.

If you see two choices: self control or lack of control (being "out of control") it will limit your life and your thinking.

When you hear or say "They will self-regulate," think to yourself: "They will learn to make choices."

SandraDodd.com/self-regulation

Self-control and other control

"Control." Control is always something to fight about, something to balk at, to rebel against. Being controlled deprives people of opportunities to make decisions or to consider alternatives.

If school is not going to control your children, who will?

There are benefits to moving away from the idea of "control." Even "self control" implies that someone has to control that person.

If you are your child's partner, then the two of you together can figure out ways to be, and neither of you will need to control the other. You can reason through situations and make a fresh decision each time, after considering the particular factors of that moment.

What about safety issues, though? If I were about to hit someone with a stick, I hope my husband or one of my big sons or my loud daughter would prevent that crazed decision and save me from such an urge. If a sharply spoken "Hey!" or something didn't stop me, one of them should disarm me without worrying about my feelings. If you're on a baseball team and the catcher seems perhaps about to take his mask off to beat someone with it, you'd stop him.

I'm not proposing a rule against control. I'm saying it should be saved for emergencies. I have not found I ever needed to control what my children ate, or to control when they woke up or where they slept. I don't control what they wear, though I do make suggestions sometimes, and they consider them, usually. I don't control where they go, and yet they always let me know where they'll be.

In case you're waiting for me to get to controlling what they learn, no one can control what anyone else learns.

People who love having control might transfer that urge away from the minute details of their children's lives and toward controlling the yard or the closets or their own hobbies.

SandraDodd.com/control

If your children are older, skim on through this section and maybe the next one.

Infants

As no infant is required to be in school, this isn't strictly about unschooling, but there are families in which the desire to unschool comes before the pregnancy or adoption, and so it's worth pointing out a few things.

La Leche League is many people's first intro to attachment parenting, and that has led many people to unschooling. The problem is generally that once a child reaches "school age," parents can justify dropping the attachment parenting idea entirely. Some drop it when the baby weans. The principles, though, are as true of three-year-olds and six-year-olds as they are of infants. And once a child and parent have a close and solid relationship, why dissolve that unless it's unavoidable?

Attachment parenting isn't "an unschooling concept," but it is something many unschoolers consider, although some come to it late. You can find more with a web search or asking at the library. There is an organization separate from La Leche League now, with a magazine and a great deal of literature.

Basically, they advocate holding babies as much as the babies want, letting them be with adults day and night, gently, and sweetly. If people can breastfeed they should do that instead of bottlefeeding. If people can sleep with the baby, they shouldn't use a crib.

From a learning standpoint, when babies are carried they see more, they hear and smell more. If they are given things to touch and taste besides just a few baby toys left in the corner of a crib or playpen, they will learn by leaps and bounds. They will spend less time crying and more time being in the real world.

The parents will know the child better, and the child will know the parents better. They will be building a partnership based on trust.

SandraDodd.com/attachment

"Partners and not adversaries"

Although it might have been standard La Leche League rhetoric in 1986, one statement lives in my head in the voice of Carol Rice who was one of my first two La Leche League leaders. The other leader was Lori Odhner. I credit and thank them frequently for giving me beautiful new tools to use to be a better mother to Kirby than I might have been without their generous and creative volunteer leadership.

Carol said, **"Be his partner, not his adversary."** She was speaking to the group, but it was like God was speaking directly to me. That was huge. Though the mothers at the meetings were sweet, others outside of there were treating their babies like alien invaders, like enemy creatures, or like evil grubs. Mothers were whining and complaining more than the babies about the cruel trick the world seemed to have played on them because they were "stuck" with this baby.

So what kind of partner did baby Kirby Dodd need? He needed someone to pay attention to him if he was uncomfortable, and to make sure he was safe. He needed someone to help him access the world, to see it, to experience it safely. He needed a quiet, soft place to sleep. Maybe it was on me or on his dad, in a carrier of some sort, or a sling. Maybe it was right next to me in the bed.

Because La Leche League is a volunteer organization, people's experiences with local meetings differ greatly, but I was fortunate to have had some phenomenal leaders who were also unschoolers. Although I wasn't considering homeschooling when I met them, knowing those families certainly made unschooling an easy choice four years later.

I am still my children's partner two decades later.

SandraDodd.com/partners/child

Saying Yes to Infants

If an infant can't even ask a question, why would a parent say "no"? But some of the first words many babies hear are "No!" and "Don't" and "Stop." Even without the words themselves, if a baby reaches out and the parent pushes his hand back or ignores him, that is a big "no." If a baby cries and the parent ignores him, or puts him down roughly, or leaves the room and closes the door, that is not even nearly in the realm of "yes."

When one of the partners is in pain, the partnership isn't doing very well. And it's not a fifty-fifty partnership; nor is anything in the whole world. In the case of a mother who can walk and talk, access water and maybe drive a car, she can't expect a newborn baby to do half the work. If she gives him everything she can, he will give back as much as he has, not just then, but for years to come if she doesn't screw it up.

What do babies *want*? They want to learn. They learn by touching and tasting and watching and listening. They learn to be gentle by people being gentle with them, and showing them how to touch hair nicely, and to touch cats and dogs gently. They want to learn which foods taste good. They want to learn how to walk, but you don't need to teach them. They'll want to know how to go up and down stairs at some point. They will eventually want to know how to get things off shelves and out of boxes. They will want to see what else is in the house, and in the yard, and you can help them do that safely.

A baby doesn't want to look at and touch the very same things day after day after day any more than you would want to watch the same movie every day for a year, or sit in the same place in your house all the time. Sing different songs with him. Play different finger games. Change what he can see in the bedroom sometimes.

A rich world for a baby is similar to a rich world for anyone else. A baby is a person. A lucky baby has an adult partner who understands that.

SandraDodd.com/yes

Communicating with Babies

Someone came to a discussion and assured us all that children under five were like scientists from an alien world. That sounds good at first, until you remember that they are natural parts of their own world. A sixty-year-old man is no more a human, no more a person, than a newborn baby.

Children don't need to be taught to speak, if they have a fairly normal range of faculties. Making the exception for children with deformities or who are deaf and blind, let me talk about the other children who can learn to talk.

The same mom wrote, "Not only have they never seen, touched or experienced anything in our world—they also have no way of communicating thoughts, feelings or desires with anything more than frustrated cries, screams and babbling."

I responded:

> There is touch. There is gaze. Have you never just looked into the eyes of your child, communicating? Have you not touched them soothingly, and felt them touch you back sometimes? They can tell the difference between an angry look and a gentle look.

Parents who didn't know touch was a real way to communicate could practice on babies, and then use it with older children, and partners.

For children to learn language, they need opportunities to hear words, and for people to pay attention to the sounds they make. Mimicry is good, with babies. Even before they can articulate consonants, they can probably copy your voice going up or down, and you could copy them back. Singing little made up two-note songs can be a good tool for communicating with babies. Copying touch is good, too. (Don't return rough touch with rough, though.)

Let them hear you speak, and find opportunities for them to hear others speak. Although there are justifications and theories about what babies like and respond to (high voices and sing-songy voices seem to appeal to babies), don't revert to a whole babytalk language with them. Some is fine, but talk to them about real things, too. Tell them what you're doing with them, and what they're seeing, when they're out and about. Don't quiz them, just talk. It's fine if they can't understand you for months and months. They'll be learning your tone and your moods and the speech patterns of the language even before they have vocabulary. You will be building a relationship that is not based on the meaning of the words, but on the sharing of the time and attention. You're paying attention to what the baby sees and touches and hears. The baby is paying attention to you.

If you can keep that up for eighteen years, you've got unschooling!

SandraDodd.com/babytalk

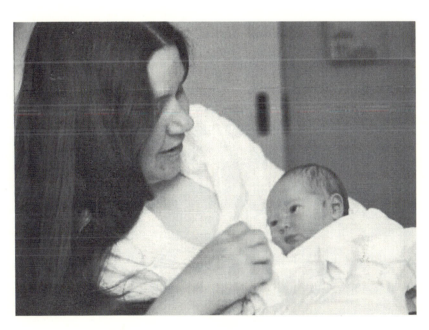

Sandra and Holly Dodd, November 1991

Co-sleeping

Part of gentle parenting is being available. If children can sleep with the parents or at least in the same room, there won't be as much panic or sorrow.

There is a book called *The Family Bed* by Tine Thevenin you might want to get if you need encouragement or ideas about this.

This isn't "part of unschooling," but many unschoolers have found it helpful in maintaining or re-building relationships with their children.

Some older children are as happy to sleep with a brother or sister as with a parent, but please don't require one of your children to comfort a sibling all night, nor to be responsible for the safety of a younger child. It's too much to put on a young person, and it will move you away from, rather than toward, parent/child bonding with both of those children.

Babies need parents all the time, not just during daylight hours.

Sometimes parents think they won't get as much sleep. It's easier for a nursing mom to roll over and nurse the baby than to get up and walk and be wide awake to pick up a baby who's been wide awake and crying even longer. That's too much disruption of peace and sleep for everyone.

If the dad has to wake up in the morning, the mom and baby could sleep in another room on work nights. Some families put more than one bed in the same room. Some use mattresses on the floor so babies and toddlers can't fall. It can help to have different covers for different people, too.

Some families never got the chance to sleep as a group early on but it might be worth considering, even later or occasionally, depending on your temperaments and situation.

SandraDodd.com/sleep/cosleeping

Toddlers and Young Children

Younger children (sometimes called "preschoolers") are not really being "unschooled" unless the parents would absolutely have put him or her in school without the unschooling intention or philosophy. When a child is below the age of compulsory schooling, there are ways to encourage his curiosity and to strengthen the parent/child relationship, even if he attends school.

If you don't intend to send your child to school, the less you do to him, the less you have to undo. The more you do *with* him, the closer you'll be to seeing what natural learning can do in and for his life.

Instead of teaching him the colors or the alphabet, play games and sing songs and speak casually about what color things are, or what's bigger or smaller. Instead of buying him only "age-appropriate" toys, consider other real-world things that would be safe for him to play with. Let him touch some of your things, in gentle ways, rather than keeping them all up high. (Hide the truly fragile things for a while.)

Let him help decide things about his own environment or the family's plans. Don't make it his responsibility, but get his input. Take an "I don't care," for what it is. He might not care! The more a child trusts parents to make fun decisions, the less he will feel he needs to whine or cry to ever get "his way." Avoid things he doesn't enjoy when you can.

When you're talking to young children who are figuring out their new language and their new world, avoid saying "always" or "never." Instead of making rules for him or dire predictions, explain your concerns and thoughts. Give him some "why" to go with his "what" and "where" and "when." Even give him some "why" to go with his "who." Don't forget that he won't know what "aunt" and "cousin" mean. He won't automatically figure out "neighbor" or "co-worker."

You're like a docent in the Museum of Everything.

SandraDodd.com/youngchildren

Guests in your home, and in your life

Some people enjoy the idea that we choose our parents when we're in some incorporeal waiting room somewhere. Others get a kick out of the idea that they will meet the same souls they "knew before" to work things out. Sometimes those beliefs become justifications for bad parenting or slack friendship, because one can always say "Well this is the way it was fated to be." I'm not interested in helping anyone justify the mistreatment of others, so if the beginning of this paragraph is the way you see your relationship with your child, please skip to the next page.

If you're still here, this is what helps me when I am stuck for how to act: I think of my child as a guest in my home. He didn't really choose to come here; I brought him here myself. When there were siblings, he didn't choose to have them. Even a child who says "I want a sister" rarely knows what he's talking about; by the time you can produce one he's on to wanting a motorbike or something. No child has a nine-month attention span, and by the time a newborn is a playmate, a year or three have passed. Don't ever blame a child for having a sibling regardless of how much he expressed a fantasy wish for a playmate who lived there.

Being new to the world, and you being his host (and partner), any light you can shed on the mysteries of the world, and any clues you can give him on what's likely to happen and what's expected of him would be good for all concerned. Advise him what might happen at a wedding reception, or a birthday party, or at a place he's never been to before. Show him how to eat a new food he hasn't seen. Help put him at ease if he's nervous. Provide him all the coaching and reassurance he wants, and no more than he wants.

Find ways to accommodate his everyday needs. Step stools, low drawers and shelves, a low hook for his coat and hat, a small chair and table, some snacks he can get to without asking—consider those to be requirements rather than luxuries. Be courteous and generous.

SandraDodd.com/guest

Attentive Parenting

Some families operate as though from a script, by default. The parents deal with the children as though they are generic, interchangeable children, or bad children, or irritating strangers. The children deal with the parents as little as possible after a while, having given up on actually being heard or respected.

If you are part of a disconnected relationship, or if you remember one, or have such examples in your life, think of the elements that created those sad situations. Make that your checklist of things not to do.

What is "attention"? Attending. To attend means both to be there, and to take care of someone. Tending a garden. Attending to a child. Being present in a focused and meaningful and useful way.

Sometimes a child is trying to get help and an adult says, "Don't interrupt." In such a case the adult has been inattentive two ways. Years ago I stopped hanging out with friends who wanted me to put my children second to them.

Sometimes a child wants to discuss or explain, and a parent says, "It doesn't matter what you think," or "I don't care why you did it." That would be a good move to be able to take back. It's not too late for you to do something different, from now on.

Sometimes attending to someone means giving them space and quiet and waiting until they have rested or calmed down or thought about what they want to say before you press them to listen or speak. Inattentive parents miss those cues sometimes.

If a child has to say "I'm hungry," it's likely the parent wasn't paying much attention half an hour or an hour before to how long it had been since food, and how much energy the child had been using. If a child is thirsty, parents shouldn't stall or argue; they should probably apologize as they get that child something to drink.

SandraDodd.com/attentiveparenting

Saying Yes to Toddlers

Children who can walk and talk feel powerful and they love their new ability to affect the world. As a parent, you probably were eager for them to speak, and you probably took notes and photos when they walked, and ran, and climbed. Now what?

Children need to explore the world. Don't go to the same park, the same grocery store, the same movie theater every time. Change it up. Take a different route. If you walk the dog, maybe go the opposite direction on the loop, or leave early and go more slowly. Go at sunset so the child can be outside for the transition from daytime to twilight.

Find safe places for him to run, and things to climb. Be right there. Help him. Cheer him on. Be patient and encouraging.

Avoid "no" when a situation isn't actually harmful or dangerous. Even if "yes" isn't the answer, try variations on "Let's see if we can," or "I'll put it on the list," or "I wish we could, but let's try this instead." Be positive and cheerful as often as you can be.

When your young partner is tired, find him a comfortable place to rest. When he's afraid, help him feel safe. When he's sad, try to be sympathetic and comforting. It all sounds obvious, I bet, but you won't have to look far to see parents doing the opposite things and being angry with children just for being children and for expressing their physical and emotional needs.

Practicalities with toddlers

Always have snacks with you.

Whenever possible, let children wear something they could sleep in. Or let them sleep in something that wasn't really for sleeping. Put sleep above tradition or appearances. The purpose of sleep doesn't require special equipment or costumes.

If baths are scary, let kids play with toys in the tub without the stopper in. Find a plastic dishpan and fill it with sudsy warm water and let them wash their toy dishes, or some other toys. Put in another pan with rinse water. Somewhere in all that, the kid will get cleaner, and be a little less afraid of the water next time. And every day he gets older. If you think back to a single argument over a bath in your life or anyone's, it probably seems silly from a distance.

Ice is a good tub toy. You don't have to wash it or store it later. It's a good toy for a warm sidewalk, too. It's fun to pull around in a wagon. Ice cleans itself up. (Have water nearby to pour on in case ice sticks to a child; ice is safer wet than not.)

A tent made of a sheet over a table or some chairs should not be rare or unusual.

Offer food and water more than you think they'll need it; don't forget sunscreen or shade; have something soft to lie on and maybe that sheet, for a tent, to hide under. For the child to hide under, I mean—though you might want to hide *with* him.

Heroics

Protect your child from bad guys. Anyone who wants to break up your team or bring your relationship into question is a bad guy. Be your child's protector and defender. Be a hero.

When your child does sweet and tender things for you, don't brush her aside. Pay attention to nurturing gestures. Acknowledge them. Let your child be your hero sometimes, too.

Holding hands in parking lots

A common question is how to "make" children hold the mom's hand. It helps to live in such a way that the child wants to hold the mom's hand. "You have to hold my hand" is both a "have to" and a rule. If the purpose and intention is to be safe, there are other ways.

Instead of requiring that my kids had to hold my hand in a parking lot, I would park near a cart and put some kids in right away, or tell them to hold on to the cart (a.k.a. "help me push", so a kid can be between me and the cart). And they didn't have to hold a hand. There weren't enough hands. I'd say "Hold on to something," and it might be my jacket, or the strap of the sling, or the backpack, or something.

I've seen other people's children run away from them in parking lots, and the parents yell and threaten. At that moment, going back to the mom seems the most dangerous option. Make yourself your child's safest place in the world, and many of your old concerns will just disappear.

SandraDodd.com/toddlers

Special Education

"Special Education" is a school term, and you may not need it even if you have a child who would have been certified "special needs" in school. Learning isn't "education." Education is done to someone, on the teacher's schedule.

Unschooling works the same way whether children are quick to make connections and to try things, or whether the child has trouble in one area or another. Each child still learns inside himself, by connecting something new to what he already knows.

In school, the goal is to create a standard product insofar as possible, or at least to document twelve years of trying so that it's not the teachers' fault if a child isn't ideally "educated" at the end of his school years.

With unschooling, the goal is for a whole person to stay whole, and to move gently toward a greater facility with and understanding of the world around him.

Of course there are exceptions and problems and extremes. There are also "problems" that aren't really problems outside of school.

When deciding what to do with a child whose needs are unusual or whose learning might be difficult, don't forget to factor in whether school would have made things better or worse, and whether the risk of "being behind" without also being taunted and shamed and branded "special ed" for life might be the best thing you can provide. Special ed kids are always behind in school.

Some kids who aren't in school "catch up." If it takes them a few years to learn what other children learned at a younger age, and if the parents can remain kind and patient, by teen years it might not show at all. I've never seen a special education student in school survive to the teen years unscathed. I have seen unschoolers who would have been labeled severely or behaviorally this-or-that grow up in peace and remain whole.

It might be worth thinking for a moment or two about what the non-special education might be. Plain? Average? *Nothing-special?* "Mainstream"? It's not a good way to think of your children.

SandraDodd.com/specialunschooling

School's special needs

Since the 1960's and 70's, schools have moved steadily in the direction of special programs and specialists for children whose learning won't be optimal in a "regular classroom." These considerations involve funding, hiring, facilities, materials, programs, accountability, considerations of legal liabilities, and maintaining a pleasant and protective environment (troubled kids not with cooperative kids; mean kids not with susceptible, sensitive kids).

What can homeschoolers do that school can't?

What can unschoolers do that school-at-homers can't?

Although schools spend a great deal of time and effort creating individualized programs, even when there is a child who is provided with a full-time teacher of his own and an aide, the program was still not created just for him. And few who vote for school bonds and new taxes are aware that there *are* students who have two employees with them almost all day.

The range of "special needs" is very great, and parents with children who have been in programs have been assured that the program was the only good way, the best way, the "no choice" way. It might take a while to regain the child's trust, but if a child can learn at his own pace, in his own way, without all the side burdens of transportation, avoiding tormentors, being pressured and tested and kept isolated, few to none of the school's trappings will be necessary.

I don't hate school. School was a haven of goodness for me when I was a kid. I don't want to glorify school, nor to promote and encourage any family life for which school, with all its frustrations and real dangers, is more desirable than home and family.

SandraDodd.com/unschool/difference

Seeing your child, rather than a label

If you are the parent of a child who has not been labeled anything past his own name, please try to keep it that way as long as you can, and once you see the importance of that, you might be able to maintain it until he's grown.

Dozens of parents have come to unschooling discussions insisting that the labels are good, that the labels don't hurt anything, that the parents don't *use* the label except in discussions with other parents, etc. In extreme cases the label is used without even a name. I knew a mom who called her children "our bio daughter" and "our Russian" and "our little Korean." Some moms have siglines on their e-mails that identify their children as "aspie" or "high-needs" or "gifted."

The parents have been assured that those labels "need" particular treatment or resources. They "have to" do this or that because their child is autistic, or has delayed speech, or has processing problems.

Here is the deal, about unschooling: Unschooling works the same way for any child, regardless of his particulars. Each child is met in the moment by a partner interested in making his day safe and interesting and in helping him do things he might like to do. If one wants to spin around for half an hour while another wants to take a radio apart and put it back together, that's not a problem.

If the parent finds ways to present options and choices and the children can say "Yes, more!" or "No more now," then each child will learn every day.

A label will put a wall of words and fears and filters between a parent and a child.

SandraDodd.com/words/without

Giftedness

Words, words.

Years have passed since I first objected to labeling a child "gifted." Years of my life, the lives of others who grew up with me, labeled and maybe wishing they had been, because the opposite of "gifted" is "not gifted"—*nothing special.*

My own first epiphany concerning labels, growth curves and permanence came one day when I went home from college and saw a friend I'd gone to school with since we were in elementary school. She was tall, no doubt about it. In fourth grade, she was taller than the teacher and taller than any of the boys in our class. Just tall. Really tall.

Years passed without me thinking of that label, and she stepped off her bicycle and was shorter than I am. I'm 5'4" so she was 5'2" maybe? Neither of us was tall. But I had never been tall, so there were no expectations on me. Nothing but the words in my own head made her short that day.

Expectations and "goals" and assumptions about other people are not direct seeing. They're not direct being. They're threats, and dares, and challenges, and relief and joy writ large, in dust.

Of course some people are better at things than others. Some can write a first draft and it's publishable. Some can make up a song and it's worthy of recording and selling. Some begin in the middle, even on their first day, of a sport or art or handicraft. Some think in patterns from birth, and so mathematics will seem obvious to them. Some dream in emotions and see people's hurts and potential whether they're raggedy and homeless or all dressed and made up and on stage. Psychology will seem elementary to them. Some have photographic memories, which is good if they're remembering a map, and bad if they've seen a serious injury. These things are not necessarily "gifts."

I believe that the idea of "talent" and "giftedness" comes from the Bible, and the idea that when God gives a person a gift, the person owes that service back to God. How that came to be measured by "IQ tests" and turned into government policy could probably fill its own book. The school didn't "gift" your child, though, and he doesn't owe the school.

To peek at school for a moment, there are gifted programs so that schools won't lose some of their students to private schools and so they won't be sued for failure to educate all their students (or that was some of the reason fifty years ago). Then there came to be teachers for the gifted and talented. That created jobs, programs, special equipment and more specialists. Those jobs need to be protected.

Turn away from school now, and back to your own children at home.

It is possible that a child who reads at the age of three will be tired of reading by the age of ten. It is possible that a child who first really reads at the age of ten will become a professor of literature and a great author.

A child who can recite prime numbers or reel off the infinitesimal pieces of pi might not be able to wipe his own ass. What kind of gift is that for anyone? It's just a thing, like being able to pogo stick for an hour, or to learn all the dialog and songs in "Monty Python and the Holy Grail." It will neither save nor destroy the world.

Parents complain about children living in fantasy worlds sometimes, and not growing up and facing reality. I think probably in every single one of those cases, it was the parental fantasy of what the child *ought* to be doing that was really the problem.

Now, unschooling: The principles of unschooling work the same way no matter how quick or slow or skewed-in-talent any particular child is. Helping each child do/see/experience what is near and interesting, helping him understand it if he's curious, leaving him alone until another time if he's not interested, will help each of those children to learn. Some might learn less in a day than you'd be happy to report. Some might learn more in a minute than you had ever known about some object/process/topic in your life. That first of those two might grow up to be rich and happy. The second one could be a crack whore someday. Don't take your "learning moments" to the bank.

Respect and acceptance are more important than test scores and "performance." Understanding is more important than recitation.

My recommendation is that if you have a child you're sure is fantastically superior to other beings, keep quiet about it. She might grow up to be literally or figuratively 5'2", if you're lucky enough that she grows up. Don't be so ecstatic now that you can't help but be disappointed in your children for being the people they are.

Many gifted children grow up to be "normal" or "average." In terms of the learning, growth and earning curve laid out for them by school and parents, they are failures. Normal is "failure." Extreme success isn't extreme success. It was to be expected, and the parents and teachers take credit for it.

When a once-labeled "average" child grows up to be a great success, some people will look askance, as though he cheated, or maybe they'll praise him in the backhanded insult ways: "I didn't think you had it in you!" or "None of us would have predicted this!"

It means "Pretty good for a guy who's not so bright."

If your child is having a slow week or month or year, don't worry. If your child is having a zippy brilliant period of life where everything's coming up roses and the backswell of music seems always to accompany his glorious exploits, don't expect that to last day in and day out for sixty years. It won't. It can't. It shouldn't. People need to recuperate from stunning performances.

Life is lumpy; let it be.

Make each moment the best moment it can be. Be where you are with your body, mind and soul. It's the only place you can be, anyway. The rest is fantasy. You can be here clearly, or you can live in a fog. Defog.

Here's a gift for you as a parent: Life will be better for all involved if you don't label your children's intelligence, or processing speed, or likelihood to reverse numbers, or ability to pay attention to something deadly boring. Don't drug your children into being still enough to sit on an assembly line. It has nothing on earth to do with natural learning or unschooling. Neither does "giftedness."

Many times parents have assured me that I just don't understand because I "obviously" have never had a gifted child. I don't argue with them. Some of them end up back in cahoots with school again, and others end up coming back and saying they wish they could undo having labeled one child over the others, or having treated a child differently because of a test score.

They would like to undo it, but they can't. Maybe it's not too late for you and your child.

SandraDodd.com/giftedness

Howard Gardner

Howard Gardner published *Frames of Mind* in the early 1980's, revolutionizing the way people see "IQ" and intelligence. Thomas Armstrong expanded that work into the field of education, recommending that teachers use different kinds of experiences. Unfortunately, some of that was diverted into educators (and home educators) trying to "identify learning styles" and going back to doing as little as they "had" to do for each student.

It can feel good to begin to understand the idea that there are other intelligences than verbal and mathematical, though. For those trying to understand themselves better, these ideas can be soothing and illuminating. Gardner wrote, "Knowledge is not the same as morality, but we need to understand if we are to avoid past mistakes and move in productive directions. An important part of that understanding is knowing who we are and what we can do... Ultimately, we must synthesize our understandings for ourselves."

Linguistic intelligence involves language use and understanding. It's not about multilingualism, though some people have a talent for learning other languages. Talent in one's own language is linguistic intelligence. Writers, poets, witty conversationalists, those who can win arguments or inspire others with words, or those who can learn well from ideas expressed in words (heard or read) are all showing linguistic intelligence.

Logical-mathematical applies not just to straight-out numbers, but to seeing and thinking in patterns, and of being scientific and analytical. Clarity of thought involves logical/mathematical intelligence as surely as being a number-whiz does.

Musical intelligence doesn't need to apply only to accomplished musicians. Appreciation and understanding of music, being moved by music, hearing tones and rhythms, as well as the ability to compose or create music fall into this category.

Bodily-kinesthetic covers dance, body-awareness, physical talents that might be used for sports or knot-tying or woodcarving or physical therapy. Some people are only slightly aware of how their bodies work and what their capacities are. Some people seem to be born knowing, or using their bodies well without even thinking about it.

Spatial intelligence—what's where, how far away, how does it fit together? Those who can solve physical puzzles or put things together that have fallen apart are probably high on this scale. Gift wrappers who can spot the right size of box and wrap it beautifully might not have considered it a special intelligence.

Interpersonal intelligence is about understanding other people—their non-verbal expressions, their motivations and desires and moods.

Intrapersonal intelligence is understanding one's self in those ways. How are you feeling and why? What are your capabilities and problems and fears and what will help you move toward goals?

Naturalist intelligence involves recognizing and categorizing things. Birds and clouds, certainly. Trees. But it also applies to flags, heraldry, automobiles, computer components... the ability to recognize a widget or a seed seems to involve the same skills.

Existential intelligence, or spiritual intelligence—this is under consideration and being discussed, but not fully accepted by Gardner and others yet.

A "kid-level" version used by Thomas Armstrong in his book *You're Smarter Than You Think*, and other places:

word smart	logic smart
music smart	body smart
picture smart	people smart
self smart	nature smart

"Picture smart" doesn't seem nearly sufficient for the 3-D modeling involved in spatial intelligence, though.

When I was in elementary school the lowest grades I got were in "conduct" or "deportment." Turns out my greatest gift was interpersonal, and I was able to help other kids with their problems. School didn't encourage that in those days in any way, and so once I had to write "Unnecessary talking in class disturbs others" 2400 times or so, and other times I just got a C in conduct for being too social. "You're not here to socialize," I was told. All the more ironic for me that most people's first question about homeschooling is "What about socialization?"

SandraDodd.com/intelligences

Abraham Maslow

Abraham Maslow, or Abram Maslow (same psychologist, different forms of his name), studied mental health rather than mental illness, which was a departure from most other research in those days.

Maslow discovered that people who are afraid don't want to eat. Those who are hungry can't learn. He wrote about what he called a "hierarchy of needs." The applicability to learning is that one's physical needs must be met before other things can be considered.

In schools, they used it to get funding for breakfast programs, and to show more patience with sleeping in class than had been shown in decades previous to the 1960's and 70's. School reformers figured someone tired enough to sleep couldn't learn anyway, so there was no sense punishing them or even waking them up.

After physiological needs, Maslow says people need to feel safe and secure. Next comes the set of belonging, affection, and positive regard.

The application to unschooling is that if the child isn't hungry, tired, afraid or feeling unloved, there should be no problem with curiosity and the desire to experience other things.

Next up the pyramid of Maslow's theory is feeling unique and well-regarded. Any time one gets tired and hungry, the other "needs" are less important. Once they've built back up through the fulfillment of the more basic needs, then they can think about their place in the world, and what they might like to do with their thoughts, words, time and energy.

SandraDodd.com/maslow

Piaget

Jean Piaget was a Swiss professor/scientist who studied how knowledge develops—how learning works. His "theory of cognitive development" is studied by aspiring teachers, psychologists and by parents. It's worth having a general idea of what he discovered.

The ages are general. Some children take longer at one stage than others, the same way some get taller sooner, some walk earlier, etc.

"Sensorimotor" stage, birth to two or three (some children longer): Children need to touch and play and see, and the feedback they need can be of a "getting warm" and "getting cold" nature: looks, encouraging or discouraging tone of voice. Don't expect them to understand anything complicated or to follow directions. One big thing babies learn after a while is "object permanence"—that parents or toys still exist even when they're out of sight. *It's peek-a-boo season!*

"Preoperational" stage, language use to the age of seven, more or less: Ideas begin to form about things that can't be seen. The names of things are sorted out, and differences and similarities are important to them. Speech can get ahead of concepts, though. A child who can talk about time in hours or days or weeks can't really conceptualize it or use it as well as he will later. Too often, parents expect too much of children this young. Try to respect their imaginary friends or their theories of how the world might work. Don't discourage their fantasies.

"Concrete Operations," age seven to puberty, give or take: Ideas start to be more realistic and logical. They might want to discuss things longer than the parents like. Parents should tough this stage out. A huge amount of learning is taking place, and the child's internal model of the universe is starting to form up. You can help!

What Piaget termed "Formal Operations," comes perhaps at puberty or at some point in adulthood. For one reason or another, some people don't develop logically as well or as early as others do. Don't worry about it, though. There won't be a test. And if Howard Gardner is right, then Piaget's set of developmental stages might only work ideally for those with a high logical intelligence.

Parents can make a big difference by helping children work through their thoughts and theories without scoffing or criticizing.

Awareness of this pattern of development can help parents avoid expecting young children to think in ways of which they are incapable, and avoid holding children responsible for "understanding" or "agreeing to" things they can't really comprehend.

Some parents will say, "I explained it and he said he understood." What probably happened was the child heard "blah blah blah blah, okay?" and said "Okay."

SandraDodd.com/piaget

Marty stabilized baby Holly in the sandbox. What a nice guy.

Subjects

Kirby was five and not going to go to school that year when I decided to keep the whole idea of a structured curriculum divided into subjects secret from him for a while. So we carefully and purposefully avoided using these terms: science, history, math.

He was too young for us to need to avoid terms such as "social studies" (which doesn't come up outside of school anyway) or "grammar," but I was prepared to rethink my list of terms to avoid as he got older, if he continued to stay home.

By the time his brother and sister were unschooling, some of those "names of subjects" (in school parlance) had been discovered on TV shows about school, or in jokes or songs. *Don't know much about history; don't know much biology...* By then, though, I was ready with confident answers, and we were all sure natural learning could work.

If you can avoid using school terminology, it will be helpful in many different ways that you will figure out if you don't already see them.

SandraDodd.com/subjects

History

Studying history in chronological order seems to make sense. It has the word "logical" in it and everything! But natural learning isn't chronological, nor is it distant or abstract. History is about how old your house is and why your town exists, and why it's where it is instead of ten or twenty miles another direction. History is about where your grandparents grew up and why, and if any relatives are or were in the military, why and where have they gone because of that and what did they do? (Keep details light and general on that, for young children.)

History is happening now. By the time you read this book, it will be a part of history that in 2009 Sandra Dodd tried to summarize the webpages she had started building a decade before that. If you read this a long time from now, you might add, "When Sandra Dodd was still alive…"

History is where your car came from, and what car you had before that, and how far back in your family it was when they didn't have cars, and what did they use?

History is why people in different places speak different languages. Why are there different accents in different parts of the same countries? Why are they speaking French in Québec and Louisiana? What's with Hawai'i? Why isn't South America all Spanish-speaking? What's with Brazil and Belize? How long did it take to get from Europe to those places back in the day? How long now?

Why are there milestones in Massachusetts? Why are there milestones in England? What the heck is a milestone? (OH! Milemarkers, like on the highways; road signs, like on the highways.) How did they measure miles in Roman-soldier days? Why are children said to "reach milestones"?

Why are the costumes better in newer movies than older ones? What's with the hairdos and make-up in movie westerns from the 1950's and 60's? 1980's? Why did cowboys wear bandanas?...

SandraDodd.com/history

Geography

Because of school, many people think of geography as maps and nothing more. There is a story in every line on every map. There's a story in the name of each nation and region, and in the difference between what they call themselves and what the neighbors call them. When a map is in a certain language, it affects the names of everything. The English word for "Germany" is not what will appear on a map in German, nor in French, nor in Icelandic. Looking at those names is a study in the history of Germany. People who speak any language in Europe have a relationship and history with what English speakers call "Germany" (which we have from the Roman "Germania").

Geography can be about people and what they do, and believe, and wear. It can be about mountains, rocks, rivers, and where the rivers empty. The stories around a river that flows to the Hudson Bay will be different from the stories of rivers that flow into the Mediterranean. And with what you know of language and history and geography, can you look at "Mediterranean" and figure out why they called it that?

What animals and plants are where and why? Who has oil, diamonds, gold, or uranium? Where do we get bananas, pineapples, oranges or dates? Why are some cities big shipping centers and others not? Where are the hub cities of railways and airlines and why? What parts of the world are crowded and which are relatively unpopulated? What makes a place dangerous for tourists?

Why are some places more technologically advanced than others, and what is lost when native knowledge and traditions are supplanted by high-powered this'n'that? Is it true the aborigines of Australia could once communicate telepathically? How did smoke signals work? What are "talking drums"?

How does weather prediction work? What knowledge did space travel add to knowledge of the planet we were already on?

SandraDodd.com/geography

Science

When one person says "I like science" and another says "I don't like science," I remember school science textbooks that had geology, astronomy, chemistry, botany, biology, agriculture and physics all in one book. And even if someone "likes animals," what does that mean? Biology covers so huge a field that few people could "like" all of it. Are they interested in bugs or in human anatomy? Redwoods or plankton?

If a child loves dinosaurs he might not (yet) care about chickens or jellyfish. Okay. But studying dinosaurs will involve geology, too, and geography. Studying dinosaurs directly uses chemistry and spectral microscopes, which comes back around to physics and chemistry.

Learning about the range of fibers from which thread or yarn can be made is science. Knowing how to polish silver or copper involves science, if one wonders how it works and what might keep the tarnish from returning so quickly.

"Scientific knowledge" changes, and so understanding is vastly more important than memorization. When I went to school a platypus was not a mammal. Now it is. Nothing changed about the platypus. Pluto? Not a planet. Messed up the song I learned.

Some people want to believe science "facts" without being scientific about it at all. What is "validity"?

There are many fun things to do and explore that could be called "science," but why not just call them skate boards or miniature golf or basketball or piano or water play or rescuing wounded birds or making goop or collecting rocks or swimming or drawing pictures of clouds or taking photos in different kinds of light or growing corn or training a dog or looking through binoculars or waiting for a chrysalis to open or making a sundial or making a web page or flying a kite or chasing fireflies or building a campfire or finding out which planet that is by the moon on the horizon, or wondering why snowballs take so much snow to make, or how a 4-wheel-drive truck works.

The fundamental core of science is learning, and by definition it should involve discovery! Learning directly and indirectly about what people know and how they know it and what they do with it that has been helpful and harmful to themselves and the planet is much more than just science. It's history, geography and ethics.

SandraDodd.com/science

Music

What I love most about music is the history of it, the physics of how the instruments work and the very different sounds they make. I like the mathematics of different keys, and the intervals that are "wrong" in western music but beautiful in Egypt or Japan. I love song lyrics. I love the similarities in religious music in different parts of the world. I love folk instruments like steel drums. Music associated with different wars or social movements can be mental triggers for dozens of things I might not have thought of if the song hadn't reminded me of what the musicians looked like and who danced to that music, and how, wearing what. Lyrics are the most practical use of poetry ever, and when a song is translated from or to another language, it's rare that it can mean the same thing and still be musical.

Learning about music can be as happy as dancing in the back yard, singing in the car, or going to watch a bluegrass band at a street festival. Listen to different oldies stations. Play with online song sites. Rent videos of concerts or operas and musical theatre. Don't "make" anyone watch them. Watch them yourself, and others might come to join.

You might visit music stores or pawn shops and see what they have up on the wall or in glass cases. There are video games involving music: Donkey Konga, Karaoke Revolution, Guitar Hero, Rock Band, Lips, Drum Mania (in arcades; the others are home games). Dance Dance Revolution is moving to music—rhythm and patterns are music, too.

A parent doesn't need to be a musician to bring more music into the house, or to take the family out to more music. Start finding music where it lives and breathes, and share stories about what you're hearing with your child just conversationally. Walk more slowly when you're around live musicians. Watch them. Listen.

There are games and music sites galore on the internet, and some are linked from:

SandraDodd.com/music

Art

When I was a kid we had art classes in school, and the most memorable lesson for me was repeating patterns, in 4th grade. We were designing something, maybe, like tile, or wrapping paper, or wallpaper, or cloth. Unclear. But I liked it.

A younger friend of mine went to school in England for a year and the art class was clearly commercial art. Each student designed a logo for an imaginary store, with a sign and a paper bag and a business card.

Most American students, when they hear "art," think "painting." That's less true of people in the rest of the world, as far as I know.

When children arrange their action figures or Barbies, they're doing what window dressers in stores do, and what moviemakers do when they storyboard a scene, and what theatre directors do when they decide on stage design.

Encourage your child to recombine clothing outfits, to organize toys in interesting ways, maybe to display clothing on a shelf or in a drawer in arrangements that create art even when they're not being worn.

Consider how the table is set when you eat, and how foods are arranged on trays or plates.

What's on and around your front door? What about photographs, blogs, giftwrapping, flowers (growing or cut and arranged), sculptures, or cartoons (animated or still)? Do you keep album, CD and DVD covers? (Some people don't; they keep the media in binders or cases.) Can you date photos somewhat by the frames of people's glasses, or their shoes or ties or hem lengths? Do you prefer busy picture books with more than you can see in one sitting, or books with one clear picture on each page and plenty of white space? Do you know more than one way to tie shoelaces? Have you ever used a scanner for anything besides paper? Ever photographed something flat?

When you're out and about, look at architecture, fences and gates, lamp posts. Consider automobiles—not just the overall form, but details like tail lights and rearview mirrors. Restaurant façades, décor, furnishings, dishes, presentation. What are the waiters wearing?

Newspapers, magazines or advertising flyers—look at advertisements and covers and layouts. Maybe for two seconds, maybe for half an hour. If your child isn't interested when it first comes up, she might be later on. What about books? Maybe you could judge a few books by their covers! Look at some older bindings, and newer ones if you have both or if you're at a library with older books. Look at the art in books from the early twentieth century, and from the 1950's or 1960s. Styles change. Printing technology changes.

Some families take sketch books with them on hikes and draw pictures of animals or plants, or maps, or take notes. They don't need to be great art, but if you practice recording what you see and think in ways other than words it will broaden your range of thought and abilities. And the updated version of the sketch book is the digital camera; the new field journal is the blog!

Maybe look at purses or wallets or shoulder bags. The shapes of intersections and overpasses and the railings on bridges. Public gardens and fountains. Street signs and traffic lights. The texture of concrete in different forms and uses. Wall coverings (paper or cloth; marble; paint; brick; tile…). Landscaping. Doorknobs and handles. Stairways and elevators. Waiting areas for the bus or train. Billboards and marquees. Clocks and watches. Hair clips. Key chains. Drinking glasses.

Even when more schools had art programs, they were limited. Unschoolers are not limited in their exposure to art in the vast everyday world.

Although it shouldn't be the starting or ending place, don't forget that the real world includes books and videos. There are museum sites online, too, with images of art you can zoom in on.

SandraDodd.com/art

Reading

Reading is one of "the three R's." People love it and fear it and misunderstand it. People will say things like "Once you can read, you can learn anything!" They didn't mean how to ride a bike, though, or to throw pottery, or to know which colors look best with teal or to tarp a truck. In school, children need to know how to read so they can see where to put their name on each worksheet, and so the schools feel justified doing what they're doing.

In school, young children read specially created, limited "reading level" materials. The parents feel good that their child is reading, but most of the children can't read a newspaper or recipe or menu. They can only read "school books" or "readers." Some of the children can't even read the readers. Some will never read regular outside materials.

When learning to read happens naturally, it doesn't look like school's reading lessons. It doesn't take years. It might take only days, but the tricky part is when those days will come. If you plant watermelons, picking at the leaves and threatening the vine will not get you a watermelon before one was going to naturally grow and mature. It's the same with children.

What parents can do by picking at and forcing and threatening a child is to keep him from ever wanting to read. They might persuade him that reading is hard, and certainly too hard for him. Or that he's lazy and "not a reader." They might happen to be "doing lessons" about the same time he figures reading out, and then they'll assure themselves and their child that the parents taught him to read; he couldn't have done it on his own.

Don't rob your children of the experience and of the knowledge that they can learn to read without help. If someone can learn to read, surely he can learn other things. I don't mean to say that after he learns to read he can learn other things by reading. I mean that reading is complex, moreso in English than some other languages, and if your child knows that he learned to read, he will have great confidence in his ability to learn. (So will his parents.)

SandraDodd.com/reading

But what if a child doesn't learn to read?

When I taught Jr. High, when I was young, there were kids who were 12 and 13 years old who couldn't read. I didn't know how to help them. There were reading specialists who knew a few tricks, but nothing that could undo six or seven years of failure in school, with six more already scheduled up ahead of them.

I have never known a single unschooler who didn't learn to read. One I know personally was a preemie, very slow to speak, slow with all language-related learning, but he was strong and coordinated and goodhearted and helpful. Had he been in school, the crushing of his spirit would have been a matter of the reading course. He was not in school, though. He might have done better had he not had a twin sister who was not premature, who was zippy-quick at learning those very things that came so slowly to him, but his mother was a marvel and he had many friends, my children among them.

When he was fifteen years old, reading clicked for him. He read novels immediately, and regularly thereafter. If you met him in a group of young adults you would be struck by his physical strength and appearance (he's a U.S. Marine, as was his dad), and by his confidence. You wouldn't know he "read late." It doesn't matter anymore.

This boy was at the community college one term when my oldest, Kirby, was too. They had known each other since they were babies. Neither went to school. Both received certificates at the end of the term, for being interested and interesting and doing what was asked of them. It wasn't a big deal for them, but compared to the other people their age and older who were at the community college, they were both impressing their instructors. And it didn't matter that one had read earlier than the other. While others were in reading classes every day for years and years and years, these guys were playing games, building things, running, climbing riding bikes, going to the zoo and the children's museum…

Unschooled children learn to read without fail, as far as I have seen over nineteen years of involvement.

SandraDodd.com/r/deeper

Where and how do unschoolers learn to read?

When Kirby, my oldest, learned to read in the early 1990's, it was from a player's guide for Nintendo games. When his brother, Marty, learned a couple of years later, it was from the player's guide to a particular video game called Breath of Fire III. Holly's reading didn't come as easily, but she was playing Harvest Moon, which had a great deal of reading, and we used to read it to her until she could read on her own. Holly's first "real reading" was a Judy Blume book. Her second reading choice was "The Body," by Stephen King. She bypassed all baby books and easy readers, as had her brothers.

Mine are not the only ones who have learned to read in the course of playing games, electronic or otherwise. Many learned from Pokemon cards, or Yu-Gi-Oh. Some have liked subtitles on DVDs. Some have watched others read to them and caught the code from seeing and hearing the words, without "lessons" or phonics drills or memorized rules.

SandraDodd.com/game/reading
SandraDodd.com/r/threereaders

Yeah, but...
Here are some quotes from the dozens of accounts you may read on my site if you wish to.

From Yorkshire:
"My 10 year old hard-of-hearing son, who I was told would never learn to read by osmosis cos of his hearing loss is reading! He learnt from Runescape and his Xbox he plays daily. He read off the screen to me today cos he wanted to tell me what it said."

Southern California:
"I've been amazed at how quickly reading progresses when they're ready—one of my kids went from barely reading to reading Harry Potter and the Little House books in what seemed like overnight."

New Mexico:
"Then something happened. I have no idea what. They both just started reading. Maybe it was the incentive of online chatting. Maybe it was long boring days at home. Maybe it was just the right time, and the parts of their brains that can process the written word had a growth spurt. It doesn't matter."

Others:

"Pokemon was the rage...and his birthday gift of a GameBoy was all it took. He sat in his room for about three days playing furiously...came out for air only to eat...and in those three days he learned to read well enough that the first book he read cover to cover was one about the stock market a few days later. His first required test from our school district placed him in the 99th percentile. All that worry for nothing!"

"I completely credit the computer game, The Sims, for my daughter's discovery and love of reading."

"When my friend's son was around 10, she told him that she had a really sore throat and that any more reading that night would have to be done by him. (As far as she knew, he wasn't yet reading.) He picked up the (hard) book and started reading. When she looked at him in shock and asked him when he had learned to read he said, 'I only just figured out that I could.'"

"Did I mention our friend who could read Harry Potter before she learned the names of all of the letters? As a matter of fact, I'm still not sure she knows all of the names."

"Rosie was reading Shakespeare—we were all involved in a Shakespeare company production—*before* she knew all the letter names and sounds. She could read the script—she could read it with great expression—having learned it by reading along with the actors, in rehearsal after rehearsal."

"Jared is intensely interested all of the sudden, and he's READING!! I do trust natural learning. I do, I do. But to see a child go from reading almost nothing, to reading whole sentences virtually overnight has been most amazing to me."

"My older son began reading just before he turned nine. Within six months he finished *Robinson Crusoe*."

SandraDodd.com/reading
(There are several links with such stories.)

Thoughts on How to Read, and Why

Someone wrote about having learned in school that fast reading was good reading. A recent discussion came to mind—whether juggling three balls elegantly and with originality is inferior to juggling five balls.

Is speed reading good? What IS "reading"? It's not such an easy question. School measures reading speed and comprehension separately. If it's possible to read without comprehension, then I can read Spanish and French and maybe German. I haven't tried, but if I could sound out German at a pretty fair clip, would that be reading? What if I could just run my eyes left to right, line by line, and *think* the sounds of German. Would that be reading?

When I was a kid in the 1960's, there were advertisements everywhere for Evelyn Wood Speed Reading. It's still there, and the site says "Finish the newspaper in five or ten minutes. Page through magazines, reports, and trade publications in record time. Polish off entire books in one sitting."

If one "polished off" *Pride and Prejudice* in one sitting, she would miss descriptions of countryside, and clothes. If one polished off *Lord of the Rings*, I'm sure he would have missed Tolkien's descriptions of sounds and thoughts.

At speed-reading rates, no doubt some people finished this page LONG ago, two seconds, went on to other things. Comprehension? Good enough for some.

If life is all competition, then finishing first is "winning," when the stopwatch is out. But what if the goal is thinking new thoughts, and enjoying the artistry of someone else's words? What if it were museums we were talking about? Would moving through an art museum and seeing all the paintings and sculptures in fifteen minutes be better than taking two hours? What if someone could train you to retain memories of what you had seen, and to comprehend it, even though you had walked as fast as you possibly could have and looked as briefly as possible at what took the artist months or years to create? Would you "win"?

Forget the hoity-toitiness of da Vinci and Jane Austen. How about a car show? If you run through the lot and see all the restored antique cars faster than anyone else *ever has*, are you better at going to car shows than those who look closely at details and talk to the owners?

Another speed-reading site offered this promise:

> "Whether it's novels, newspapers, magazines, or just any materials, reading can be very relaxing, interesting and often, breathtaking."

If someone doesn't read well enough to be fluent, reading won't be very relaxing or breathtaking, that's true. Maybe the speed reading courses are more to get people who went to school and were told they could read to the point that they're *actually* reading, in a fluent and relaxing way.

SandraDodd.com/r/speed

When is reading "REAL" reading?

Schools assert that children are reading at six, or seven, and George Bush's advisors thought that a presidential edict can guarantee that all children read by eight, but if they can only read at school (meaning they can read the lessons and the "readers" their reading group is memorizing at school, or can read other materials carefully constructed to contain the same few dozen words) is it really reading?

Yes, and no.

Yes, for the school's grading purposes the child has mastered (or probably "passed") the reading lessons put forth. But for most English speakers' definition of "reading," they are not reading.

Homeschooling parents get frustrated and press their children out of fear of comparison to schooled children, but it's quite possible that the parents don't remember (stress and trauma will do that) being six or seven, and what they could and could not independently read. Parents can be intimidated (sometimes pointedly) by professional teachers and their proclamations about how reading works.

Sometimes I've been criticized for saying that I won't say my child is reading until he or she can pick something up and read it. Not something I planted and that they've practiced, but something strange and new. If I can leave a note saying "I've gone to the store and will be back by 10:30," and if the child can read that, then I consider that the child is reading.

Others want to say "My child is reading" if he can tell Burger King's logo from McDonald's. I consider that more along the lines of distinguishing horses from cows. Yes, it's important, and yes, it can be applied to reading, but it is not, itself, reading.

Schools have a term for this preparatory, related stuff: "reading readiness." And many of their six- and seven-year-old students are "getting good grades in reading" because they're cooperative during reading-readiness drills.

If parents are unaware of this, they will waste emotion and energy worrying or pressuring young children about reading. The problem is, reading is something that can take years of slow development. It requires some maturity of mind and body.

My recommendation to worried parents is to smile and hold your child lovingly and to do no damage to his happiness while you're waiting for the day he can really read.

SandraDodd.com/r/real

Phonics and Whole Language

Schools have experimented over the years with phonics and with what they call "whole language." Children have been taught to read by sight, by the shapes of words, and by learning phonics rules and sounding words out.

None of those is the magic one-and-only or best way, because different children learn differently, and because English is one of the worst languages for learning phonetically.

Because phonics treats written English as a simple code when it is not, many children are frustrated very early on.

Whole language involves language as communication, rather than separate parts (writing/reading/spelling). First language; details later.

With unschooling, children will learn from the language you use and they use, from the words they see around them, from using games and computers, from signing greeting cards or playing with words. There's no need for any school-style structure at all. For those who have worried about phonics and reading and spelling, please don't press that on your children.

Some languages are simpler than English in that the letters and sounds match pretty consistently. French and Spanish come to mind. German. But because of something that happened in 1066, and because of the history of The British Isles, and because of the isolation of some English speakers and the migration of many others, English has complexities and a crazy-large vocabulary. Our basic grammar and language are Germanic. The majority of our vocabulary is from French (look up 1066 if you don't remember what happened) and Latin, though the everyday words we use are from Anglo-Saxon, which had borrowings from half a dozen early dialects of various early Germanic tribes.

If that was a painful paragraph to read, never mind it. If it was fun, then you can help your children spell by looking up what language a word is from and figuring out why it looks the way it does in written English.

If you have games or books at home that deal with phonics, that won't hurt as long as you tell the kids those "rules" don't always work. And if you do no phonics at all, the kids will figure out the patterns on their own.

SandraDodd.com/phonics   SandraDodd.com/spelling

Writing

Because it's a "three R's" term, most people assume they know what they mean by "writing," but most of them haven't thought about it.

When people ask me "What about writing?" I ask "What do you mean 'writing'?"

The first reaction is often irritation with me for not understanding a simple question. I've taught writing. I know what it is. I want to know if my questioner has thought about it nearly as much as I have.

Writing ranges from endorsing a check to writing a novel, and from lettering place cards for a wedding to creating a stirring toast. People write to persuade, to strike fear, to explain, to sell. People write to inquire, to request a job interview, and later to quit the job. People write recipes and directions. Policemen write traffic tickets. Legislators write laws. Graffiti artists write in code sometimes, it seems, and in color, and with depth.

When you think about writing, think past the word to what your real concern is. Handwriting/Penmanship? Forming letters and copying is a kind of writing. Putting one's name on one's own things is a kind of writing.

E-mail involves writing. Some young people don't use e-mail; it's old-timey already. They use text messaging, and maybe instant messages online. There are online games that can be played with writing. Sometimes there's an option of using a head set or typing messages in text at the bottom of the gaming screen.

Much of the exchange of information among unschooling parents is on e-mail discussion lists or on message boards or on "social networks." That sort of writing is very real, and can be quick, but there is an option to edit before sending (and occasionally shortly after sending).

Text and instant messages are real and immediate, writing in real time. This is not something I was ever taught in school, but my children are all very good at it without "training"—simply from having access to the tools, an interest, and the opportunity to practice.

SandraDodd.com/writing

Book Reports; School Reports

Sometimes what parents explain they mean by writing is writing reports. Then I ask "a report to whom?" And once again they're stuck.

"They won't learn to write reports," I hear. Perhaps they will have nothing to report. If they do, they will report it.

Book reports in school are a horror for all involved. If your children are home and have read a book because they wanted to, I'm pretty sure they'll discuss it with you if you ask, and maybe if you don't. Holly sometimes talks about books she read years before, or picks one up to read it again, because she thought of it. I have never once assigned a book or pressed a child to read one nor tried to obtain proof that they finished and understood a book.

When I taught English it was on the list of things to do, to encourage them to read books and then ascertain their compliance. So I used to sit down with the child and the book and talk about it, one-on-one. Even that is more than unschoolers need to do, ever.

How do you know if your friend has read a book, or your spouse or your mom? I doubt you ask them to report.

There is a place, though, where people write real reports, regardless of age: the internet. Readers' sites such as Amazon.com, WeRead.com, and LibraryThing.com don't ask how old their readers are. There are movie reviews and commentary on sites that rent or sell DVDs. Video game players will know of places to read reviews about new games or peripherals from third-party vendors. Gamers read (and write) "walkthroughs." Ask one what that means if you don't know.

Yet parents whose children are involved in those things will ask how unschoolers learn to write, or whether they can write a report.

The first report Kirby wrote was when he was fourteen. It involved a summary, an inventory, and recommendations for a schedule for future purchases, concerning the Pokemon League at the gaming store where he worked. He didn't have a problem writing it, because he was reporting what he actually knew to people who needed to know it. That was a real report, with a purpose and an audience.

School reports are practice reports. They are people reporting on things they don't know or care about, to people who didn't want to know anyway.

SandraDodd.com/myths (halfway down)

Letters

In the 1950's, my granny used to worry that I wouldn't know how to milk a cow or use a fountain pen. Fifty years later, people worry about whether kids will know how to write a paper letter, get it properly into an envelope, get the address on there, buy a stamp and mail it.

I learned to use a fountain pen, and a dip pen too, and to do calligraphy, but that was because I wanted to, not because I needed to. If one of my kids gets the urge to write a formal letter in a traditional format they can use Google to find a sample to follow. They understand format and folding, and envelopes with addresses and stamps on them come in the mail all the time, so they could use one of those as an example.

Letters can be wonderful things, but forcing a child to write a letter is a step toward having a child who will not willingly write letters later. And the world is moving away from writing and mailing paper letters, slowly but surely.

Handwriting

The term used for forming letters carefully and artistically, when I was in school, was "penmanship." That's a great old word. My own mother had beautiful, by-the-book penmanship. I remember some of my friends and teachers whose cursive writing was glorious.

For most purposes anymore, people are asked to block print anyway, when they're not being required to "input data" with a keyboard, or recite and spell it to an "input clerk."

Stressing over penmanship in the 21st century is like worrying about whether a child will know how to yoke an ox, or crank-start a Model T. Your kids don't even need to know how to use a cassette player.

SandraDodd.com/handwriting

Cursive writing vs. printing

Last things first: Pam Sorooshian, who teaches at a college, brought a note to the Always Learning list recently:

> Pam: That reminded me ... only 15 percent of students who took the recent SAT college entrance exams wrote their essays in cursive. The rest printed.
>
> Sandra: Are they marking down for it? REALLY interesting.

Pam: No marking down. I know someone who was a grader. She said the graders are thrilled–the printing is easier to read, in general.

"But cursive is faster," you might think or say. That's what John Holt thought. He thought it because that was the justification given to him as a child when people taught cursive (though he was old enough to have used fountain pens not just for fun).

In his book *Learning All the Time*, John Holt tells of having taught fifth grade and having explained to them what he "knew" about cursive writing. But three of those ten- and eleven-year-old children could print faster than the teacher could write in cursive. They raced. They timed it more than once. He discovered he was the fourth fastest writer in the room.

Holt wrote, "Later I learned that school cursive, called in my day Palmer penmanship, had evolved from an elaborate decorative script invented for engraving in copper, a very slow and painstaking form of writing that had nothing to do with speed. Someone, somewhere, decided that it would be nice if children learned to write like copperplate engraving, and the rest, as they say, is history."

Later he raced the clock against himself and discovered that his own printing, even after decades of cursive writing, was faster than his own cursive, so he took to printing, except for his signature.

I have friends in their twenties who went to school and who can't read most of the cursive writing they see around them. Life is changing. Don't worry if your children don't want to learn cursive, and don't be surprised if at some point in their teens they do want to learn it.

SandraDodd.com/cursive

Language Arts

What's that, "Language Arts"? It's a school term for what "English teachers" will be teaching, in an "English class," to people who already speak English. It includes oral and written language arts. Artsy language arts. Reading, understanding, appreciating and perhaps creating different forms of language manifestations. (That's not the wording of any professional educator, not counting me myself.)

An easier definition is "Playing with and using words."

Poetry

Poetry can be studied for years or appreciated in passing. I wouldn't press it, but it might help if the parents are on the lookout for possible strewing opportunities. Many young boys love Shel Silverstein books because they're both cute and gross. Mother Goose rhymes are available in many editions with beautiful art. Song lyrics might be the most accessible and common poetry in these early-twenty-first-century days, and they're easily found with a web search. Don't trust every text you find. Check it against your favorite recording and be open to slight variations.

"Aural poetry" is poetry beautiful for the sound of the words in the air. Reading sonnets aloud was popular in Jane Austen's day, and it might return again, but you might try poetry for bedtime reading sometimes. One easy introductory source might be *The Sneetches and Other Stories*, by Dr. Seuss, or *Yertle the Turtle*. The stories have depth, and the words are fluid and beautiful.

"Visual poetry," or word art is newer to the world of language arts. Until the 1970's or so, it was prohibitively expensive to put illustrations in grammar or language arts books, but now images are plentiful in books and on the internet. You will find animated word art, too, online.

SandraDodd.com/smallwords

Theatre

Just as music doesn't live on paper, theatre doesn't live in a script. Find opportunities to see puppet shows, plays, or musicals, live and on video.

Follow your children's cues about finding more things, or different, or waiting a while.

In school theatre classes, there are discussion of the physical layout and facilities of Greek, Elizabethan and modern theatres. They talk about the audiences and purpose of the performances, and related traditions. They discuss particular genres of plays, but probably won't talk about musical theatre. That would be the music department's job.

As your children aren't in school, though, you don't need to carefully sort out the opera from musical theatre from plays with incidental music. Everything's connected.

Speech and Debate

Formal debate societies and competitions are on the wane, but it's worth knowing they used to be very common. Presidential debates and some other political processes still are structured with timed presentations and rebuttals. Court trials have similar structures and rules/limitations. When this comes up naturally, it will help if the parents have some knowledge of the terminology and history.

Speech is still very useful, but doesn't need to be "taught." One way to practice is by speaking on video, and watching to see whether one's speech is rushed or clear, or hesitant. Many digital cameras and some cellphones have video capability. A MacBook with Photo Booth can be used, too, and the videos can be easily deleted.

If you or your children become especially interested, there is an organization called Toastmasters that provides ideas and the opportunity to speak to other members, at meetings that also involve buying a meal (generally, as they meet in restaurants, sometimes for early breakfasts).

As to debate itself, that has effectively moved onto blogs, discussion lists, radio and television. Casual conversations about the talents and tricks of various writers or speakers can be illuminating and entertaining, and will help you or your children if and when you are moved to jump in and defend unschooling or something.

Fiction

Writing fantasy stories is fun for children, but if they're telling them rather than writing them down, don't worry about it. Maybe you could write down what they've told you so it can be kept for the future. Pressing a happy, playing child to stop and write isn't good for the happy, the playing, or the writing.

Within "fiction" are historical novels, fairy tales and fables, mythology, science fiction, short stories and novels of all other sorts, manga and graphic novels, screenplays...

Non-Fiction

The dreaded "expository writing" you might remember from school can be put in simpler, smaller words. "Exposition" is showing (exposing), telling or explaining. Writing a game walkthrough or the directions to your house are the kind of non-fiction writing schools call "exposition." Magazines, newspapers, book reviews, *TV Guide*, descriptions of albums on iTunes—all of those are expository writing. I don't want to spook you, but you're reading exposition right now. Don't be afraid.

Vocabulary and Spelling

"Vocabulary" is another big Latin word for a concept that doesn't need to be so intimidating. All the words a person knows are his vocabulary. All the words about music are musical vocabulary. Learning more words or caring more about the ones you already have is what vocabulary is all about.

All children collect words and add to their collections. Help keep it fun and lighthearted, rather than weighty and intimidating.

SandraDodd.com/spelling

History of English

English has a more interesting history than many other languages have, and if you dip into those stories sometimes it will shed light on why English has such a variety and number of words.

Just looking up where the word "English" came from and what it means will get you started. English is one of many languages that came from early Germanic, but because a mixed-Germanic-language land was conquered by the Norman French (who had another part-Germanic but mostly Romance/Latin-based language), our common words and grammar are "Germanic," but a majority of our "fancy" words are from French and Latin.

Parents don't need to know all of that, but as it's all made of geography and history, it will come up from time to time.

Some fun word-toys for beginners are the names of the months and of the days of the week. Place names and people's surnames are also fun to take apart and compare.

SandraDodd.com/etymology

Traditional forms

There are folksongs, nursery rhymes, children's games, "sayings" (in Spanish, "dichos")—proverbs, or everyday commentary recited in the same way for generations. Traditional riddles and jokes will come up in the course of normal days, and each could be a source of other connections, if you or your children are interested in looking such things up.

This section of the book is a little menu or preview. My website is the feast, with links to other word-festivals online.

SandraDodd.com/language

Two bits written in other years, about

Shakespeare

2003: ~~This week~~ [Once upon a time], Marty, a macho 14-year-old American boy, watched Othello with me.

I studied Othello in college, meaning it was one of the plays I had to read and talk about and pass a test on. Then I saw it when it came out with Lawrence Fishburne and Kenneth Branagh. I haven't watched the other two Othello movies.

So... I had read it once in the 70's, seen a movie in the early 80's, and that was all. Seems like a lot. (Plus all my familiarity with other Shakespeare plays, and being raised reading the King James Bible, and the cherry on the top of "I have an English degree.")

So I asked Marty if he wanted to watch it with me since it has Lawrence Fishburne. Marty and I have been Lawrence Fishburne fans since he was Cowboy Curtis on PeeWee's Playhouse, and we rooted for him in Searching for Bobby Fisher, and so Marty said "Sure."

I warned him it wasn't a happy play. Definitely a tragedy.

Well. Marty understood what was going on perfectly well. He learned the characters' names as it went. He was having NO trouble. A couple of times when it seemed least like English I'd look at him or ask him if he got that, and he had.

He made comments that were as good as anybody would have made. He talked about Iago being the main character, and I thought about saying "antagonist" and "protagonist," but decided not to. We watched half and quit 'til the next day.

I talked to Keith about it. He said "Well, it's because they've been exposed to Shakespeare their whole lives, and nobody's told them it's supposed to be hard." I told him I hadn't said "antagonist," but maybe I should the next day.

What I HAD said (I told him) was "But if they called it 'Iago the Shit,' it would have given away the story." He said it might be because they want to focus on good guys instead of glorifying evil.

So the next day we made an especially good lunch and sat down with it to watch the rest.

Oh! The night before, after we had quit, I put on the Reduced Shakespeare Company, right to the Othello part, and showed Marty up to the part in the movie we'd seen. It was funny, but I turned it off before they would give away what Marty didn't know. He had been about to go up and play video games, but said he would stay to see that. It was two minutes or less.

Then he said, "Do they do ALL the plays?"

"Not really. They do all the histories as a football match, and they combine the comedies into one big story."

"Do they do Hamlet?"

"Yeah."

"I want to see it."

Hamlet's the longest one, but he said yeah, he'd rather see that and then go play.

By the time Hamlet was over, Kirby was back and took over his own video game, but Marty didn't really mind.

That was a pretty great Shakespeare "happening." It was more fun for me to see it with Marty than alone.

After we watched the second half, Marty watched quite a bit more of the comedy disk.

They were both rented and have been sent back, but I recommend if anyone has Netflix getting that "Complete Works of Shakespeare" by the Reduced Shakespeare Company.

I saw them perform in Albuquerque the year before they went permanent in England, but as explained on this DVD, they have three companies, one in London and two touring. The commentary track is interesting, and there's a video (one camera home video) of one of their shows many years ago at a Renaissance fair in California, where they used to do Hamlet and Romeo & Juliet separately and then pass the hat. One of the guys has been doing this for twenty years now. A Renaissance Fair skit became a lifelong career.

Somewhere in there I had a momentary flash of Marty becoming a Shakespeare scholar or professor or actor. WEIRD. Marty is *not* the kind of guy I would think would want to go academic, but he understood that effortlessly, and discussed it intelligently.

It didn't hurt that the acting was good and the enunciation was clear.

2004: Having just watched Pride and Prejudice (again, the BBC mini-series which is on DVD) with Colin Firth, the first thought that popped into my mind was to recommend that everyone here immediately rent or buy the DVD called "Black Adder: Back and Forth." It was the last (most recent, maybe not always last) installment of the Black Adder series, involves time travel, and Colin Firth plays Shakespeare.

I like Black Adder, and Colin Firth, and Shakespeare.

Of my kids, none fear Shakespeare. When Marty stayed with Anne Ohman's family, they saw a production of The Tempest, with an actor who's a friend of Anne's and Marty had met him beforehand. As soon as Marty got into the hotel room at the conference, he told me lots about it, and showed me the program. When we were packing to leave, he couldn't find that program, and was as close to grouchy as he had been all weekend when I didn't know where it was either. We searched, it was located (in my pile of papers) and he was happy again. He's talked to me about the play a couple of times since then. I have a Classic Comics or some other kind of illustrated version of it, and I intend to locate that and leave it on Marty's bed at some point soon.

But "studying" Shakespeare is quite different from enjoying and appreciating Shakespeare if my kids are any indication.

Another wonderful thing to get if you yourself are afraid of Shakespeare or marred by previous "exposure" or you didn't have much exposure and would like more is "The Complete Works of William Shakespeare," also on DVD, by The Reduced Shakespeare Company. There are only two plays they do at length, but they... well, you'll see.

Luckily for us all, we can see Shakespeare in our own homes, done by professionals, and we can pause or rewind or fast forward, we can eat chocolate chip ice cream or hamburgers (neither of which were known to anyone at The Globe Theatre), sit on soft couches with kids in our laps, have subtitles playing... I love DVDs. And I'm grateful to anyone who has ever made a film of Shakespeare. Netflix has a DVD of some of the earliest silent movies of Shakespeare plays. Sometimes it's only one scene of a play, and some were very experimental things with interesting special effects.

I can't leave this without a curtsy to Kenneth Branagh, or without telling you that he is mentioned in the conversation between Black Adder and Shakespeare in *Back and Forth*.

SandraDodd.com/shakespeare
SandraDodd.com/strew/Shakespeare

This was written for the German magazine *Unerzogen*,
and appeared in their 4/2008 edition (Fall 2008)

Mathematics

"But what about algebra?"

I think that's the second-most-asked question, after "What about socialization?"

Years before we had children, I was telling my young husband-to-be that in school the only math I liked were the "word problems." He said those are the *only* real math problems in text books. That was the real math. The numbers sitting already in equations and formations were the solutions to unstated problems, with only the arithmetical calculations left to be done.

I remember that moment vividly. I was in my late 20's and hearing for the first time what "mathematics" meant. I had asked my teachers all through school "What is this for?" and "How is this used?" and they rarely had an answer beyond "Just do it," or "It will be on the test."

Another ten years passed, and we were starting to homeschool our first child, in the way John Holt advocated, without formal instruction, without a curriculum, but by finding learning all around us.

We have three children who have not been to school. As I write this, they are 22, 19 and 17 years old, but when we started unschooling, they were five, two, and about-to-be-born.

I think in words. My husband, now an engineer, has always thought in patterns. We both play instruments, sing and read music, which involves patterns, proportions and complex graph-reading in real time. Genetics do play a part in the talents and intelligences a child will have, but then nurture can enhance or harm his development.

I had been a teacher of language arts when I was young, and in college had studied English, psychology and anthropology. New research has come out affecting the way intelligence is considered, largely by Howard Gardner and his theory of multiple intelligences.

In thinking of mathematics, I operated on the assumption that our children might be more pattern-oriented than I am (spatial and logical intelligences) and that they might be more word-dependent than my husband. We provided games involving patterns—board games, video games, dice, cards, and singing games—and played them with the children. One of the most memorable games was Bazaar, a game with exchange rates and values but requiring no numbers or reading. (In Germany there is a similar game called Bierbörse.) Math was a fun part of the fabric of life. It was the structure of games and of music and of Lego and Ramagon. We talked about proportion and perspective in art and construction, but only in words, not with numbers. They found patterns; I found patterns, and we shared them without me saying "this is mathematics."

Deductive reasoning was covered early, when I helped them figure out how to pass the bonus round on Super Mario 3 with the charts in the player's guide. What seemed to be a random matching game only had eight permutations, and they were all shown in the book. I copied that page and mounted it on cardboard. We kept it near the TV. They all learned how to choose their first plays in ways that revealed which pattern it was, and then turn all 18 cards without error. It didn't need terminology. When they heard the terms years later, they had something to tie it to.

They grew up with exposure, context, experiences and knowledge of those things mathematics is designed to describe. Our oldest son, Kirby, worked in a games store from the time he was fourteen, and was running tournaments for Pokemon, Magic the Gathering and other such structured strategy games, in the store and at hotels in town for several years. The knowledge required to play those games and even more to organize, judge and score tournaments, is huge.

When Kirby was 18 he took his first math class, at the community college. Like a musician who can't read music, he was baffled at first, but once he understood the notation, he soared, and had the highest test score in the class.

To some people reading this, it might seem there was no "higher math," but what we have done is create a home in which algebraic thinking is a standard part of conversations. Our interactions are analytical and involve factors and projections. They see the concepts and they use them.

Meanwhile, in school, children their age have been plowing through rows and rows of solutions to unnamed problems, preparing themselves for the long-gone days when calculations had to be done by men seated in rows doing arithmetic. Half of those in school have been declared below average. A third or so have been declared average. They will fear and avoid math for the rest of their lives. Very few have been told they are "good at math," and most of those probably don't really understand it.

If you took a group of those who made top marks in algebra, for example, and put them in a room and asked them to give you examples of algebra in everyday life, they would probably have no idea. They know what equations look like on paper, but they don't see it in the world. When I overheard my sons at the ages of 9 and 11 figuring out how long it would take them to save both of their weekly allowances to get an expensive game, and how long it would take if they combined their allowances disproportionately as opposed to if both contributed equal amounts, and who would own what percentage of the game if they went the quicker route over the equal-shares route, I knew that mathematics was neither scary for them nor difficult, and later experiences have confirmed that.

Because of the discount Kirby got at the gaming shop, he learned to calculate 30% (and so 70%) of any number. His discount for things he bought for gifts was 15%, which was already what he was using to tip at restaurants.

When he was 15, two notable things happened. He had been sent to a regional Magic tournament to run a sales table for the store. He sold things all morning without the cash register he was used to having. He was figuring sales tax in his head (5.8% or so), and was creating a tax chart on scrap paper. I picked him up at lunch to carry the cash to the bank and to take him back to the hotel, because he couldn't drive yet. He told me in the car that they were going to bring him a tax chart that afternoon. He hadn't known such things existed. They were bringing him a calculator, too. Most people would have said hours before that, "I can't work without a calculator and a tax chart," but Kirby just did it, because he wasn't afraid. He had not gone to school to learn that math is difficult.

That same year, he was overheard explaining to some other teens at the gaming shop how to multiply by 18—to do it by 20, and subtract two for each one you have. No pencil, no paper, and his school-labeled "learning disadvantaged" friend totally understood his explanation. The adults who overheard this expressed amazement. The other homeschoolers who heard about it were amazed that adults had been amazed (and came and told me about it).

Kirby is now 22 and works for Blizzard Entertainment, in Austin, Texas. I called him about this article and we talked about math's applications in his life. He talked about running Magic tournaments in those game-store years, and the considerations involved in planning to finish a tournament within the allotted time. He talked about things I didn't understand—elimination systems and "Swiss rounds" in which wins and losses all receive points. He talked about the logistics of styles of play, and of the social factors in running tournaments and in teaching karate (which he also did as a teen). "It's not enough to know how it could or should play out, because there are human factors that will affect the time required," he said. "I apply the same things with my job now, helping manage a team."

Unschooling is simple but not easy, and it's not easy to understand, but when math is a normal part of life then people can discover it and use it in natural ways and it becomes a part of their native intelligence. All that's left is for them is to learn the notation, later, when they need to.

SandraDodd.com/math
*a link to the German translation is there, too
and in the archives at unerzogen-magazin.de*

SandraDodd.com/intelligences

"Methods"

Some unschoolers say, "Unschooling is not a method of homeschooling." Others say, "Unschooling is a form of homeschooling."

Can it be a form without being a method? Does it matter? Is that "just semantics"?

Unschooling is a form of homeschooling; it's a way to homeschool. The method is to create and maintain a full-time learning environment in which learning happens at home and away, from as many sources as the family comes across.

There are many more bad definitions of unschooling out in the world than good ones. Here's a description that's getting it wonderfully right, but goes bad at the end: "The philosophy behind the unschooling approach is that the child learns and retains much more when allowed to follow interests, share in real life experiences and exploration. The adults within this approach recognize how imperative it is for children to have access to the things that interest them. Because of this, the unschooled parent is always seeking materials, classes, and other teachers that can take the child to deeper depths and broader horizons."

I read it thinking at first Yes, Yes! and then *ACK!*

If real-life experiences and exploration are "getting warm," why the jump back to "always seeking materials, classes, and other teachers"? "Other" teachers suggested that the unschooling parent is teaching. I help people learn all the time without "teaching them."

If there is a method to unschooling it's certainly not a simple one. It involves changing one's stance and viewpoint on just about everything concerning children and learning. That's not "a method." That's a life change.

There are aspects of method in the period of seeming-madness that leads to clarity.

SandraDodd.com/unschool/definition

Curriculum

The word "curriculum" is from a Latin word meaning a course, as for horse racing. So a "college course" is a path from a starting point to a finish line. Course and curriculum both have to do with a pre-determined trail that the horse, hound or student should stay on to the end.

Unschooling is a departure from a curriculum, but not a rejection of everything that could be seen along that course through the meadows and woods.

Based on the successes of the Winchester and Ford assembly lines, American schools wanted to have interchangeable parts too, so that children who moved to another district or state could still "get an education." If all third graders were learning the same things in all their courses, then a third grader could be moved from one assembly line to another. This plan never quite worked, because states and districts are always tweaking their courses, because one teacher might love poetry and another prefer prose, and so even children in the same school didn't learn the very same things.

No one needs an assembly line to make a single item, nor to educate a single child. Rather than seeing the curriculum and then trying to wrap that around your child, or insert all the parts, it works better to see your child and help him learn as part of a busy life, considering occasionally whether maybe you should introduce other topics into his life, or introduce him to other people, places and things. This can be done casually, though, and doesn't need to be scheduled or methodical.

If "at the end" (let's say for the moment that "the end" is one's 19th birthday) one horse has finished the course and another horse has meandered through the valleys and hills, followed rivers and crossed them, wandered by the track and watched, explored, rested in the shade... which horse "won"?

If "at the end" means at the age of 30, it will depend on the individuals. Few people know or care which 30-year-old graduated from high school early, late, or not at all.

If "at the end" means retirement or death, then what a child was reading or doing at the age of ten or fifteen hardly matters anymore at all.

That all having been said, a few unschoolers have written unschooling in the style of a curriculum, and you can find that on my site. Pam

Sorooshian has written an elementary and secondary description. Carol Narigon wrote one for Ohio's requirements, and Melissa Dietrick has adapted that one into an Italian version. Another mom named Shell sent her version, which she submitted to the Ministry of Education of New Zealand. I've provided those, but they should be kept for emergency and formal uses rather than as a primary tool for learning how to unschool. They divide the world into subject areas, and unschooling works better when explorations involve many senses and "disciplines." More commentary and ideas can be found at the first link below.

SandraDodd.com/curriculum
SandraDodd.com/unschoolingcurriculum

Learning, not Teaching

This whole book is about learning rather than teaching, but as an intro to a page I have actually called "learning," here is a story.

Marty was invited to a party. Holly wanted to go with him. He wasn't even sure he wanted to go. Holly was agitating. I told her to chill, because she was tertiary in the situation.

Holly said "Okay, but I don't know what 'tertiary' means." I held up two fingers and said "Marty's secondary." Then I added another finger and said "You're tertiary."

I'm sure I had to write out the definition and use it in a full sentence, in 8th or 9th grade, so I have cursive writing and my kids don't because I spent many years writing and writing and writing in school, but my kids have the vocabulary with NONE of that writing, which is honestly pretty remarkable.

I didn't use "tertiary" in order for Holly to learn it. I was trying to persuade Holly to be calm so Marty wouldn't reach the point of saying "I don't want you to go with me even if I *do* go." In the course of a conversation that wasn't about language or mathematics or vocabulary, Holly got that word, by my only saying it twice and holding up fingers.

Children don't need long explanations to learn something if it's something they would like to understand better right at that moment. If you can learn to live at the edge of knowledge and curiosity, learning will be like breathing.

SandraDodd.com/learning

Connections

"That reminds me..."

That's all it takes. If one thing makes you think of another thing, you form a connection between them in your mind. The more connections you have, the better access you have to cross-connections. The more things something can remind you of, the more you know about it, or are learning about it.

Flat representations can't show these connections. Neither could an elaborate three-dimensional model, because when you consider what a thing is or what it's like, you not only make connections with other concepts, but experiences and emotions. You will have connections reaching into the past and the future, connections related to sounds, smells, tastes and textures. The more you know about something, the more you can know, because there are more and more hooks to hang more information on—more dots to connect.

I got the idea for this kind of graph from *Trust the Children: A Manual and Activity Guide for Homeschooling and Alternative Learning* by Anna Kealoha.

Here's a simple mathematical example:

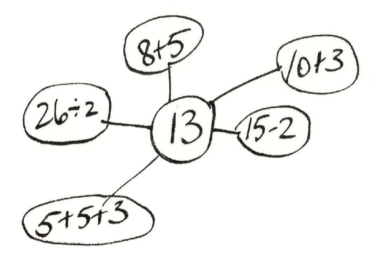

But being more "cross-disciplinary" about it, not limiting to just one area, we've played with them more like this:

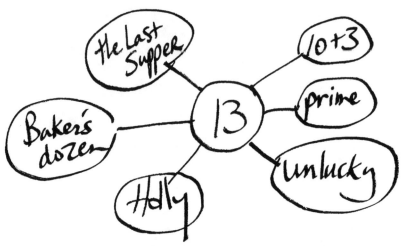

And any of those can become "the center" and branch out to everything else in the whole wide world. But at the heart of this exercise is what is and what isn't: What *is* a thing, and what is not the thing? What is like it and what is unlike it?

(Those were drawn when Holly was thirteen. She's seventeen now.)
SandraDodd.com/connections

Thinking and Knowing

Thinking's fancy name is "cognition."

"Think" and "thought" are very old English words. Those actions happen in your mind, in the realm of ideas and feelings.

The older English word for that sort of thing is "ken" which survives in a few drinking songs and some phrases in Scottish dialect. It's the root word of "know" and "knowledge." (Now you can tell your kids why they're spelled with a "k"—being forms of "ken," so that the "k" was pronounced in those sword-yielding days of yore.) Knowing is more related to seeing, recognition and perception. Maybe its nearest Latinate equivalent is "awareness"—familiarity with a thing from direct experience—but "knowing" is stronger. It can be muscle deep when you know how to do something physical.

Learning

Where do thinking and knowing turn to learning? Right at the edges, where you think something new, or know something different. Learning comes from connecting something new to what you've already thought or known.

Associating one thing with another

What scents, stories, emotions, visions do you associate with your mother? Your first pet? Your newest car? Ohio? Candy canes?

Each idea, object, concept, person, song, motion—anything you can think of—has personal associations for you. You have an incalculable mass of connections formed in your brain and will make more today, tomorrow, on the way home, and in your sleep.

What you know can be added to, or amended, but rarely deleted. Some things are best not learned, which is why it's so important to be careful what you say and how you say it (and to drive carefully, and all that).

Some people do try to encapsulate ideas or experiences and forget them. Sometimes other memories are shut off along with that. That's a good reason for analyzing traumatic events and sorting through instead of trying to encase it. Too many "do not enter areas" in your mind will slow down connections, and also will inhibit the biochemicals that help make learning fun and easy.

Happiness helps learning. Biochemically, joy is better than dismay. Optimism is better than negativity.

Parents can practice seeing connections as vital, even if it's "after hours." This is a follow-up to comments on an article called *Late-Night Learning* (link to follow):

From my point of view and from my experience, if art and music lead a kid-conversation to Italy, and they make this connection at 10:30 at night, I could say say "Go to sleep," or I could get excited with them, and tell them the Ninja Turtles were named after Renaissance artists, and that all the musical terminology we use, and most of early opera, came from Italy. That maybe the Roman Empire died, but Rome was not through being a center for advanced thought. Or however much of that a child cares about. And some of that will work better with an art book out, and maybe a map of the world. Look! Italy looks like a boot for sure, and look how close it is to Greece, and to the Middle East. Look who their neighbors are to the north and west, and how much sea coast they have. Look at their boats.

Maybe the child is seven, though, and Italy isn't on the state's radar before 8th grade geography.

So I don't look at the state's requirements. I look at my child's opportunities. And I think the moment that the light is on in his eyes and he *cares* about this tiny bit of history he has just put together, that he wants me to say "YES, isn't that cool? I was much older when I figured this out. You're lucky to have great thoughts late at night."

And if he goes to sleep thinking of a camera obscura or the Vatican or gondoliers or a young teenaged Mozart seeing Italy with his dad, meeting people who thought they would remain more famous than Mozart... I think back to the circumstances of my own bedtimes as a child and I *want* to fill him with pictures and ideas and happy connections before he goes to sleep, if that's what he seems to want. I could be trying to go to sleep and being grouchy and he could be in another room trying to go to sleep and being sad, or we can go on idea-journeys and both go to sleep happy.

SandraDodd.com/latenightlearning

Substance

"Transubstantiation" is associated with sad medieval scientists who failed to transmute base metals into gold, and with Catholic Mass, pretty much. I want to share something totally without magic but with a special kind of substance.

I wrote the piece below on a discussion list in 1997 or so, so the description is the back yard at our old house. Italics are the words of a new unschooler in that discussion.

Trust, Free Time, Compost

The best of my personal deschooling, I think, was to still the running commentary I had been keeping up about what was educational about what they were doing at the moment. To justify for my husband and me, and later out of habit, I had an analysis going every moment. That has stopped.

At least I had never been saying it to the kids. I was determined from the beginning not to distinguish what was "good for them" (educational) from what was "just fun" and in the course of treating it all the same, it became all the same—not only in reality (which I think it was already) but in the eyes of my children (because they didn't know any different) and in my own gut.

For about the last week and a half I have been feeling like we're just not "jiving"—if you know what I mean. We get along great when it's fingerpaints and playground time, but whenever learning tries to raise its ugly little head....well, my children are not too happy with me.

Banish the ugly-headed little learning situations. Stay at the playground. Play with sand and water. Find seeds. Sit in the shade, and in the sun. Set ice in the shade and in the sun. Write with ice on a sunny sidewalk. If there's a brass plaque at the park you can set a piece of ice on it when it's hot and get the letters in reverse, melted into the ice. Don't talk about WHY those things happen unless the kids ask. Just let it happen. They'll figure it out.

Once they get the hang of figuring those things out, they'll be able to figure out harder things. If they practice on cheap and easy stuff (ice is great—in the bathtub for floaty toys, crushed ice for snacks...), they'll be calmly confident about figuring out increasingly harder things.

(Wow—I liked what I just wrote. I'm saving it. You might see it again someday.)

...Free time with Lego, etc. until about 9:00 PM bedtime.

It probably doesn't affect your children directly, but I'm guessing that inside your head there are voices and schedules causing you distress and agitation. If after dinner is free time, what was the rest of the day? What if they want to browse through encyclopedias at 8:30 p.m.? 8:30 a.m.? No doubt you let them, but maybe in your mind you're ticking off the time clock. "Overtime."

A typical busy day might be that someone is coming over and we're taking her (usually a her, not always) with us to do something "out there"–movie, museum, playground, theatrical-something-or-other. We go out to lunch maybe, or bring something back, and a rented video, and watch that and the kids wander off individually or in clumps to do whatever—make up games in the yard, play with the dog or cat, color paint, play with a game...

I don't know anymore what they do.

A typical boring downtime day is kids in bed until 9:00, one gets up to watch TV, one gets on the computer to play something, one sits in "the toy room" (a storage room/ passage way) and plays alone. We eat some boring lunch, do some laundry, put some stuff away (never as much as we've taken out, it seems), Keith comes home, takes us to dinner because everyone was so comatose there's no plan, and we come back and split into ones or twos at games, video, computer, lying on the big bed talking or telling stories, goofin' in the yard.... something.

We have a great big covered patio in back with a couch, two 6' folding tables, various mis-matched chairs and benches, and a concrete floor. That's where chalk is, and Lego. That's where a lot of summer art is. We have swings, a funky little tree house, and a big sandbox.

Out front there are bikes, a pogo stick, a pogo-ball thing, lots of rollerblades, a skateboard, a "taxi bike" (a tricycle with another seat behind), and those are used in waves, and left alone in waves.

Kirby takes karate three times a week.

Marty skates on Saturdays. He's up to Basic IV and will start hockey in April, I think. Holly skates too, unfortunately not at the same time. She's in Basic I, having finished a little-kid Snowplow Sam class.

All three kids are in swimming lessons three days a week.

We have a compost pile, and it's kind of amazing how it seems at first that the food and leaves and sticks and banana peels and dog poop will never do anything but sit there looking like garbage, but when I stop watching it, it turns to solid black, rich dirt! I can't find any parts of the elements of which it's made. It's kind of like that with my kids. It took me a few years to quit watching them and trust that it would compost. It did.

(end of 1997 quote)

What is substantially different?

People still look and sound the same before and after becoming unschoolers. The difference is in their beliefs and expectations, in their experiences and in their positive attitudes.

When one is flailing and worrying about how and whether and when learning will happen, there is an irritating and contagious negativity. When one truly knows that learning is happening all the time, emotions can move into the calm-to-joyful range.

SandraDodd.com/substance

Strewing

Someone asked, "What exactly is strewing and how do you do it? I think it is leaving material of interest around for our children to discover. Is there more to it?"

That's it.

I said it years ago in an AOL discussion and the visual stuck. What I was referring to was leaving things around and changing them out. Some of our most successful items have been toys or objects for playing around with:

- pattern blocks
- castle blocks
- magnets (or some new magnet toy where something swings or moves)
- a prism
- odd little crafts things with some tactile element people will just HAVE to pick up and mess with (fuzzy, furry, slippery, gummy...)
- printouts of good cartoons or little articles or humor lists (generally taped inside the bathroom or left on the counter there, or on the dining table)
- new foods, snacky stuff, in a bowl, out
- interesting rocks, rinsed, in a bowl, on the table

There's another element which isn't physically "strewing," but involves instead taking the children out and about with the idea of their seeing (hearing, tasting, smelling, touching) things they might not have come upon otherwise and that you can't lay casually about the house.

Sometimes it's just as simple as driving another route to the same old place, or going to a different grocery store than usual. Other successful outings of note which I consider in the same category as strewing (though not the same action):

- construction sites
- any public doing like racing remote control things in a parking lot or vacant lot—just passing by is sometimes sufficient without even stopping

- concerts
- fleamarkets
- garage sales
- new stores just opened
- old stores in danger of closing (take them in before it's gone)
- prairie dog towns
- vacant lots with wood we can pick up for firewood

And with ALL those things, we get time together, shared experiences and conversation.

SandraDodd.com/strewing

The charge of "manipulation"

There have been a couple of discussions in which people said strewing was manipulative and sneaky. I don't see it that way at all. If I know what kinds of things my children could use being exposed to in order to be more well rounded, or to "fill in gaps" in what they know, or to take them to another level of understanding, bringing those things up in physical or conversational ways is no more "manipulative" than bringing more fruit into the house if there hasn't been much fruit consumption lately, or bringing them bottles of water on hot summer days. I don't need to force them to eat oranges or drink water, but I can notice it might be good for them and make it appealing.

Some unschoolers seem to make it more difficult for kids to find "academic" topics. It seems to be evidence that those parents are still dividing the world into academic and non-academic.

I've had friends interested in things I knew I owned or had access to, and I would bring those things out, or take my friend where the things were. When my husband expresses a desire for something, I don't make him ask specifically for it in detail. If I know what he might like and I have it easily available, I will provide it because I love him (if I have time and if I don't forget). Examples lately were he said his undershirts were getting too old. I bought him some more. He wanted to take bananas to work, and he fell asleep. I got him bananas. He said he used to have scissors on his desk but they were gone. I found some scissors and put them there.

These are the kinds of things parents can and should do for their children. If you think they might like something, or you know they would like something, if it is easily within your power to hook them up, why would you not do that? I have heard some reasons parents have given, ranging from "I don't have to," or "They'll learn that at school," or "I don't want him to be spoiled," to "He can get a job and buy his own."

When you decide to provide an item or experience, consider relationship-building as a goal, along with learning.

When you have a twinge of worry about whether you're doing the right thing by putting something where your child might find it, think of "conversation pieces" or magazines left on a coffee table, specifically so that others might pick them up. An interesting rock or a conch shell or something left out for guests to see and pick up is not "manipulative."

SandraDodd.com/strew/howto

Strewing for teens?

Someone asked about strewing for teens, and I wrote:

Well, it's the same thing.

Your family needs to be interested and interesting. Go places. Bring things and people in. Visit friends of yours who have cool stuff or do interesting things. Ask him to go with you if you take the dog to the vet. Drive home different ways and take your time. Putz around. Go to the mall some morning when it's not at all full of teens, and window-shop.

If you can at all afford it, find something in another town like a play, concert, museum, event and take him there. Stay overnight.

Go touristing somewhere not too far from you. Like if you had out of town guests, but just go with your son. Watch DVDs together.

Is there something you do that he might want to learn? Is there something you could learn together? Maybe the two of you could take a class or join a group that does... photography, hiking, quilting, scrapbooking, pottery, woodworking...

Last week Holly and her boyfriend went with me and Marty to the credit union to get money for a used Jeep he wanted. That was a learning and sharing experience for us all.

There are suggestions by other moms at
SandraDodd.com/strew/teens

Experiences

This includes one of my favorite memories of Kirby, and I'm glad I wrote it up when he was still very young. But the intro has to do with direct experience as opposed to formal learning, or even informal but school-style learning.

Some people see experienced unschoolers ("experienced" meaning in this context people who have done it well and effortlessly for years, who aren't afraid anymore, who have seen inspiring results) mention classes, and they think "Ah, well if the experienced unschoolers' kids take classes, then classes are good/necessary/no problem."

But if beginners don't go through a phase in which they REALLY focus on seeing learning outside of academic formalities, they will not be able to see around academics. If you turn away from the academics and truly, really, calmly and fully believe that there is a world that doesn't revolve around or even require or even benefit from academic traditions, *then* after a while you can see academics (research into education, or classes, or college) from another perspective.

Once there was heavy fog at our house. Kirby was four or five. He had never seen it at all, and this was as thick as I have ever seen fog. He wanted to go and touch it. I yelled, "Let's go!" and we ran up the road, and ran, and ran. About seven houses up we got tired. I said "Look" and pointed back toward our house, which was gone in the fog.

I did NOT say, "See? You can't touch it, really, it's touching us, it's all around us." I didn't say, "Let's don't bother, it's just the same wherever in there you are."

I let him experience the fog. He learned by running in fog and smelling it, and losing his house in it.

For someone who has been out of and away from school for six months to take a class will not be the same experience as someone (child or parent) who has been out and away for eight or ten years. It will be different in very, very profound ways. And "profound" doesn't show from the house. You have to run until you can't see the house, and then profundity kicks in.

. . . .

There are several sayings about the journey of a lifetime beginning with a single step and such. One step isn't the beginning of a journey if you keep one foot in the yard. You have to get away from the starting point completely.

Let your children make discoveries with their own new eyes. Don't show-and-tell them into a helpless stupor. Be with them, pay attention to what they're seeing for the first time and be poised to explain if they ask, or point out something interesting if they miss it, but try to learn to be patient and open to their first observations and thoughts. Like bubbles, or dandelion puffs, they are beautiful and fragile and if you even blow on it too hard, it will never be there again.

Practice being. Practice waiting. Practice watching.

Let them experience the world with you nearby keeping them safe and supported.

SandraDodd.com/peace/newview

Building an Unschooling Nest

"Building an unschooling nest" is a phrase that has come to mean maintaining a safe, rich, happy environment in which learning cannot help but happen.

What will help to create an environment in which unschooling can flourish? For children to learn from the world around them, the world around them should be merrily available, musically and colorfully accessible, it should feel good and taste good. They should have safety and choices and smiles and laughter.

There is some physicality to the "nest," but much of it is constructed and held together by love, attitudes and relationships. Shared memories and plans, family jokes, songs and stories shared and discussed, all those strengthen the nest.

It seems people want to know exactly HOW to unschool, but the answer is not what they expect. The best recommendation is to open up to the expectation of learning. It helps if the parent is willing for a conversation to last only fifteen seconds, or to go on for an hour. Remember that if your "unit study" is the universe, everything will tie in to everything else, so you don't need to categorize or be methodical to increase your understanding of the world. Each bit is added wherever it sticks, and the more you've seen and wondered and discussed, the more places you have inside for new ideas to stick. A joyful attitude is your best tool. We've found that living busy lives with the expectation that everything is educational has made each morning, afternoon and evening prime learning time.

If you think you haven't done enough for your children lately, do more. The richer and safer your children's environment, the more interesting and open to input and entertainment and encouragement, the more learning will happen, whether you're at home or in the car or on another continent.

Maintain and replenish your children's learning environment.

SandraDodd.com/nest

Playing

Children learn by playing. Parents can learn about unschooling by playing. Parents can learn about their children by playing, too. Don't try to control the play. Be the guest in your child's play sometimes. If you've forgotten how to play or he doesn't want you to play, just watch, then. See if you can help by providing more of whatever he might need: space, materials, a surface, boxes or bags or tools or a photo of what he's done so he won't feel so bad about taking it apart, maybe. Maybe he needs a light to keep playing outside at night, or maybe a darkened room in the house to play with something that glows.

When you're working in the garage, maybe find something your child could play with there. If you're in the kitchen, maybe let him play with plastic dishes, or old spices, or the water in the sink. If you're in the grocery store, let him hold something interesting from the groceries while you shop. I used to put one child in the big part of the basket and let him arrange the groceries around him, while another rode in the baby seat.

Watering the yard could involve play. Sorting laundry can become a game. If you can blur the line between work and play, you'll find more togetherness, more peace, and more learning.

Consider your resources and be on the lookout for more necessities like these: balls, flashlights, cloth for capes or tents (over tables or chairs or couches), containers, bathtub toys (ice is good), costumes, hats, blocks, magnets. Think of yourself, as a child, and what might have caught your attention. Provide for the child inside you and the current child, too!

SandraDodd.com/playing

Games

According to Stephen Nachmanovitch in his book *Free Play*, the difference between play and a game is that games have rules, and play can be freeform. Sometimes with younger children it's good to let them play *with* a game rather than actually *playing* the game. It's not worth arguing with a young child about the rules. If they want to move "the wrong direction," so what? Learn to relax.

But as to playing games with children, don't press anything to the point that it isn't fun anymore. Playing to the end just because you started isn't a good thing for games. They should be about fun, and the loving or friendly relationship between the players, and about learning maybe, but should not be the cause of antagonism or anger or frustration.

There are traditional games like checkers, tic-tac-toe, and hangman, that can be played without much equipment. There are games that have existed for a long time, in part because of the aesthetic appeal of the game boards and their playing pieces: chess, Chinese checkers, backgammon.

When children are young, find games that don't require reading. There's one with colored markers and cards called "Bazaar," which has been in and out of print. You might find one used. It has no words or numerals, but can be played by adults as well as children.

Some of the board games that were popular in the mid twentieth century are still around. They might be the only ones the grandparents know, but consider looking at some of the newer games by companies like Ravensburger, Rio Grande Games, or Set. If you live where there's a gaming store, perhaps ask for ideas there. Department stores or toy stores might not be the best places to get games these days.

Some games have historical settings, some have maps for game boards, some involve deductive reasoning (Clue, Scotland Yard, Mastermind for Kids, Battleship), some involve drawing or patterns. Be brave about new games! (And check thrift stores, charity shops and yard sales.)

SandraDodd.com/gameplay

Humor

Given a choice between something funny and something somber, go with funny if your goal is peace and learning. Very few things need to be still and serious.

Surprises help with learning, and so a humorous situation is more likely to be memorable than a humdrum one.

Reminder: Frightening and sad situations are memorable too, so avoid those. Humor can be cruel, so take care not to make fun of a person in a way that makes him feel small, or less than, or afraid, or ashamed.

Funny songs, stories, pictures and poems amuse babies and adults all. Amusing food and unusual table settings can be fun. Comedy movies or TV shows are good for relaxing, passing time, and for exposure to different geographical, social or historical settings.

Smiles and laughter involve safety and trust. Those emotions are good for families, for relationships, and for learning.

SandraDodd.com/humor

Typical Days

Because the primary "method" of unschooling is living a rich life with a focus on learning and relationships, it's difficult to photograph. I've had newspaper reporters want to come and photograph my children unschooling, at our house. I told one reporter once that if she wanted to send a photographer, my kids were at various places around town, and I named places and times for the next couple of days. The gaming shop; Kirby teaching karate; Holly playing Harry Potter at a comic book store. I told her if they came to our house what unschooling would look like was a kid on the computer, or watching TV, or playing with toys. She was certain I was missing the point of what she "needed" to have photographed.

Depending where a family lives and what's going on that day, and how old the children are, and how early the mom wakes up naturally (if she doesn't have infants or toddlers to wake her up), the children will probably get up as they wake up, and eat as they want to, and find some clothes, if they didn't sleep in something they can continue to wear, and pick up where they left off the day before on some game or project or activity.

To some people that might seem like "nothing's happening." Those people are looking for something to look like school.

It's possible the family, or some part of the family, will go outside, and walk to a store or a pond or into the woods or to a vacant lot, depending where they live and what's out the back door.

It's likely that the family will leave their home on some days. Some families leave every day. Where they go will depend on where they live.

This doesn't keep people from asking "What is a typical day for unschoolers?"

I do understand the question, but I'm also sure the answer is too varied to summarize. I've been keeping a collection for many years of accounts of particular days, though. Snippets from some of these (because I can't find all the authors anymore to ask to publish full accounts anyway):

I just wanted to share the great day I had with my 2.5 year old son Logan....I never had this much fun, or got so much out of a day in school.

[Singing subway "A" train, elevator, water play, curly slide, Central Park, ducks, Shakespeare, sword fights]

—Meryl

This leads to a discussion about the body and how an ear infection would cause one to be off balance and about moms need to take it easy and mainly sit down a while...

[Mom falls, WoW, exorcism, wind tunnels, Pythagoras, computer graphics, cake, dinner, cooking and then some more cooking]

—Nicole

One of my great joys in this world is watching my children run through the pastures. It's one of those mental snapshot moments where I just try to burn that image in my brain because it's perfection here on earth.

[reading, chess, games, piggies, grass whistles, meadow, moonrise, pizza, costumes, domino effect, electrical short, video and peaceful sleep]

—Danielle

I took the big plunge with unschooling, and I'm still finding little things I didn't realize I was ruining for everyone. We stayed up swimming until midnight...

[dollar store, fries, coloring books, glowsticks, FLUXX, 100 degree heat, nighttime swim, noodle chairs lightning bugs, babies, video games and storytime]

—Melissa

Unschooling WORKS!! A day in the life of…us

[sewing, tricks, comics, ants in the field, a vole, salad, shopping, budget, Fantasia, computer games, tarsiers, chapter books and a doll hat]

—Tamara

Early Spring day: We had a friend sleep over last night…

[overnight friend, playing, pancakes, girl scouts, secret codes, dance, comics, super-hero origins, seeing kids in different lights, "Castle in the Sky," playing, party preparation, voting, hair dye, leapster, volcanos, news, food]

—Lori

Pi to calligraphy - awesome day

[square and a protractor, race cars, angles, drawing and measuring, circles and pi, history, Arabic script, calligraphy, paints, peanut butter sandwiches, and wall decorations]

—Becca

Funny how the happiest days are full of small joys instead of major undertakings.

[Seahawks game, mail, calculator, playing bank, neighbor-baby, nineteenth century nautical history, hangman, sharing, relaxing]

—df/dragonfly

Enjoying My Kids

[Magic School Bus, bikes, Harry Potter, computer, arrows, treasure hunt, Lego, peg boards, Lord of the Rings, ooblek, air guitar, fantasy, fancy dress and joy]

—Julie

One morning... *(all before lunch)*

[early light, photography, hot air balloon, heat and physics, hot chocolate, lake, dock, waterfowl, international adoption, Erica Enders and geography, tangled guinea hen, veterinary aspirations, Norwegian relatives, dusting—all before lunch]

—Mary T.

I WILL NOT GIVE UP THIS KIND OF LIFE.

[Smithsonian, foam, paper airplanes, business mail, Delta, "blitz," roof rescue, sand box, grape picking (all that before lunch!), nap, antiques, jamming and joy!]

—Paula L

A magical afternoon right when a tired frazzled mom needed it.

[regional park, river, rocks, water, wind, sticks, birds, minnows, deer poop, moose poop, magic and awe]

—NancyBC

My heart is just bursting with joy this morning. I had to share this with someone.

[money saved, relaxation, experiments with electricity, mapping dinosaur finds, reading, punctuation, love, science, life, peace and freedom]

—Lannie

Dustin our 11 yr. old taught himself how to skim board. He wanted to surf but the water is still a bit cold here. We attended a homeschool meeting, the kids played and had a blast.

[skim boarding, homeschool meeting, X-men, the dump, yard sale, Brittany Spaniel, VCR, swim suit, trampoline, rocks, bookstore Spanish, impressing a stranger, and The Man in the Mountain]

—Laura D.

Here we reside, adjacent to the den of the mother bear and her two cubs, lingering on the shores of a large deep lake with 22,000 miles of shoreline, cradled by pines, poplar, birch and maples, atop rocks of the Canadian shield. We embarked on our unschooling journey, with enthusiasm, as well as some feelings of uncertainty...

[Aspergers, bears, iced lake, sauna, firewood, a squirrel coat for Barbie, web design, nutrition, outdoor skating, ice fishing, building shelters, games and swimming]

—Minna

This evening we have some friends coming over who are going to help get a piano into our basement. We've had one in our garage for a year and we finally get to bring it in!

[computer, animals, toys, books, gameboy plants & dirt, trampoline, scooter, bike, yoga, Toonami, friends, and a new piano!]

—Kelli Traaseth

Today, while Abbie was at Drama, Katie and I played in the park. You know, this group has been good for me, because I'm seeing "say yes to your kids," "spend time with your kids," "be there beside your kids working and playing and talking."

[glop, lemonade stand, signmaking, treehouse, painting, hummingbirds, glass beads, slides, sand]

—Heidi C.

We play. A lot. And most people would say that's all we do. We're a happy family.

[snuggling, visiting grandma, movies, computer games, spelling, prices, Animal Planet, paints, play dough, toys, playing in the yard, food, showers, encyclopedias]

—Mary B.

I thought "Our days are never typical and we don't really do anything much." Then I thought about what we did yesterday and realized this is the essence of unschooling and I love it when I realize that."

[Making maple syrup from their own trees, appointments, x-rays, physics, biology, physiology, bird poop, photo-reactive dyes, hydro-engineering, and other fun and games.]

—Heidi R.

I'm sure on any given day I could look at what we're doing and say "We haven't done much today" and I could choose to freak out about it and panic. But when I look back over a week or a month I can see the rich tapestry of fun and learning that is our life.

[Lego, Bionicles, cooking, writing, painting, computer, music lessons, gymnastics, playdate, Hogwarts, hiking, library, bikes, cooking, swimming, movies, reading]

—Robin

There are times when unschooling just happens and life goes by and it doesn't strike me how cool it all is…

[sleepover, unschooler etiquette, infinity, chess tutorial, möbius strips]

—Robin (another cool day, same family)

[U]nder the drawing was the scrawled word "brachiosaurus." His passion for dinosaurs had prompted him to write that long word better than all my efforts to get him to write "cat!"

[dinosaurs, art, food chain, travel, geography, maps, online research, measurement and math, sharks]

—Amy

My son is six and he watches what he wants. Even though the TV was on when he woke up yesterday, he walked right past it to ask me to take him to the park.

[Harry Potter, identifying poop, worms, train tracks, doves' nest, demo games, Blues Clues, doll house, Franklin, classical music, stars, and the sad inability to fly]

—Mary J.

[T]his morning she got dressed and went back out to her bike. Michael (5) decided he wanted his training wheels off as well.

[bikes, wrenches and bolts, ebay, financial planning, internet research, Gameboy, new teeter-totter, fulcrum and balance, pizza, Mario Party, Harry Potter, Scooby Doo and a heated blanket]

—Pam L.

The full accounts of those and many other days:
SandraDodd.com/typical

TV

There is a kind of magic thinking that says television can rob people of their imagination, but that if parents sacrifice televisions, children will be more intelligent.

I think I have probably heard, read, and been reminded of (repeatedly) every argument made against television since the 1950's. They pale and dissolve into the airwaves next to the arguments for letting go of TV fears and restrictions.

The discussions involving television are among the top three issues that challenge parents' thinking. The other two are food and chores.

It's nearly impossible anymore to separate television from movies and videos, so when I say "TV" I'm talking about the box that shows programs from whatever sources. Over the next few years it will become harder to separate that from a computer, or a gaming system such as Xbox.

Parents fear brainwashing. The word "zombie" is bandied about. They are told to fear children becoming corporate pawns, and drones. Children will want everything they see on TV, parents are told. Children will have short attention spans, teachers say. Television will keep families from eating together, or talking to one another.

Those arguments are false and they are wrong. But you don't have to take my word for it. Look at your own children directly, and not through the lens of a decades-old anti-TV book. Don't be swayed by the arguments of schoolteachers who would love for your children to think teachers' classroom lectures are mesmerizing.

There's no missionary like a convert, as they say, and among unschoolers there are many who once prohibited or measured out TV time, and who changed their stance. Learning became a higher priority than control, and joy replaced fear in their lives. I can't quote all the accounts I have collected, but I invite you to read them.

SandraDodd.com/tv

Economics of Restricting TV

This was posted on a discussion list originally, so "we can talk about them" was directed to other list members.

Economics of Restricting TV Watching of Children
Pam Sorooshian

Conclusion: Restricting TV-watching time increases the marginal utility of TV watching and causes children to become extremely strongly attracted to it and to value TV-watching above other, nonrestricted, activities.

"Utility" is a word used by economists to mean the pleasure, satisfaction, usefulness, or whatever other value a person gets from a product or service. Gaining utility is the reason why a person buys a product or engages in an activity. Just like businesses make decisions in such a way as to maximize total profits, individuals make decisions in such a way as to maximize their "total utility." Economists view people as "utility-maximizing" agents. Through an economist's eyes, we're all going through our lives making constant comparisons—choosing minute-by-minute what to do, what to eat, what to buy, what to wear, what to say, and everything else, and every time we choose, we do it so as to increase our total utility as much as possible.

Imagine you are standing in an ice cream store and choosing a flavor—what an economist sees is that your brain is rapidly going through all the choices, figuring out how much utility you'd gain from a scoop of strawberry versus a scoop of rocky road and so on, and then picking the one that gives you the most utility. (Notice that utility has to be predicted—we could be wrong in our pick, but we do our best given the information we have. I could decide that strawberry is my pick for today—that's the flavor that I prefer right now—the one that will give me the most utility. And then I might discover, to my dismay, that it doesn't live up to my expectations and I might WISH I could change my mind. It happens. So, our choices are actually based on our "expected" utility gains.)

Okay—there is a lot more I could say about "utility" and if you have objections to this way of seeing the world, we can talk about them. But I'll leave that for later and, after introducing one more idea, I'll move on to what this has to do with children and television-watching restrictions.

First, imagine you're in that ice cream shop and you've bought that strawberry cone because it had a high utility value to you. You eat it up and it is delicious and you compute the expected utility of *another* ice cream cone and decide to buy one. You eat it. *Yum.* Now you compute the expected utility of a third ice cream cone. So–what do you think? Is the 2nd ice cream cone going to give you as much *additional* utility as the 1st did? Will the 3rd one be expected to add as much to your total utility as the 1st or 2nd ones did? What's going to happen as you eat more ice cream cones? After you've had one, the expected utility of the next is lower than the expected utility was for the first. And after you've had two, the expected utility for the third will be lower than the expected utility for the second one was. They still might have value to you, they still give you utility, just not as much extra utility.

The "extra" utility you get from having "one more" of something is called "marginal utility." Marginal utility goes *down* as you have more and more of the same thing.

Even if you chose different flavors for each of your ice cream cones, you'd have chosen the highest-utility flavor first and so subsequent cones would provide lower and lower marginal utility.

This way of looking at choices is applicable to almost everything we do.

What's your favorite thing to do? Watch movies? Read a book? Garden? Go to Disneyland? Why don't you just do *that* all the time and nothing else? I mean–if it is your favorite, then doesn't it give you higher utility than anything else? Why do you ever stop doing it?

The answer is that as you do more and more of something, the marginal utility of doing even more of it, goes down. As its marginal utility goes down, other things start to look better and better.

But when you restrict an activity, you keep the person at the point where the marginal utility is really high.

When you only allow a limited amount of TV, then the marginal utility of a little more TV is high and EVERY other option looks like a poor one, comparatively. Watching more TV becomes the focus of the person's thinking, since the marginal utility is so high. Relax the constraints and, after a period of adjustment and experimentation to determine accurate marginal utilities, the focus on TV will disappear and it will become just another option.

SandraDodd.com/t/economics

Gilligan's Island and *Star Trek*

Watching *Gilligan's Island* as a kid triggered hundreds of thoughts and connections for me. I wrote up a list of some of my thoughts in 1993, and someone sent it to *Home Education Magazine*. That made it easy to find again, so it's in my TV pages (and appeared in *Moving a Puddle*). When something is online, it can attract similar accounts and so I learned of these:

Dr. Robert Sapolsky, a professor of neurology at Stanford School of Medicine, wrote: "How did I wind up as scientist? By all logic, I should start with *Gilligan's Island*, a sitcom that entranced me when I was an eight-year-old growing up in Brooklyn."

Dr. Mae Jemison, a medical researcher and astronaut, credited watching *Star Trek* as her inspiration to study science even though she was an African-American girl from Alabama.

Parents didn't plan those inspirations. It's likely they thought their children were wasting their time, or taking a break from learning, when they were watching TV.

Even if you don't decide to unschool, keep an open mind about where and what your children could be learning, and where they might find the inspiration to become something like world-changing scientists.

SandraDodd.com/t/Gilligan

Learning from Cartoons

Each family discovers the value of choices in unique and wonderful ways. Well, not every family—only those who actually do start giving their children choices, and in which the adults work to see the choices they are making as well.

One surprise is that programs the parents had thought were "stupid" have led to discussion and research on the autobahn, the metric system, classic movies, technology, international sports, geography, segregation, famous speeches, sportsmanship and ethics, live theatre, opera, oil and mining, hygiene, reproduction, Australian food, life cycle of frogs, hurricane formation, trust, cooperation, classical music, Vikings, religion, art, how different animals survive the winter, Galileo, Japanese mythology, cooking, geology... this list could be twice as long without leaving that section of my website.

One trail went from a mummy cartoon to Egypt, to Pharaohs, to slavery, to the Civil War, to Abraham Lincoln, and to other presidents. The Simpsons' parody of Schoolhouse Rock led to a discussion on Thoreau and *Walden*.

Accounts of those discoveries in the enthusiastic words of the parents involved are online, and new stories are added frequently.

After the parents become comfortable with television as a resource, some also find their children would rather do something else: "I suggested we watch a movie. My eight-year-old said please can't we play a game instead? So we played Yahtzee. When one child got a Yahtzee, the other joined her in dancing for joy."

SandraDodd.com/t/cheesy
SandraDodd.com/t/learning

The following was written one day when Holly was younger, and is at the link below:

TV, dead rat, insurance, young girl, theology

This is hard to convey, because it was quick and sometimes two or three people were talking at once. Sometimes I couldn't quote, and there was laughing and gesturing, but here it is for the sake of its punchline:

My husband brought papers for me to sign. He's moving my IRA to the Navy credit union (his dad was a WWII pilot, and his brother was on a submarine years later)

We were talking about insurance policies his dad has for the kids, which are paid for by interest from an IRA that's in Holly's name, bought by her grandparents. Holly wanted us to tell her what we were talking about. I said it would be enough money if she died that we could bury her and have a party. She acted like that sounded good. I said maybe we could put her out between Purple and Luna (a cat and rat of hers, both in the flowerbed out back). I said maybe we could pay the house off with the insurance money so we wouldn't ever have to sell it and lose Holly's grave.

Illegal to bury her in the yard? Maybe.

I suggested that we could get a stone that says "Luna, beloved rat of Holly," and underline Holly, so God would know it was actually her.

Holly said God is a genius and would know anyway.

"Why's God a genius?" Keith asked. He just is. I suggested "butterflies"; Holly concurred.

Keith said God's omnipotent, so he knows everything.

Will he turn us in to the city? Probably.

I said, "That's omniscient. Omnipotent means he can do anything, all-powerful. And (to Holly I said) the question that goes with that is whether God can make a rock so big that he himself can't pick it up. If not, he's not omnipotent.

Holly, without missing a beat: "I thought the question was whether Jesus could microwave a burrito so hot that he himself couldn't eat it."

I HOOTED!

Me: "Well yes, that's the same question, updated. Where did it come from?"

"The Simpsons."

"Who asked it?"

"Homer."

>SandraDodd.com/strew/simpsons

Shared Experiences are Important

If watching TV is your child's thing and complaining about TV is your thing, you've spoiled a chance to have a shared thing.

Children in school might have so little in common with their parents that there's nothing to discuss, but when children are home there is a great deal to know and share. If a movie or a television program or cartoon or music video or concert film can be shared, there are dozens of jumping off places right then, and things to think back on later, or to connect in another year.

The more experience and information you have in common, the greater your relationship and bond.

If the child loves a program the parent can't bring himself to watch, or if the child wants to watch a show over and over and over and the mother's tired of watching it, there are other things to do in way of sharing. The parent could find websites or magazine articles or games related to the program or movie. Maybe the child would like related foods, or costumes, or articles of clothing, or toys. Maybe the parent could research something of interest about the voices or music or art or story, and have that to discuss sometime at dinner or on a car ride. If it's an older show and there are others of the series on DVD or available online, the parent might share that information with the child or buy more as a gift.

>SandraDodd.com/t/sharing

Movies for Unschoolers

Parents worry about movie ratings sometimes. Different countries have different rating codes and criteria, and that's worth knowing. Understanding how those movie ratings are derived might be fun to research, too. Although theaters might have legal or franchise restrictions, parents can decide what's watched in their own homes, and their own "ratings" might be very different from the movie rating board's.

I myself don't like movies in which young children die, or people are hit with fists. I'm okay with machine guns. Snakes don't bother me. Wanton or comic destruction of musical instruments disturbs me. My relatives know that.

If you know your own family that well, you'll be able to decide which movies would be pleasant or bearable or fun for which others, and that will help when deciding what to go to a theater to see and what to rent for in-home viewing and so on.

It's rare now that a family will be watching a movie at home without the ability to mute scary music or to pause to discuss something. When a scene can be replayed, the urgency to try to make people pay attention and the temptation to be angry at interruptions is gone. That adds to peace and togetherness. Even if it takes two or three sessions to get through a movie together, it's nothing to argue about.

There are some movies that can help parents consider natural learning and unschooling, at the same time that they're sharing something fun with their children. Or you could watch them alone.

- *Mary Poppins*
- *Heidi* (with Shirley Temple)
- *The Sound of Music*
- *Searching for Bobby Fischer* ("*Innocent Moves*" is the title in the UK)
- *Ferris Bueller's Day Off*

Other movies could be useful for particular purposes, such as initiating discussion about relationships between children (*Stand By Me, Christmas Story, Holes, Madagascar*) or teens (*Mean Girls, Breakfast Club, 10 Things I Hate About You, Tuck Everlasting*) or between children and adults (*Fly Away Home, About a Boy, Dead Poet's Society, Billy Elliot, Mrs. Doubtfire*).

There are movies with relationships and dance (*Strictly Ballroom, Footloose*) or sports (*Karate Kid, The Mighty Ducks*).

Some movies are rich with images, characters, history and ideas:

- Spartacus
- El Cid
- Ben Hur
- Monty Python and the Holy Grail
- Star Wars (all)
- Karate Kid (all three in marathon maybe!)
- Hamlet (the one with Mel Gibson is easy to follow)
- Romeo and Juliet (I like the Zeffirelli from the '60's)
- Joseph and the Amazing Technicolor Dreamcoat
- O Brother, Where Art Thou?
- The Music Man
- The Last Starfighter
- Last Action Hero
- The Patriot

It's easy to see the wealth in those. When you get better at it, more comfortable with what your child likes, knows, and wants to know, you could find lots of value in just about any movie. We had plenty to talk about the other day with *The Little Princess*, with Shirley Temple. We talked *lots* about characterization and motivation and plot detail after the first Ninja Turtle Movie, when the boys were little. They have learned to milk a movie for all it's worth, and I helped. Marty came in halfway through *Joe vs. the Volcano* (which I bought at the flea market after someone quoted it in an online discussion), and though I offered to rewind it, he was happy to just pick up where it was and fall into it.

How NOT to watch movies:

Don't be cynical and critical and dismissive. Find the good acting, the good sets and good props. Don't say "Oh, brother." If there's a movie you really don't like, don't watch it with your kids. For me, that is *Robin Hood, Prince of Thieves*, which I think is atrocious. I walked out of it in the theatre. It was on TV the other night, and I watched some I had missed that first night, and *tried* to watch it to the end, but the script and the acting and the whole concept just irritated me beyond bearing, and I turned it off. If someone else had been watching too and been interested, I would have just left the room instead and let them watch in peace.

Many movies with particular recommendations are listed here:

SandraDodd.com/t/movies

Movies as a playground—as tools, as portals

Movies touch and show just about everything in the world. There are movies about history and movies that *are* history. There are movies about art and movies that *are* art. There are movies about music and movies that would be nearly nothing in the absence of their soundtracks. Movies show us different places and lifestyles, real and imagined.

I rented *Clash of the Titans* because it had Judi Bowker, whom I'd seen in *Brother Sun, Sister Moon* 30 years ago (and many times since). Looking up Harry Hamlin after that, I read about and bought a copy of a San Francisco state production of *The Taming of the Shrew*, and that will lead to something else as well. Because of the directors' commentaries on Lord of the Rings, I knew Peter Jackson was influenced by Ray Harryhausen and so when I added *Clash of the Titans* to my Netflix list, I knew it was going to help me understand Peter Jackson's artistic influences too.

In an interview on the DVD, Ray Harryhausen told Arnold Kunert:

> The cinema was made for fantasy rather than normal type of stories, mundane stories. It gives you a feeling of wonder, for one thing. It stimulates the imagination and I think adults like fantasy as well as children. Most people feel it's rather childish to have an imagination. I don't agree with that. I think you should go through life and imagine the very best.

In talking about creatures and special effects, he named Dennis Muren, George Lucas, Steven Spielberg and James Cameron. I know nothing about the first and last, but in the course of finding links for the webpage, I learned a great deal. Harryhausen said one of his greatest influences was the art of Gustav Doré. That name (and art) I do know, from storybooks from my own childhood and I've bought and studied (meaning looked at until I disappeared into that world) as an adult, too.

On my site and elsewhere on the internet are other lists of movie trails you could explore. Follow a movie's leads, whether they're mental, conversational, research, comparison or eventually involve new hobbies or travels or writing/art/music. Come back to movies after a couple of years and you and your children will have new knowledge to connect and a new point of view from which to understand different aspects of the movies.

I love historical fiction, and true stories in movie form, but they're rarely documentaries of the actual buildings and clothing, if they're about anything older than 50 or 100 years, and they'll always have actors portraying the famous personages. History can be learned by absorption, from seeing the props and carriages and weapons and such, but it can be even more useful to discuss how the time in which the movie was made, and the budget, and the purpose, can affect the way in which characters are portrayed, and the degree of the attempt at authenticity in manners, dress, hair, make-up, facial hair, shoes, horses' bridles and saddles, etc.

Rather than hooting and saying "stupid" when you find historical mistakes, maybe discuss why they might have made the choices they did. If you look at westerns, for instance, the women's hair often reflects the styles of the day. There were westerns made in the 1970's and '80's in which the men had their hair kind of fluffed and blow-dried. It can be amusing, but it doesn't have to be condemned, just observed and noted.

Depending on your interests and your children's, you could go movie to movie by favorite actors or directors, or you could look at award winners for cinematography or sound editing or soundtrack, or other factors that could lead you on unpredictable learning trails. Don't commit to a longterm route. If you start watching Sam Rockwell movies but you get to *The Green Mile* and decide to go to another Tom Hanks or Michael Clark Duncan film, or to look at another Stephen King adaptation, don't feel like you didn't finish a project. Don't create opportunities for obligation or failure when you're creating a learning-for-fun environment. Sam Rockwell movies will still be there in five or ten years.

Everything is connected.

SandraDodd.com/movies

Books

"So you don't use books?"

"Like fingernails on a chalkboard (something my children might never experience) that question breaks into a calm day from time to time. By books many people mean school-style textbooks designed for one subject area, one school year, one level. They mean school books. . . ."

That's the beginning of an article called "Triviality," which is in *Moving a Puddle*, my previous book. Books, books, books. There will be some people who will be excited about this book even though it's a black and white summary of a full-color, full-length, ever-growing website.

I love books; they were my childhood friends, rescuers and escape routes. My children don't love books as much as I did, but it's partly because they've had many friends and didn't need to be rescued or to escape.

Many people who ask about books haven't thought very much about them. They're vaguely sure that learning comes from books, and that school subjects live in books, and so homeschoolers ought to have those books, whichever books they might be.

I am so certain that learning comes from experiences and touching, hearing, seeing, smelling and tasting that in light of natural learning, books seem flat and dry.

There are times when books are a comfort and a gateway to new ideas. There are times when books are adventure. Kirby always has a fantasy novel. Holly likes to read books that have been made into movies so she can think about what they changed and why. Marty likes zombies, but he's the least bookish of mine.

Some other families have kids who read and write as primary activities. My kids do more gaming and art. Some are musicians or athletes. In the absence of school, reading and writing don't create an upper class of humanity.

The books that have helped us with unschooling have been things that amused or intrigued or provided answers to questions. How-to and trivia books have been popular here. Real-life combined with humor makes for easy learning.

SandraDodd.com/bookandsax
SandraDodd.com/triviality

Book Worship

More and more, I'm thinking our culture puts too much glory on books.

There was a time when the only way for a kid to get information from outside his home and neighborhood was books. (Think Abraham Lincoln, log cabin in the woods far from centers of learning.) Now books tend to be outdated, and an internet search engine can be better for many kinds of information. If Abraham Lincoln had had full-color DVDs of the sights of other countries, of people speaking in their native accents and languages, and of history, he would have shoved those books aside and watched those videos.

When someone thinks books are the one crucial step to any further learning, then books and school have crippled that person's ability to think expansively, and to see what's unfolding in front of him in the real world.

Reading equated with "Wisdom"

I was off reading speculation about the next Harry Potter book, and on a discussion board I found something in passing that I added to my book-worship collection. It's not a gem, but it's a fairly good rock. Written by some Harry Potter fan somewhere in 2005:

> When Dumbledore mentions him to Hagrid, he implies that Aberforth might not be able to read which means its likely that Aberforth, while his intentions are good, might not have inherited Dumbledore's wisdom.

Equating the ability to read with wisdom seems a jump.

This isn't the first time I've heard this.

And on a slightly-related (in that both involve teens, I suppose) thing, on Neopets, "intelligence" points come from reading books, not from being good at the math puzzles. "It's just a game," but it points to book worship as sure as anything.

Among my boys' friends, when they were teens, a role-playing game was being initiated. The gamemaster was assigning attributes to the characters in advance of the game, based on their real-life attributes. He gave Kirby and Marty low intelligence "Because they hadn't gone to school and hadn't taken chemistry and stuff." He gave Kirby a 20 in charisma. But intelligence, single digits.

In many people's minds, intelligence and wisdom and books are all wadded up in a confusing mess they seem unable to think about clearly.

It's another reason that for purposes of deschooling with the hope of unschooling it's good to forget about "intelligence" and not worry about "books." Go toward things that don't look like school so you can come back to the schoolish-seeming ideas and materials with a clearer outlook later on.

When people ask me if we use books, I most often say "What do you mean?" Often they have no idea what they mean. Sometimes they say "You know. Text books."

"*Text* books? Books with text?"

I've only gone to that step twice, when the tone of "You know, text books" seemed particularly insulting. Because I did indeed know exactly what they meant. I was checking to see if they had any idea what they meant.

And to "You mean books with text?" the answer was a withering and exasperated "SCHOOL books." Once I said, "They don't go to school."

I've been too kind to do that more often.

I own school textbooks—mostly mid-twentieth century music books and New Mexico History textbooks aimed at seventh graders over several decades.

I have textbooks as the history of education, of the tone and prejudices and hopes of different periods of twentieth century history. When my kids ask about music or the history of New Mexico, I bring out other things.

Online I have examples of book-worshipful artistic motifs and some odd side topics, but the words aren't all mine and I will leave it for you to discover if this topic has stirred any curiosity in you.

May you be saved from The Black Spot, whether you've read Treasure Island or not.

SandraDodd.com/bookworship

Video Games

In 2002, three adults and three kids did a presentation on video games at a large homeschooling conference in California. The room was packed to overflowing. Some people came to ask pointed questions to the point of disruption. The parents, Dan Vilter, Kathy Ward and I, were telling stories of the benefits to our children from games, while three of our children–Jonathan Ward, Matthew Vilter and Holly Dodd– demonstrated and described some of the games they knew well in such a way that the game showed on a large screen as they played and narrated (thanks to Dan's AV expertise and equipment).

That seems like twenty years ago, though it was only seven. I came home and started a pro-video-gaming page on my site. It was about the only one out there, then, and I used to get grateful but sad e-mails from teens whose parents were horrible to them about video games, and hopeful e-mails from young adults who had played despite pressure not to, and who just wanted to say they were glad my children wouldn't need to suffer through what they did.

Of course games are engineering, reasoning, logic, stories, art and music. More now than in 2002. Less now than in another seven years. The games out now make those 2002 games seem rudimentary, but Holly still plays Harvest Moon, which she was playing then too.

As I write this there are three young adults playing Rock Band in the next room. Anyone who hasn't played rock band should make an attempt to find a place to try it out. If it's too hard for you, that's fine; just don't disparage those who are bright and coordinated enough to play it or any of its cousins (Guitar Hero, DrumMania, Karaoke Revolution, Lips, and so forth). It's physical, it's musical, and it's not easy.

The days of justifying video games as no more than "eye-hand coordination" belong to Pong. (And even Pong had physics and geometry, in non-notated forms.)

SandraDodd.com/videogames

Educational Benefits

Books and articles keep coming out about the value of gaming, and I'm not even going to name them because it will date this book too much. More will be available by the time you read this. The kinds of things being written and published are things unschooling parents have known for quite a while. Anything that involves thought and exploration, anything that's fascinating and engrossing, is something from which a person will be learning. Things shared with other people create friendships. Learning about games from other people is the same way to learn about other things from others—networking, sharing resources, using internet tools and writing walkthroughs and reports of glitches is as real as information-sharing can be.

When Kirby was very young, he learned to follow maps without even trying to, by playing Super Mario and checking the player's guide for the locations of coins and dead ends and such. We paid for a subscription to Nintendo Power magazine when he was five. From those gaming articles and guides, he learned to read. Because he could look up a game by knowing that 23:35 meant Issue #23, page 35, later when he saw the notation for Bible verses and Shakespeare references, it was simple for him to understand them.

Solving complex puzzles creates skills people can use in any other situation, and video games are all about solving puzzles, finding patterns, making quick decisions, making the better guess and remembering how you got where you are. Deduction and inference were never so easy to play with.

In cases of children with dyslexia, developmental delays or autism, there are reports (some linked from my page) of their visual and language processing abilities improving because the games involve information presented in various ways. Because the parents and siblings can help them understand the directions of the games and to find and use charts or lists in the manual or player's guide or in online sources, everyone involved learns more than the obvious.

Most games involve points or scores or levels or something numerical, so from the lowest levels of simply needing to read numbers to higher situations involving interest and percentages and deciding which tools, weapons, seeds or potions to buy when and why, both math and language get a workout—often at the same time images are being manipulated with the controller or mouse or keyboard.

I quit counting the number of unschooled kids who learned to read from playing games. At first maybe they can only read enough to pick their name out on the "choose player" screen, and to know "quit" and "play," but all reading starts somewhere, and it beats reading about a boy and a bear who aren't going to actually do much. Red fish and blue fish just sit on the page looking at you. These video fish and boys and bears get up and go! Reading has an immediate and real affect on players' lives and their ability to play. No one else needs to tell them "Oooh, good job! Now you're starting to read!" And what they're reading was written for normal people, not for beginning readers.

Vocabulary, spatial reasoning, morality (Knights of the Old Republic, for instance), critical thinking, physics (rollercoaster building games, Tony Hawk games, Monkey Ball, Gran Turismo and others), military history and strategy, geography, mapping, following complex directions including distances and compass points, decisions in complex situations… All these things become a part of a child's native skills painlessly and effortlessly if you let them play games. If you play with them, you'll appreciate their knowledge and abilities. If you can't begin to play with them because the game's too hard, there's a different kind of appreciation.

I played some games, but many were beyond me or not interesting, so what I did to support the kids was to help keep their equipment in good shape and be willing to replace worn or broken controllers when I could, and be on the lookout for sources of used games, or of player's guides or helpful sites. As they got older they could do those things for themselves and each other.

Some games require writing. For a few years my boys played a text-based role-playing game on AOL, in chat rooms and by IM. It was quite an elaborate "world"—several kingdoms with intertwining storylines. Much spelling and keyboard speed came from those. With World of Warcraft, some players might be using head sets and speaking, and others might be texting at the bottom of the screen, all at the same time.

One of the best things about video games is that when someone's no longer having fun, there's an off switch. He doesn't need to "finish what he started" or "wait for the bell" or ask if it's okay to continue later. They can play when they want to and stop when they want to.

SandraDodd.com/game/benefits

Family Benefits

Gaming System:

Shared experiences are as good with Mario Kart as with Monopoly or Parcheesi; they're probably much better. Shared experience, knowledge and memories are an important part of relationships, and playing games together can create pleasant lifelong memories. Playing a game at which the children might have equal facility or even an advantage over parents is even better. They won't be little kids in that moment, nor shorter nor weaker, if they can operate the controller better than an adult.

When they have friends over to play games, they probably won't be bored. Bring them something to eat or drink every couple of hours, make sure they have comfortable places to sit and that the room is a pleasant temperature, and let them play.

Online multiplayer games:

Having a way for children to be with friends and be home at the same time is good. Having a way for them to be home and with friends you don't have to feed is even better! And you don't have to drive them home or make them a bed, because they're already at their own homes.

Frequently members of a family will play games together on a designated evening, and maybe distant friends or family members join in. It's a way to visit and communicate and interact within a game all at the same time.

I have adult friends who have kept a one-night-a-week gaming group going for over fifteen years. It started in person, playing Doom at one guy's house, and as they got older and moved around the country, it has become a weekly World of Warcraft meet.

Some games are quite international, such as Halo. Holly used to play with Australians and with people from all around the U.S. She loved the accents from Arkansas. Because they're communicating by headset/voice, there can be two layers of activity—conversation and game playing at the same time.

Jill Parmer's children have had international experiences from home, thanks to voice chat programs such as Skype and Ventrillo. They've played WoW with people from Brazil and Algeria and all across North America. Details and stories on that here:

SandraDodd.com/game/tales

Courtesy and Responsibility

"Play when they want to and stop when they want to" brought to mind guilds on World of Warcraft. That's a different deal, and a bigger one. There are opportunities for teamwork and leadership strategy on WoW. Interpersonal relations skills are valuable in gaming guilds or teams. There are certain "dungeons" or "raids" in games that require a team of five, or ten, or even twenty-five at advanced levels of the game.

Guilds have leaders and commanders and though they're not all organized the same way, if there are scheduled raids people are as expected to be there as if they were on a sports team or in a play. Sometimes if they can't make it they find a substitute, or guilds might have alternate players or might invite one for that session.

There are responsibilities that go with having access to tools and "gold" owned in common by the guild, and even though the player might be at his own house the whole time, he still has the opportunity to succeed gloriously, to be considered a great organizer or mediator or leader, or to prove himself to have been irresponsible or negligent. The emotions and need to follow-through socially will be as real as if he were outside the house, even if he hasn't met the other players in person, but moreso if they have relationships outside the game.

Smaller opportunities for courtesies come even in sharing a gaming system with other people, or in playing two player games that aren't online. When there is shared memory storage or players have access to other players' accounts or games, the etiquette and actions are real and can make or break relationships and trust. When a more experienced player helps a newer player, that rarely has to do with age. When an adult can take advice and assistance from a kid, or a teen can take advice from a young child, that's an all-new opportunity for humility, respect and courtesy, all three of which are lacking in many lives.

People have long valued the character-building sportsmanship and integrity involved in athletic games. "You never really know a man until you've played golf with him," I've heard. Tennis courts, swimming pools, public greens and sports fields all have rules and traditions.

Multi-player games provide opportunities to practice, improve and use one's interpersonal skills in many ways, with a chance to earn real-world respect and admiration.

SandraDodd.com/game/tales

Sleeping

When our children were babies and others would ask "When does he go to bed?" Keith used to say "About half an hour after he goes to sleep."

For the first MANY years of their lives, our kids fell asleep being nursed, or being held or rocked by dad or mom, or in the car on the way home from something fun. They slept because they were sleepy, not because we told them to. So when they got older, they would fall asleep near us, happily.

We never minded putting them in the bed after they were asleep. It was rare they went to sleep in the bed. They would wake up there (or in our bed, or on the couch or on a floor bed) knowing only that they had been put there and covered up by someone who loved them.

Going to sleep wasn't about "going to bed."

In contrast to my own childhood and that of many other people I know, that is a fantasyland of love. I cried myself to sleep hundreds of times, in the dark. It didn't make me a better person. It didn't make my mom a better mom. It certainly didn't create a more restful night nor improve my health.

For my children it wasn't a fantasy. It was just the way life was.

The cost to relationships of the parents thoughtlessly doing what they think others are doing is real and lifelong. The damage from letting babies cry, alone, unanswered, because a magazine article said it was okay is something you can't undo if you buy a thousand magazines. Loving, compassionate regard for your child's feelings in the moment should be primary. If your children are young, you can avoid distress and regret by making sleep part of a gentle, peaceful life.

SandraDodd.com/sleeping

Opportunities

As my kids were growing up they had many friends who couldn't come over because of a scheduled naptime, or couldn't stay the night because they could only sleep in their own beds.

There were park get-togethers interrupted because someone's child couldn't sleep there in her mom's lap, nor on a blanket under a tree, but could only be taken home to sleep in her own bed, by the clock, because... "Because" was never very well thought out, it seemed to me. Because that was a rule at their house. A rule made by... the mom? A book. A grandmother? "Just because."

My children saw live music, dancers, comets, eclipses, falling snow, midnight movies, and newly-arrived out-of-town guests because we considered experience and learning to be more important than "just because" schedules. And because our children rarely needed to be anywhere very early in the morning, the times that we needed them to be asleep early were also rare.

Then there were opportunities to sleep, on blankets at parks. In the car while we were traveling. In tents at the house. On couches or floor beds while movies played for the other kids. In the laps of parents.

Unschoolers have found that the very best questions and ideas can arise late at night when other stimuli are dimmed and muted, and the child is peaceful and thoughtful, or in those moments of waking up naturally after a satisfying sleep.

SandraDodd.com/latenightlearning

Future Jobs

I wish I had collected all the statements ever spoken or written to me about the irreparable damage I was *certainly* doing to my children by not scheduling their sleep, and by not requiring them to wake up at a certain time every morning. I was assured that a horrible fate awaited them all:

They would never get a job.

Or they might be hired, but would certainly lose the job from their lack of discipline and their total inability to get up early in the morning.

Kirby's first paid job involved running the Pokemon tournaments at a gaming store every Saturday morning from 8:00 to noon. He needed to be there early, to set up. I used to help him wake up, at first, but usually his alarm had gone off by the time I got in there. He was fourteen years old.

As more days were added to his schedule over the years, the most common hours were four to midnight or 1:00 in the morning on Friday and Saturday when the store closed and the Magic players went home. It was a good thing he hadn't been trained to get sleepy at 8:00 or 9:00 every night.

He worked at that store for four years. Not many nineteen-year-olds can say they've had the same job for four years. I guess the dire warnings were wrong.

Marty's first job was noon to four, helping make boots and pouches for re-enactors and medievalists. He was cutting out and hand sewing leather, mostly. Those hours were no problem for anyone, and the predictions could have been true, for Marty.

His next job, at which he stayed for sixteen months, was working Monday through Friday, 6:30 a.m. to 3:00 at a grocery store. He was late one time, about two minutes. I never had to wake him up. It was a two-minute walk out the back gate, but he got up an hour before he was due to start work.

How could he possibly have "learned to do that," having gone to bed whenever he wanted to for sixteen years!? He didn't "learn to" do anything except to make responsible choices for good reasons, and that covered all such situations.

Holly worked one night until 4:30 in the morning, restocking a clothing store in a mall during the Christmas rush. Sometimes she was scheduled for 8:00 in the morning. She never knew how late it would be. Good thing she was flexible about hours.

Kirby's "adult job" is with a company that operates twenty-four hours a day, and he's able to do any shifts, due to the way he was raised and his variable work hours before.

Those whose parents trained them to nap at 2:00 and sleep at 9:00 and get up at 6:00 will be disadvantaged in many jobs.

SandraDodd.com/myths
SandraDodd.com/teen/jobs

Peace

Peace is a recurring theme with unschoolers, and sleeping in peace is a luxury that costs nearly nothing.

In the larger culture, sleep isn't always peaceful. People pay for sleeping pills, and more expensive mattresses and pillows, and then they pay counselors or psychiatrists to help them untangle their dreams and fears and panic attacks.

I've noticed my children report peaceful, cheery dreams. It is possible to go to sleep contentedly and comfortably, to sleep gently and to wake up glad to be in that place on that day.

It's easy to screw that all up for someone, too, so when you're making any sleep-related decisions, keep peace in mind.

If a child is peacefully asleep and doesn't have to be somewhere at a certain time, let him sleep! If he stayed up late playing video games because it was the only time he could get a large block of uninterrupted access to the game, let him sleep as late as he needs to.

Going to sleep and waking up shouldn't be about the feeling of control the parent can gain from demanding and commanding.

SandraDodd.com/bedtime

The Purpose of Sleep

Sleep is beneficial to mental health, physical health and safety. It restores and refreshes us.

Psychologists have said for some time that during sleep the day's experiences and thoughts are added to long-term memory, or connected to other memories and "cross-referenced" in ways the conscious mind didn't consider, and that the distractions of the day prevented from happening earlier. Your brain isn't asleep just because your body is asleep. Sometimes the sorting of the new information causes dreams, or the mind's reconsideration of biochemical/emotional stimuli triggers similar memories.

Dreams seem to disturb sleep sometimes, but preventing dreams disturbs the daytime thoughts and functions. Balance is good!

Bodies can function calmly during sleep. Digestion, healing, growth—those don't stop, and might work best when the body can relax and the muscles can be still.

Being alert and waking up ready to stretch and move and explore some more will help children to learn. If they're comfortable and healthy and happy, learning will come more easily.

Some people have more difficulty falling asleep than others, so anything parents do that makes it even more difficult to fall asleep should be considered a bad plan. Lean toward happy hopeful thoughts and reassurances at night. If your child can fall asleep holding your hand or lying next to you, you're way ahead of the average nighttime parenting.

As children get older, they will probably need less sleep than they did when they were babies and toddlers. An eight-year-old might rather be up and running than sleeping. But when he's twelve or thirteen (give or take a couple of years for variations in the onset of puberty) it might be back to ten or twelve hours of sleep for a while. Let that be. And if you don't believe me, look it up. Pubescent and teen folks need more sleep. Their bodies are growing like crazy in ways you can see and ways you can't. Don't screw that up by treating them like younger children, or like full-grown adults. Accept and support their physical needs.

SandraDodd.com/sleep

Food

Food is *The Big One* for some people, the insurmountable obstacle, the place where awareness stalls. (For others, that's television.)

The more one's reaction to "food" (the word, the idea, the substance) is strong and emotional, the more evidence there is that the way in which that person was raised to see and deal with food should *not* be repeated.

The food section of my website is called "The Full Plate Club." Its intro says:

> "The empty plate club," referring to kids who successfully clean their plates, sounds so sad.
>
> "Full plate" sounds much more nurturing.

On questions of whether a cup is half full or half empty, consider a plate. If a child has a feeling of abundance he will stop eating when he's had enough and be healthier and happier than if anyone presses him to take one more bite.

Just as the topic of food can be a hurdle or a brick wall to some trying to get unschooling, it can also be the source of the epiphany that sheds light on all other principles involved in natural learning and parenting peacefully. Consider a child who has been told what and how much to eat, and told how his body feels by someone trying to manipulate or control him. That is not about learning or choices. If a parent understands that a child can learn about food by trying it, by eating it or not, by sensing how his own body feels, the parent understands something so profound that all their lives will change.

SandraDodd.com/food

The Clock isn't Hungry

Perhaps "eating by the clock" has roots in European manor houses filled with servants, where the lady of the house got to choose the times of meals (within the narrow window of what was considered right and proper). In more modern times, eating by the clock has to do with factory lunch breaks and with school bells.

Don't be the clock's mother. Don't watch the clock to see if it's time to eat. Watch your child. Or watch the clock to see if it's time to offer another snack, but don't let the clock say "not yet" or "Must EAT!"

It isn't good parenting or self control for an adult who has reproduced to be looking to a mechanical device to make decisions for her. Clocks are great for meeting people at a certain time, but they were never intended to be an oracle by which mothers would decide whether to pay attention to a child or not. Your child knows whether he's hungry. You don't. The clock doesn't either, never did, and never will.

SandraDodd.com/eating/peace

Not forcing

Perhaps it was The Great Depression, or the fears of WWII scarcity, rationing, blackout drills and bombings. Maybe it was a byproduct of the way the nineteenth century tended toward crushing children's spirits. By the late twentieth century, though, there were parents and grandparents who thought they would be good parents if they tried to force their children to eat everything on their plates. Every bite.

Perhaps it was intended to be scientific balance and measurement. Perhaps it was control for the sake of control. Maybe it was because some of those grandparents remembered really being hungry after a week of baking-soda biscuits and gravy and beans, and thought making sure kids got food in their bellies would help them sleep. Maybe it was training, for the sake of discipline itself, for children to eat when they were told.

I remember being told what to eat, when, where and how. Why, too, but "why" was "Because I said so," or "Because you won't get another chance until morning," or something similarly punitive and unnecessary.

SandraDodd.com/eating/idea

Not Limiting

"That's enough."

"You can't have any more."

"Just one."

Those statements lead to overeating. They lead to sorrow, a feeling of paucity, and to neediness for food, love, nurturance, compassion, generosity and money to buy more food someday. They lead to a yearning to find someone who will take them on dates where there is food. They will hasten the desire to grow up and leave.

"You can have more."

"I wish we had more; I'll get some next time I go to the store."

"Sure, you can have another one."

Those statements lead a person toward actually wondering whether he's still hungry or needy, and toward a feeling of contentment, of protection and provision, and of abundance. If someone has enough, neediness isn't likely to consume him.

SandraDodd.com/eating/control

How Does it Balance Out?

"Everything I've read about has really happened. The first couple of days, my youngest ate nothing but Twinkies and Spider-Man snacks. Then, amazingly enough, he got up the next morning and asked me for grapes for breakfast. You could have knocked me over with a feather! It truly didn't seem possible until I experienced it for myself." –Evie

After Holly had had braces on her teeth for two years, she posted this in public:

> Things to do when I get my braces off:
> 1) Have corn on the cob like all the time
> 2) Go to Shoney's and get like a ton of gum from their really cool 25¢ gum machine
> 3) Eat carrots until my skin turns orange

She doesn't chew gum much at all; never has. But she's frugal, and to spend a quarter to see that big gumball roller coaster work when she can't even chew the gum seems wrong to her. She has definitely been missing carrots, and grated carrots just aren't the same for her.

When the braces were removed, the dentist's office presented her with a balloon and a plastic canister filled with candy. No corn, no carrots, no gum. They gave her things she didn't even want, assuming *everyone* would choose candy.

In my family and others I have seen kids eat something sweet and then follow it up with meat or vegetables. Without having a hierarchy of what's "yucky" and "good," each food has as much chance to be "good." Nothing is glorified or vilified, and so children are making honest, thoughtful choices and end up eating (to name some of the things cited on my site as choices of young children): alfalfa sprouts, plums, broccoli, celery with peanut butter, milk, pizza, Chinese food, pickled garlic, cucumber with salt, grilled cheese sandwich, cantaloupe… there are more stories there, with details, but you get the idea.

SandraDodd.com/eating/balance
SandraDodd.com/eating/sweets

Advantages of Eating in Peace

If you've ever tried to eat when you were afraid or crying or someone was yelling at you, try to remember what that was like.

If you've ever tried to make someone eat something to the point that they were afraid or crying, you owe someone a serious apology.

When people are frightened, their digestive systems stop operating well, if at all. People need to be calm, for the sake of their health. A little bit of plain food in a peaceful room filled with trust and love is better than the greatest food in the world choked down through fearful tears.

Once I wrote

> Ramen in a happy environment is better than four dishes and a dessert in anger and sorrow.

Nancy Wooten responded:

> Proverbs 15:17 :-)

I looked it up: "Better is a dinner of herbs where love is, than a stalled ox and hatred therewith." In another translation, "Better a meal of vegetables where there is love than a fattened calf with hatred."

Perhaps I'm being repetitive here, but it seems people have been reciting this good advice for many thousands of years, and still there are parents threatening children with punishment if they don't *Eat*, **NOW!**

Americans, especially, spend a great deal of physical and emotional energy feeling terrible and guilty about what they have eaten in the past, what they're eating now, what they're cooking for later. They argue about it with others, make dire warnings and threats and just generally work themselves up into an unhealthy froth about the latest inkling or vague correlation concerning butter, honey, rice, corn or soy. Agitation and panic are more unhealthy than Twinkies, most likely. It is possible to avoid Twinkies *and* to lay aside the painfully frantic quest for the optimal amount of the perfect food, eaten in the best place at the ideal time.

SandraDodd.com/eating/peace

The Purpose of Family Dinner

There is an ideal of a family sitting down to eat together, dressed nicely, calm... It's a vestige of having had servants (or having *been* servants, more likely, in my own family's case and most others). When a family has strict requirements that all will sit together at the same time, it's worth examining the intent and the results. If it's working wonderfully well, carry on. If it's something to fight about, if it's stressing the mom out, if the meals are tense or forced or if the parents know there's something else one or more of the children would much rather be doing and just don't care, this family dinner might be the low point of the day for someone.

In a case in which the family has been scattered to various jobs and schools and the only chance they get to see each other is at dinner, then it's probably not an unschooling family.

Some families might have so much joyous desire to cook together and be together that sitting down together for a meal is better than anything else could be. In those cases it should definitely be done!

In those ideal, traditional family sit-downs, either the adults talk over the heads of the children, who are expected to say nothing unless they're addressed directly, or the children are asked to report on their days. If it's conversational, then it's not a report, and that could be good. If it's a report, then maybe separating work/school from eating would be good. If there is "school," then it's not an unschooling family.

Rephrase: If it's a report, then maybe separating learning from eating would be good. That doesn't even make sense, though. Why report on learning? And eating with nice conversation around is probably going to *be* learning.

Some people unthinkingly recite phrases like "Family dinner is crucial," or "Families should eat together, or..." The "or" might be that their kids will be juvenile delinquents, their kids won't get good grades, the parents will lose touch with their children, the kids won't learn how to use forks and spoons...

Whatever you decide to do, try not to make a rule about always doing it the same way every night, regardless of circumstances. There are times to eat together and times to let it slide. Make your decisions and recommendations thoughtfully.

SandraDodd.com/eating/dinner

Social Obligations and oddities

Probably in every culture there are ceremonial and social meals. There are times when eating food with other people creates or strengthens bonds, or when sharing bread or a drink has spiritual significance. One taste of a wedding cake is better than turning down wedding cake altogether, because it's the ceremonial blessing of a marriage. If people are toasting with alcohol and you don't or can't drink alcohol (ever, or at that time), at least join the toast with water. To refrain from joining a toast is worse than an insult; it's like a public curse. One who pointedly fails to toast is standing up against the crowd and saying "I hope your project fails horribly" (or whatever it might be). So let your children know those things.

In the absence of a social obligation to eat at least a token amount, let your children choose not to eat if they don't want to. If the purpose of food is the sustenance of the body and the mind, then let that principle override schedules and expectations and traditions, most of the time. Your children will be more willing to eat to be polite if you only press it on rare occasions.

Don't make it a social obligation to finish a bowl of sweetened cereal, or to eat more spaghetti than they want just because there's still some in the bowl. Remember how much the clock didn't know or care? Bowls are even less interested than clocks are.

There should be a special buffet in hell for parents who have personified foods and told their children that the orange juice will have its feelings hurt if the child doesn't taste it. No wonder some children lie to their parents!

SandraDodd.com/eating/humor

Longterm Problems with Controlling Food

If I were to be beating around bushes, this book would be twice as long, so let us move to the #1 Most Harmful Food Rule of All Time:

**You have to finish everything on your plate
or you won't get dessert.**

I don't think any other food-related issue even comes close to having done the kind of damage that can last a sad hour, a memorable year, a decade and a century. "Self control" then is expressed by people who live alone and might like to have a bowl of ice cream, but without a single witness to their actions, they will, out of a sense of self-discipline and doing what's right, eat meat, two vegetables and some bread, rice or pasta so that they "earn" the right to eat ice cream.

So let us leave my grandmother back in my memory, and whichever ancient and possibly long dead old folks you, dear reader, have conjured, and go back to children you know, living today, who will want to eat within a few hours.

You could mess them up early (which our culture applauds) or you can learn to let them grow whole and healthy and strong and free, not crippled in mind and spirit. Simple. Don't mess them up.

The title on the page is about "controlling food." People talk about it frequently, but food isn't a conscious wild thing that needs to be controlled. "Food" is a vast array of substances, many of which exist on the planet in the absence of people, and some of which are traditional re-combinations of substances, or substances altered with heat. You probably can't herd cats, and neither can you "control food."

People talk about "controlling your appetite." You might with force of will control your actions, but that generally means creating a chorus of voices in your head saying "Don't do it; you'll get fat; it's stupid; leave it alone; you don't need that; you've had enough; children are starving in Africa," while you ignore your instincts and your body's signals.

Maybe what is really meant is controlling *other* people's actions. Probably so. Parents are expected to alternately bribe and shame their children until they no longer have the ability to sense what their bodies need. It doesn't take long. It takes many more years to recover from having that instinct dulled and ignored. Some never regain it.

There are adults who eat by the clock and by the scale, measuring their food instead of eating until they feel they've had enough. Some people have no idea whatsoever what "enough" might feel like.

There are adults who eat as much as they possibly can, every time they get a chance.

There are adults who try to eat nothing at all, until they're weak and unhealthy.

There are teens who do those things, too, mostly the eating nothing. There are teens who eat what their parents "make" them eat, and then go and throw it up. Sometimes it's because they want to be thinner. Sometimes it's because they are so tired of their parents telling them what to do that the only way they can feel real and whole is to remove what their parents forced into them.

The parents did not get their way after all, and for a moment that teen feels that she won.

That cannot happen when a parent is a child's partner and the facilitator of her natural learning.

I know not all bulimics are female. My friend Vincent went below 100 pounds at the age of 16 and nearly died. He was in the hospital and then in treatment in another state, but his dad still didn't back down from his attempted control of every aspect of that boy's life. Then Vincent ran away, still turning down food. I see that family, and my neighbors, and families at restaurants, and families in magazine articles and in other cars on the highway. I know that with very simple changes in their attitudes toward each other they could see those painful, dangerous, hateful habits and actions and turn them to love and support and togetherness.

The desire to control others kills. First it kills their respect for you, and then it kills the relationship, and it can in worst cases cause the actual death of the younger person.

In less extreme cases, they might just be anorexic or might eat for comfort and self-reward to the point that they have no idea what "healthy" is or what it might be good for, because they just don't care.

SandraDodd.com/eating/longterm

Health Food / Diets

There is a growing body of evidence and research about the temporary nature of dieting. If a person chooses to follow a particular diet in a series of choices over days, months or years, that can work. If one has a diet imposed on him, or commits to a diet once and then feels helpless and trapped thereafter, the stress can cancel out any health benefits of the diet. If the food choices exist to satisfy a person other than the one doing the eating, that can build up to an unhealthy relationship and body both.

Paying two or three times as much for a health-food version of processed food is probably not as good as buying ingredients and preparing things yourself. If the parents don't enjoy cooking, explore ways to present raw or packaged foods in interesting ways. Cheese, bread and fruit can make a beautiful meal with a pretty plate and arrangement.

If you're reading labels more carefully than you're reading your own child, please reconsider. If "cheesy puffs" are neither glorified nor vilified, then they're just a thing. Not a dangerous thing or a sinful thing or an exciting thing. One option of thousands.

Diets are about control and not choices. They are about lack-of-choice. If someone chooses 100 times to eat or not eat something, he's still choosing. If he decides ONCE that it's not okay to choose, then he's deprived and powerless and trapped. This is not just words. This is biochemistry, posture, emotion. It is powerlessness, either self-imposed or inflicted from the outside.

Help your children to be powerful. Let them have all of their power and some of yours.

SandraDodd.com/eating/diets

Research

There is research in pediatrics and in anthropology supporting the idea that children's choices should be respected. I'm trying not to press particular books, nor to treat the news of 2009 as news forever. I can say it looks like the research is growing and building upon itself, so you should be able to find some easily now and much more linked off from those.

SandraDodd.com/eating/research

The Purpose of Eating

If people grow up eating when and what they want, without having attached other values to eating, then the purpose of eating for them is to maintain bodily function. They'll eat the way they drink water or use the toilet. Their body will give them physical cues.

You don't know exactly what your children need. They won't know either, if they're never allowed to live in such a way that they will learn to pay more attention to their bodies than to a book or a menu, calendar or clock.

You do know they need water, and some fruit and vegetables and protein and carbohydrates and enough oil (from nuts or meat or cheese or fish or something) to make their bodies function. If you make a variety of foods available, and if your children aren't shamed or ridiculed or controlled about what they can choose, they will deal with food in ways that most people don't believe could be possible.

People who have raised livestock or had pets who could go outside might have seen animals eat unusually sometimes. Maybe a dog or cat will seek out grass or something leafy. Sometimes a horse might forage differently than usual, or eat a little dirt. They know what they're doing.

When children have been able to choose, they can grow up knowing they need to not eat anything for half a day or more, or that they need just vegetables, or they need something salty. It does go against our cultural conditioning to think that people have instincts, but once someone has had a baby and smelled that infant's scalp and felt the reaction when the baby cries, it must be easier for them to consider that instincts are functional in people, it's just nearly taboo to discuss them.

So the purpose of eating can be medicinal. It can be for strength and health. It can be for stimulant purposes or for calming. It can be a social activity. It can be a nervous or self-soothing habit. If you can maintain a situation in which your children are usually calm and comfortable, those last few will not be needed as much as they are with some people. Be a better friend and comfort to your children than food is. That is not accomplished by shame, control or rules.

SandraDodd.com/eating/purpose

Holidays and Sugar

If you've turned to this page in random Ouija-Book fashion, welcome! If you arrived here methodically, page-by-page, you won't be surprised at what I'm about to say.

Halloween candy gets dusty if kids' diets aren't limited or controlled. If a child goes trick-or-treating but isn't desperate for every bit of sugar he can grab, and if the parents don't take the candy away from him or make rules about how much he can eat, he'll eat some and the rest will probably be thrown away around Christmas.

Christmas stockings have candy, almost always. The Jewish kids still have gelt left. Those who've been limited will finish that stuff off within days. Those who haven't will probably have to throw their candy away to make room for...

Easter! Stores load up with a whole bunch of attractive candy on the theme of little yellow chickens and the eggs of fantasy birds and malted milk balls that look like colored eggs, and hollow chocolate bunnies.

When I was a kid I longed for just one more bite of hollow chocolate bunny. Since I've been a mom, I have thrown away several half-bunnies and lots of Santa candy, and dried-up Halloween candy from cardboard boxes stuck on closet shelves. Something's different, and much, much better.

There is a young wives' tale that sugar causes hyperactivity. There are several scientific studies that say it does not. There are young moms who would swear in court that their child was hyper because of candy, and if candy is refuted, they say food coloring or *something* has made their kids hyperactive—"Off the wall."

What the researchers say is that what the parents were seeing was the child's exuberance at receiving something that was usually forbidden, or the joy of being at a party. I think those parents aren't used to seeing their children happy. Part of the reason the children haven't been happier is that the mothers have been shaming, blaming and controlling instead of living calm, joyful lives. Don't be one of those.

SandraDodd.com/myths

Monkey Platters

If the several pages before seemed to be nonsense, you can try this one yourself. You'll need a large plate or tray, a knife and cutting board. Maybe also a can opener and strainer. If you have wooden toothpicks, bonus!

Look in your cupboard or pantry for five to eight of these things:

> cheese, apples, grapes, bananas, cherries
> ham, turkey, hot dogs,
> pineapple, pickles, olives,
> nuts, crackers, raisins, dates, currants,
> carrots, celery, raw cauliflower, jicama,
> cherry tomatoes, melon cubes,
> tiny sandwiches of peanut butter or tuna,
> blackberries, strawberries, raspberries,
> orange sections, kiwi slices...
> (you get the idea)

Arrange the food nicely on a plate and put it within reach of kids. Don't tell them it's time to eat it, or that they have to taste everything, or that you worked hard and they owe it to you to eat it. Just put it down and say "Here, if you want it" or something neutralish.

Check back to see what went first, and what stayed. Plan accordingly next time.

Taking food to someone who is reading or playing a game or watching a movie and just putting it where he or she can reach it without any instructions, warnings or reminders is a great gift. It is a simple gesture, and a profound service.

SandraDodd.com/monkeyplatters

Chores

Kids blossom and get bigger from doing adult things because they want to, instead of kid-things they have to do because they're small.

When parents see the world as a web of "have to" situations, in which the adults and the children are all powerless to make choices and everyone is trapped and helpless, the child cannot be empowered. If the parent feels like a martyr and a servant, she will resent her children, and they will feel unloved and unwanted.

It's a trap made entirely of words and thoughts.

I had been unschooling for years before a few people suggested on a message board that requiring kids to do chores could be as bad as making them do schoolwork. I perked up immediately, and everything they said has proven true at our house. The first principle was "If a mess is bothering you, YOU clean it up." Another one was "Do things for your family because you *want* to!"

It was new to me to consider housework a fun thing to be done with a happy attitude, but as it has changed my life and because it fit in so well with the other unschooling issues, I've collected things to help others consider this change as well.

In the same way that food controls can create food issues, forcing housework on children can cause resentments and avoidances which neither get houses clean nor improve the relationships between children and parents.

Also, studies of separated identical twins have shown that the desire and ability to clean and organize has more to do with genetics than "training."

I hope you enjoy and are inspired by some of the collected writings at the site listed below, few to none of which are my own.

SandraDodd.com/chores

Serving Others as a Gift

Do you like your dishes?

Would you wash your dishes even if you had no children?

I'll get back to those questions.

When a mother lives with a thought like "These kids *owe* me..." it's unlikely that she will get very far toward generosity with her time and energy. The feeling that you're giving and giving to someone who will never repay you can be deflating. Perhaps it's just not right to send our children the bill, though. I remember being told I should respect my mother because she gave me birth. The unhappier she was making my life, the less sense that made. When I learned more about where babies came from, the idea that I should be grateful made no sense at all. I started to understand that she resented my presence and wanted to get whatever work or praise out of me that she could.

With my children I turned it right around. They didn't ask to be born. I was the one who wanted children. I invited them here by my actions and decisions. I owe them. I owe them food and friendship and protection. I owe them comfort if I can arrange it. I owe them the best of me, and to help nurture the best of them.

Before I was married, I had dishes and I washed them. When I was married, I had dishes and I washed them. I have children, and sometimes they help me, but they're my dishes, and I wash them. When my children leave, I will still have dishes. I will still wash them. Should my husband and I not die at the same time, the one who is left will wash the dishes.

Where in there does it make sense to make children wash dishes?

And seriously, if you have dishes you don't like, get rid of them and get dishes you enjoy. Look at thrift stores or ask your friends, or learn to make dishes. But don't confuse the simple washing of a dish with the worth of a child.

Dishes seem to symbolize the intersection of housework and helplessness to many people. They can understand that children can learn to read without lessons. They're sure science and history can be discovered in fun ways. But they "have to" do the dishes, and their children "have to" help them. And after they fight about that, there's not enough energy or love left to make anything fun.

Over the years when people have said, "But I *have to* wash the dishes," people such as Deb Lewis and Joyce Fetteroll have made many sensible and sometimes shocking suggestions. People could get cheap dishes at garage sales and throw them away. They could use paper plates and burn them for fuel, or throw them away or compost them. They could eat over the sink or stove. They could make food that doesn't need plates, and use paper towels, or newspaper or printer paper. They could eat out.

Some people say "But cockroaches will come," or "our house has ants" or "mice."

Submerge the dishes in water until morning, and they'll be easy to wash. Get a dishwasher.

But the attitude that someone *has to* wash the dishes gets in the way of seeing options.

Wash dishes because you want to. What would make you want to? Love. Generosity. A desire to have an available kitchen, a clean slate, a fresh canvas. The wish to do something simple and kind for yourself and others. The wish to keep peace in your house. The preference of singing and feeling warm soapy water over accusations and threats and tears. The intention to build loving relationships rather than antagonism. The hope to make a haven of your home, rather than a dangerous trap everyone would love to escape.

If you offer service with the hope of reward or praise or indebtedness, it will create resentment in you and in those who received the service. If you offer service without sending the bill, anything others say or do will be an honest expression of gratitude, not the last-minute submission of the bare minimum payment for services rendered. A "thank you" that's scripted is just noise. A "thank you" you didn't expect is true communication.

As with all changes, it might take a while. If the path you're on is working really well, ignore all of this and keep on it. If the path you're on is causing rifts in relationships, or arguments, or if people are trying to avoid work or doing a crummy job so that the dishes aren't really clean, consider taking a different path.

SandraDodd.com/chores/gift

"Necessary?" No...

If a family shows up in unschooling discussions, and they're still doing school at home but they're curious about unschooling, maybe the talk about food and chores and bedtimes is just going to overwhelm and confuse them. Because there *can* be unschooling in a family where kids also have chores and bedtimes and have to clean their plates. I don't personally think it will have the depth or benefit, ultimately, as a house where the children's preferences and freedoms have high priority, but it could still absolutely be, in homeschooling terms, unschooling.

Every family I've seen where control is protected has eventually gone back to trying to control learning, or the resentment and frustration around other issues causes the parents to be disdainful of the children, and the children lose hope that they can please their parents, and eventually they go to school to escape the house.

Do you want a surly child, or a happy child? Do you want a child who wants to be with you, or who wants to avoid you?

SandraDodd.com/option

Relationships

In one online discussion, a mom was assuring us in strong terms that if we did not make our kids do chores, they would grow up like her husband. Someone defended her by writing:

> It's possible that the poster has a husband who doesn't clean up and is [a jerk] about it. (Not completely uncommon in our culture.) That can certainly color one's perceptions. (Probably color them an angry red color.) I wouldn't want to raise a son to be like that.

I responded:

> Do you think requiring chores will ensure non-[jerk]-adult-status?
>
> Was your friend's husband required to do chores?
>
> It's completely common in our culture for kids to be forced to do chores, while adults laugh at them, shame them, and tell them they didn't do them well enough. It's a Whole LOT like school. There's a curriculum and there is a schedule, and kids are expected to do things adults don't have to do, and the kids are (in many families) "graded" and either made to do again or given rewards (allowance or money), but the child doesn't have the option to quit.

Is the purpose of chores so that a child will learn to do chores? Learn not to be [a jerk]? If it's lessons, how does it not fall under the principles of natural learning?

Holly had two disposable cameras with her in England. Her hosts sent her home with a disc with 445 high-quality photos, but still.... So we got those back, each with a disc, and I downloaded one, marking the other while I was doing that. OOPS. The second envelope had Holly's prints and negatives, but the disk was a family's pictures of the Roman coliseum, and some other stuff looked like Italy and Spain. They had a teenaged boy with them. He did not look the least bit happy to be there. He wouldn't pose with the adults, but sullenly on the side. Anyone want to take a bet that he's been made to do chores and was supposed to be extremely grateful to go on vacation with people who had treated him as property (or as a very underprivileged housemate, for anyone who was about to claim that when people share a house they share upkeep)? I'm betting chores and school and shame. There was a harsh face on the boy, and they've captured it in photos (if they ever get their photos, I mean. I did go back and impress upon the photo lab to try to find them before they come in, pay, go home, and discover they have Holly's pictures of cows on the Thames. . .)

Well, we have Holly's now. The difference between Holly's face in her photos and that poor teenaged boy's is like two different worlds. Granted, Holly's younger and was off without her family, which probably lit her up some, but she WAS with a family, and she could've been surly, theoretically.

SandraDodd.com/chores/relationship
(where the word isn't "jerk")

"It Seems Unfair." "It's CRAZY."

Two examples of moms who were angry at the whole idea:

> It just feels really unfair to me, to be standing in the kitchen late at night, surrounded by cockroach-attracting mess, watching the kids play the xbox or watch TV, while I do all the cleaning up.

A tirade directed just at me:

> I have three sons, ages 8, 4, and 2. I'm starting our third year of homeschooling. I have gradually come from trying to copy the school curriculums to mostly unschooling. But when I read the comments about doing the housework for them, I want to scream! Unfair, to me, to even suggest that they should not be required to

contribute. My mother said, as her mother said, "You eat, don't you? Then you can help clear the table/clean up the dishes."

I met a woman who said to clean up after her (only) four-year-old son was like a 'gift' to him, to re-set his toys. I looked at her, wondering exactly what drugs she was on. I'll bet his future spouse will want to kick her butt.

Why should the children take no responsibility?

If you agree with those voices, you're not alone. Many unschoolers once felt that way. Most mainstream parents feel that way. Few people have seen the alternatives but are certain that the straw man of their stories is a certainty. We will create cockroach-attracting jerks whose spouses will hate them.

Having taken that risk, along with many other families, I have not seen those dire predictions play out at all.

At the links below there are long, inspiring and entertaining responses to the two quotes above, but as one is by Deb Lewis and the other by Joyce Fetteroll, I haven't brought them to this publication. They do live on the website, though, in all their kick-ass logic and compassion.

SandraDodd.com/chores/unfair
SandraDodd.com/chores/scream

Modeling Joy

Attempting to force someone to do something has never led to peace and cooperation. It creates sneakiness and avoidance. If something is so painful and distasteful that one person will bully another person into doing it, the pain and distaste are the problems.

If you're not in the mood to put away laundry, don't do it. Find alternatives, or get what you need and then find a way to get in the mood to put the rest of it away before long. If you can't make it fun, how could a child begin to do so?

Helping mom do something fun can be desirable. Being in the same room with a mom who's talking or singing can be fun. Being in the same room with a mom who is yelling and slamming things around and accusing and shaming is not fun.

If a child helps you for a while, say "this was fun," or "I appreciate that!" or something in your own words. Don't say "It's about time," or "If you can put the towels away you can do the rest of it, too."

If you live a joyful life, there will be joy in your house. If you live a grumpy, hateful life, you will be modeling hatred. Most people live somewhere in between those. If something can take you all the way to "joy," and you can share that with your children, they will have a gift some people never once have in a lifetime.

SandraDodd.com/chores/joy

True Tales of Children Helping

Unexpectedly, Beth's children vacuumed the van; Deb's son vacuumed the den once a week; Danielle's girls chopped vegetables; Kathryn's son brought in the trash bins; Deb's son did the dishes. There are many other such reports at the link below; each was a sweet surprise.

As to when these bursts of activity might appear, maturity can help. Some of the stories in the larger collection involve very young children, but most involve kids over ten. Some of the instances were "short attention" situations, and others were long-term.

Two tales of my own house, Saturday, April 10, 2004

> I had given up waiting for Kirby to bring laundry down, but I knew he was out of socks, and I happened to be in his bathroom, so I gathered up all his black socks and t-shirts.
>
> When they were dry, I just yelled upstairs and asked Kirby if he could help me do something when he got to a stopping place. He was there pretty soon, and I said I wanted help getting his stuff into his room.
>
> We sat side by side and folded ten t-shirts and paired up seven pairs of socks. We talked about the night before and the plans for the day. It was really nice.
>
> Later in the day I had the urge to clean behind the refrigerator. I was the only one in there, and I scooted it out, unplugged it, and Holly passed by. I said "You want to see something gross?"
>
> Lots of dust. LOTS, greasy yucko dust-layer and regular back-of-fridge excitement.
>
> She was doing other things in the kitchen while I was doing that, but ended up interested in a few bits. I asked if she would help me down from the chair when I wanted down (when I was cleaning the top).
>
> She got interested in doing the other side of the top, and then the walls. She moved on to cabinet doors. I hadn't intended to do those, but she was having fun. So when the fridge was scooted back into its

hole, I asked her if she'd be willing to do the ceiling fan if I'd hand her rags already set up with hot water and 409. Sure, she said. So we did.

That wasn't planned, and all I had asked for was help getting down from the chair, because I'm still spooked about falling.

I think the answer is be happy even if they don't help, and give it time.

There are many tales on the page below and linked from it, told with all the excitement and wonder of it just having happened, by many moms who had previously thought it was crazy.

SandraDodd.com/chores/tales

Service

STOP! Cover up the rest of the page past this paragraph. Don't look down before you think about the word "service." What emotions or images arise?

Feel those emotions; breathe; what are those emotions?

I know service has been mentioned before, in this book, but I also know it's something at which very many new unschoolers (and some of the older ones) balk. It stops them dead in their thoughts.

Did you really think about it? Was it difficult to even think about? If not, I'm guessing you're involved in a service organization of some sort, or a group with an emphasis on virtues. I could be wrong. I'd be interested in collecting some reactions and thoughts on this. My e-mail address is Sandra@SandraDodd.com if you'd be willing to share.

Did "service" make you think of church? Military? Servitude? Class? Martyrdom? Lunch? Tennis? Subpeonas?

"Service" is an old word in English. It's from French. They have it from Latin. The root word is "to serve." It means to present something to someone, or to take care of someone or something. It means to be useful, to do what is needed.

In an unschooling chat in April 2009, a general discussion turned beautifully serious for a while, and I've saved that part for people to read. We had talked about England, World of Warcraft, hand-knitted socks, and we were having a good time when someone mentioned that her teenager had jumped up to help with groceries. It was like finding a piece of a jigsaw puzzle on the floor and knowing exactly where it goes. The transcript and links to other things it ties in with are at the link below.

Some of it was about the enthusiasm with which several people's teens will jump up and bring in groceries, with some sweet details of particular days. Part of it was about doing laundry for people. Chat writing is pretty informal.

> SandraDodd: A few days ago Keith went for groceries to Costco. He usually comes back with a car trunk full of stuff and we all go out and bring some in and put it away, so it's usually one trip, but with three to five worker ants. One day, though, Holly heard him pull up and yelled "Dad's Home!" and ran down to be the first to help him, and it only took two people.
>
> Schuyler: No coercion, no force, just a request and the ability to say yes or no
>
> RVB: Sometimes, I'll get home from grocery shopping and Michelle will come, without me asking, to bring in the bags.
>
> JennyC: Chamille does that all the time
>
> SandraDodd: I think not many people would expect that of a 17-year-old. I just kept sitting at the computer, and nobody got mad at me for it.
>
> JennyC: she always helps bring in the groceries, I never have to ask, she just does it she'll even put groceries away sometimes
>
> SandraDodd: I've seen parents say "I shopped, you have to carry it in," and then it's not fun anymore
>
> RVB: Michelle often asks for help bringing her things from the car. I helped her and mentioned I'd have to come back to get my purse and coffee. She said "well it's a good thing I'm here" and she brought my purse and coffee in!
>
> SandraDodd: "Will you help me?" is way better than "You have to do it." Yucko.

Without choice, there can be no gifts. Without options, there can be no generosity. With expectations, there can be no spontaneity. Life becomes a test, with guaranteed failures. The biggest failure, though, is to set up such tests in the first place. I'm going to pull from the chat some things Schuyler Waynforth and I wrote:

Schuyler:

> It's amazing to see doing for others as a gift. It takes the whole angst about servitude away. There isn't any servitude in it when it's a gift.
>
> David just brought me tea He does that most nights, it is such a sweet thing. I just got Linnaea Dr. Pepper, and she thanked me. The gentleness is so overwhelming, the consideration.

I wrote:

> There's another level in medieval monastic thought that says the opportunity to serve is a gift. And I'm getting old enough to understand and feel that. It's very interesting.
>
> One place to see it is with Diana /hahamommy who realizes that when she does things for Hayden she's lucky to have a child. [Diana's firstborn, Hannah, died of leukemia and an infection in 2006, at the age of nine.] But most people can't even relax enough to think of the gift they give someone else by bringing them a cup of tea or a Dr Pepper.

It is amazing when you don't need to hear thank you. Doing it was enough. "Service as a gift" can be a gift to the server, as well.

Even with grown kids who could absolutely take care of themselves if I died or if they moved away, I'm still doing laundry for them because I want to free their time up to do more interesting things. I started running out of ways to express my affection and to support their interests when they had jobs and cars, but this is a thing I can still do. If I decided it was hurting me, I could turn around and hurt them. Lots of parents do that.

If I decide it's a way to show affection, I turn around and show them affection.

Part of creating a learning environment is creating a safe, generous, loving environment.

SandraDodd.com/service

Gratitude

Gratitude is about abundance. Resentment is about paucity. Choose gratitude. It is a choice.

Half-empty cups are substantially different from half-full cups. It's not just theoretical holy water in those cups. The half-empty cups hold a concoction of frustration and need and irritation. The half-full cups contain joy and hope and gratitude.

Ren Allen wrote beautifully about gratitude one day, and I'm glad I saved it.

> Washing dishes may not be my favorite activity, I can think of many things I prefer. But I can choose to grumble and feel bummed that I "have to" do this "chore" OR I can choose to be grateful to have hot running water, my loved ones alive and with me to use dishes, to have food to need dishes for etc...there is SO much to be grateful for in the simple act of washing dishes.

Gratitude embarrasses people sometimes. The same aspect of modern life that breeds cynicism chokes out gratitude. It makes people poor, though, to think of gratitude as something archaic or corny or stupid.

The difference between poverty and abundance is sometimes the ability to see what one has. There have been times when I didn't have a car, we had a leaky roof, and the washing machine wasn't working. There have been more times that the car and washing machine were functioning, the house was solid, and I forgot to appreciate it.

People seem naturally to want more, and to want better, and to have the urge to tweak and improve their lives and their surroundings. Don't deny the restless desire that enables people to explore and invent, but while looking ahead with hope and plans, look around with gratitude, too.

SandraDodd.com/gratitude

Focus, Obsessions, Hobbies

If it is true that everything is connected, then any hobby, interest or obsession can lead to every "subject area," and be tied in with many historical periods, areas of science, other hobbies, art, music, geography, technology, religion, photography, literature, future, fantasy, safety, sports, colors, holidays, mathematics of one sort (or of several sorts)...

The same parents will say "He can't focus" will say "He's too single-minded about... [something they don't understand or appreciate]."

WWII, Elvis, Gilligan, Barbies, musical theatre, bicycles, electric guitar, topiary sculpture, Zoo Tycoon, religion, horses, pirates, teapots, Samurai armor, hamsters, running or beading have tie-ins to a thousand things.

I have a relative who told me a story and wanted my agreement and sympathy. His son's grades in school weren't the highest, and so he was going to make him quit his job at a Civil War shop in a mall in South Carolina. I said no, I thought it was a terrible mistake—that he would learn more working in that shop than he would at school.

My argument didn't win that battle, but it can't help but win the war, as it were. Rejecting learning in favor of grades is a giant step backwards into the darkness.

Our oldest son was obsessed with games and martial arts from an early age. As a teen he worked in a gaming shop and at a karate dojo, and as an adult he works for an online video gaming company. Had we told him he couldn't play games or go to the gaming shop until he had studied his writing and his New Mexico history, it would not have helped him get a good job in Texas where he communicates in writing in real time. We would have been pulling him a giant step back into the previous decade, rather than letting him find his way into the decade ahead.

SandraDodd.com/focus

Barbie

As a hobby goes, Barbie can range from a shelf of costumed dolls to owning a museum.

One morning I came in and there were photos on the computer I hadn't taken. Holly had. They were Barbie dolls dressed and posed as the characters in a certain musical. I recognized it. She had done a really great job. I won't tell you which musical, but if you're curious, the photos are here:

SandraDodd.com/barbieholly

Meanwhile, unbeknownst to Holly, her friend Jayn in California was similarly costuming, staging and photographing a Barbie version of Romeo and Juliet. Being young and not understanding the end, she had changed the story to make more sense. The new storyline was charming all by itself.

Jayn and her mom, Robyn Coburn, have been to a Barbie convention and other doll-related events.

SandraDodd.com/barbiejuliet

Ren Allen was raised in such a way that Barbies and make-up and adornment were sinful. She became an unschooling mom and a make-up artist.

Kelly Schultz documented the play and learning her daughters were having with Barbies. Among other fun things, she wrote, "The Barbies are played with almost every day, and like others have written about, there is usually an elaborate process of setting up a designed environment for the dolls, which involves finding a location, finding all the pieces of furniture/accessories that they need, getting the vehicle they need, etc. Often this process includes creating or building some type of infrastructure that the Barbies need, which is very creative! Think paper with holes punched through it and strung up with yarn as a shower curtain, little tiny pieces of cloth strung up with yarn for hanging beds for the little fairy-sized Barbies, pools in the sink, chopped up real salad greens for food, specially fashioned clothing from little bits of fabric, etc."

In response to some people saying *"Barbies are stupid,"* Kelly wrote, "Barbie brought pulleys into our life recently, since the girls wanted to create a Barbie elevator out of a Costco-size Fruit Loops box. I can't imagine that learning about pulleys, the weight capacity of string from the hardware store, and the number of Barbies it would take to exceed that weight capacity would somehow be associated with stupidity!"

Never in my life did Barbies appeal to me personally, but I have supported Holly's Barbie interest in dozens of ways. We moved when she was six and our new house had a closet under the stairs that became Barbieland. She could play without being disturbed and she could quit without needing to clean up. All the Barbie forks and earrings and shoes have stayed safe from the vacuum cleaner.

There are many other stories, accounts and photographs at "Barbie in the Lives of Unschoolers."

SandraDodd.com/barbie

Feed Passions

Unschooling depends on children being able to follow their interests, but just as with food, it's hard to know whether they want to just taste it or finish off a case. If a child wants to bake a cake, you don't know in advance whether she just wanted to mix the batter once or whether she will end up creating wedding cakes for millionaires. You don't need to know.

Help a child experience some of what she's interested in, and pay attention to responses and mood and questions later. Don't press or force. Don't ignore interest, though. You'll get better at it with practice.

Think of your adult friends who love sports. Some love to coach, some to watch on TV, some in person, some to play, some to collect cards and articles, some only love big international finals, some like local games or pick-up sports in parks for fun. If your child loves baseball it doesn't mean he wants to play. If he wants to play, it doesn't mean he wants to be on a team. Go easy with your pressure, but be ready with your generosity of attention, time or money if what the child wants is something you can afford.

Interests come and go, but let that be natural and not because of parental discouragement or pressure. Facilitate their interests without trying to own or manage them.

SandraDodd.com/obsessions/feedpassions

Judging Interests

When books are an obsession, it's considered a virtue. When mathematics is an obsession it's considered genius. When history is an obsession, that's scholarly. When rock and roll is an obsession or folk art, or dance... maybe not as easily impressive to the outside world. But as all things are connected, let your child see the world from the portals that open to him, and don't press him to get in line at an entryway that doesn't sparkle and beckon.

Many of my friends are making socks. I don't understand it, except that I've seen their joy. I've touched the yarn and seen the sparkle in their eyes.

I write about the same thing day after day. My friends who aren't involved in unschooling probably could think of many other things they wish I would do instead—things they also like, things they could join in on maybe, or at least talk about with me.

Keith makes furniture that's only used for camping.

Some people paint pictures I don't like. So what!? There are pictures in the world I do like, and there are hobbies I do understand. Some people play music I don't like. Some people read books I don't like. But none of that is about me except the negativity I've generated being irritated with their hobbies.

Unless their joy and curiosity are snuffed out, your children will have interests and, if you're lucky, obsessions and hobbies. How negative do you want to be about those? Try to decide in advance so you're being mindful and aware when they show you their painted rocks or their plastic soldiers or their hip-hop video collection. They will trust you as long and as far as you are trustworthy.

If your children's joy and curiosity have been crippled or shushed, or if your own joy and curiosity are comatose somewhere in the older parts of you, either put your children in school or find ways (even if it's hard work) to restore and refresh and maintain joy and wonder and appreciation. I don't want anyone to buy this book or read my website and use it as an excuse to be lame-ass *sort-of* unschoolers. Do it right and do it well.

SandraDodd.com/obsessions/feedpassions

So wait, wait, wait...

Did I just "judge" an interest in unschooling? That page before, did I start off saying accept people's interests and then saying if you're just kind of vaguely interested in unschooling, put your kids in school and get a better hobby?

A vague interest in unschooling is peachy. An intense interest in unschooling is fine for a teenager who wishes she had found it sooner, or for a childless adult who is fascinated by the possibilities and by the tie-ins to current and historical movements and theories. But if you have children and they are not in school and you have custody and you intend to or are claiming to unschool them, then use the tools and tricks in this book and on the webpage. Follow links to other sites. Really try these things. Unschool right and well, with vigor and enthusiasm, with understanding and knowledge. Don't stumble along from park day to park day with the unschooling crowd, or say "I'd do better, but I'm isolated from other unschoolers."

If you're unschooling, that's not "an interest in unschooling." That's a part of your being, of your life, of your thoughts, actions and priorities.

Priorities

The most difficult part of this book has been deciding the order of the chapters. The website on which it's based goes all directions. The page on priorities is linked from and to several other pages. Here it sits between "Obsessions" and "Personal Change," which shows one plane of it but discounts the others, which isn't perfect.

Here's the deal, though, with priorities: It could follow any section in this book, and could be linked from every page on my site, and that would make sense.

Some people don't think of their priorities, or they have priorities like "finish the to-do list," or "make more money," or "exercise an hour a day." If your priorities involve principles such as "providing for others' comfort" or "learning," then your more tangible goals might still make sense, but they will have a purpose.

Some people's priorities come from religion, or clubs or hobbies. Someone might have a priority involving being Godlike, and not missing Mass. They might provide flowers for the altar every week from their own gardens, and won't schedule things that would hamper that.

My own family's priorities for a long time had to do with events of the Society for Creative Anachronism (SCA). Medieval trumped other considerations. I've just returned from the U.K. with twenty pounds (weight, not sterling) of books, and less than half of that involves the Middle Ages. My priorities have changed. That's not a problem for me. We used to plan our "real-life" events and vacations around SCA events and deadlines. We lived there, and learned tons, and have great friends from it. Keith and Marty still attend events quite often.

So you're unschooling. Learning ought to be a priority. Safety and comfort. Availability of materials (back to learning). Togetherness? Relationships. Think about the things you value and want to support with your time, energy and funds.

Someone wrote:

> Health food is not more important to me than my children's happiness. Health food is one way to promote a healthy body and the health of my children is very important to me. So is their happiness. You seem to be saying that the two priorities are mutually exclusive. I would like to find a way to promote their health without sacrificing their happiness and vice versa.

Joyce Fetteroll responded eloquently, and it can be read at the link below, but among her insights was this:

> If you've ever made your child cry because of something else that you wanted, then your child's happiness was secondary.

People don't like to hear things like that, but it is not possible for two priorities to be of equal value. "Prior" means before. One priority must (logically and linguistically) come before the other. In the case of health food, the food isn't "a priority." It might be an interest or an obsession. But if the principle is health, then it's about health of people, not purchase of particularly labeled foods from special stores.

SandraDodd.com/priorities

Personal Change

So you're your child's partner. You are beginning to see learning and family togetherness as priorities. You're becoming more accepting of your children's interests, and you're thinking of ways to provide them more choices about their own comfort and bodily functions.

Or maybe you've turned randomly to this page without reading anything else and you don't know what I'm talking about. This wasn't a good first-random-page. Maybe flip again, and come back to this page later.

What happens when you see other people differently is that you cannot help but see yourself differently. When you choose to find opportunities to give other people choices, you yourself have begun to make more choices.

When you begin to see learning from new and interesting angles, you yourself are learning about learning (in addition to all the things about bugs or food, bridges or clouds or trains that you're learning with your children, or when they're not even there).

Your softer, clearer vision of the world makes you a softer, clearer person.

Personal change has been touched upon in earlier sections, and will be found throughout my unschooling site, if you follow any of those links. The purpose of unschooling is not to change the parents; it's to provide a personalized learning environment for each child. Doing that does change the parents, though, if they do it wholeheartedly.

SandraDodd.com/change

Happiness

Dark thoughts or light? Worms or sky?

Sometimes dark thoughts are interesting, in spooky dramas or Stephen King novels. I've "raised" and kept and released worms. But if one's waking moments, meals, thoughts, bedtime stories and dreams are dark and negative, their children will be better off in school. It's one thing to go to goth night at the dance club. It's another thing to practice negativity and live (sort of live) in disdain of bright joy or humor.

If you were custom-designing a grandmother, for example, as in "I Sing the Body Electric," by Ray Bradbury, or the related "The Electric Grandmother," would you want a happy one or a cynical, whiney one?

If you're making a decision in some moment, for example, as in the next decision you make concerning your family, will you take the low road and have a low-energy, Eeyore moment? How much energy would it take to have a Pooh moment instead, or even a Tigger moment? Are you reading this from such a dark, cynical mindset that even a mention of Eeyore seems too cheery and upbeat to be endured? Prepare to go back to your black hole, then. Take your children to school, and stop on the way home for some black eyeliner and red eyeshadow. Don't say thank you at the check-out counter, either. Maybe just sleep the rest of the day, because life sucks.

Or don't! Maybe remember that every moment is precious and that you do indeed have choices and that you can for certain take joy in the sky as easily as you can be irritated about the ground.

If you were designing a parent for your child, wouldn't "happy" be pretty high on your list?

SandraDodd.com/peace/mama
SandraDodd.com/morning

Becoming the Parent you Want to Be

Change a moment. Change one touch, one word, one reaction. If you try to change your entire self so that next year will be better, you might become overwhelmed and discouraged and distraught.

Change one thing. Smile one sweet smile. Say one kind thing.

If that felt good, do it again. Rest. Watch. Listen. You're a parent because of your child. *Your* child. You should be *his* parent, or *her* parent. Not a generic parent, or a hypothetical parent. Be your child's parent in each moment that you interact with her.

Somehow you will need to experiment with trust and patience, in little ways. If it feels good, if it seems to work, try to remember what you did physically or cognitively to get to that place, so that you can induce it in the future. Was it pausing? Breathing? Posture? Lovely thoughts? Did you think a phrase or an affirmation? (I'm thinking maybe "choose peace" or "He's just a baby," or "Don't say something you can't take back," or "Be kind.") Did you smell his hair before you decided what to say to his request? It works wonderfully with very young children, and if you have that experience of letting the smell of your child's scalp trigger your instincts and memories, maybe you can form a memory or message from that so that you can use that even when the physical trigger of that scent isn't available. (That might work better for moms than dads; I've never asked dads if there's a scent-to-instinct trigger for them in the scalps of babies. It might have to do with breastfeeding.)

When you know how you want to be, the next step is to make conscious decisions in a "getting warm" or "getting cold" kind of way. Not all steps will be forward, but if the majority of steps are in your chosen direction, there y'go!

SandraDodd.com/peace/becoming

Abundance

How much do you have? Not enough? Enough? Plenty? Too much? Unlimited amounts?

Of what are you thinking? Money? Space? Food? Bedding, toys, books, music, dishes, paper, space to run, peace or love? Time?

How much do you need for the next interaction with your child?

If you feel you have too much time, you're lucky. If you feel you have too much house or too much yard or too many beds, think how fortunate that makes you, on average, on a planet where so many people feel needy and crowded and unsafe.

If you feel you don't have enough, think of your next interaction with your child. How will you feel to him if your body and posture and voice and words all say "I'm needy"? You will not be a comfort to him, but a drain. He might feel he needs to comfort you. But in any case he will not have been nurtured.

How much do you need to own to touch a child gently? How much money do you need to have in order to smile?

Look at what you have rather than what you don't have. Look at what is in the world beyond your family and your neighborhood, and rejoice that your child might be able to go out someday and experience things you've never seen or heard or touched or tasted.

The world is big. Your life is big. Your child is as big as you help him to be, or as small as you make him feel.

Move toward finding and feeling abundance.

SandraDodd.com/abundance

Phrases to avoid

"Have to…"

"I was forced to…" or "We forced him to…"

"No choice but to…"

Your thoughts affect your body. Your moods change your health. Your attitude shows in your face. Negativity will be contagious and harmful to your children.

When you speak or write or hear the words that paint your life as powerless and harsh, rephrase. If you have time, think about where those things came from. If you can trace them back to a certain voice or incident in your memory, remember that, and be prepared the next time.

Part of people's minds involves what Freud called "the super-ego." It's that part of you in which you store "the rules," and where you save messages for the future. Remember the holographic Princess Leia that R2D2 showed Luke Skywalker? I don't know about you, but I have both my grandmothers like that in my head, and many other people besides. Sometimes they hop out and try to shame me, or sometimes they say something nice to me. One of them sits on my shoulder when I'm sewing and tells me all kinds of early-20th-century stuff about hemming by hand and tying off machine-stitched seams, and clipping my curves. She just goes on and on. The other one tells me I have no common sense, but I think it's because she wasn't well supported as a child, and she didn't understand or value all my interests when I lived near her when I was little. Some she did, though, and I remember her smile and the smell of Jergen's lotion on her hands.

So in your head, you have some repeating-loop messages. Some are telling you you're doing a good job, but I bet some of them are not. Some are telling you that you have no choice, but you do.

Your children are developing a holographic internal image of you, complete with voice and emotion. The things you do and say are being recorded for posterity; make them sweet and good. What you choose to say and do now will affect what your children say to their children, and what your great grandchildren will hear after you're long gone.

Live like you're their last hope.

SandraDodd.com/phrases

Words

It takes practice to separate thought from words, especially while one is reading. There are other non-verbal ways to examine and communicate, but for the analytical thinking involved in learning about something new, or deciding how to react, we often use words, even if only in our thoughts.

Words have the power to harm, to limit and to sadden. So be careful with words. Use the good ones, the happy ones.

Words are like all the oceans and rivers in the world, like the rain and snow. They are insubstantial in a way; they can become solid, as these on this page are, or they can be flowing, as in a song or rhyme, or they can dissolve into the air. They can come crashing against you or knock you down. They can erode trust and love, as water can erode a cliff. They can soothe and heal and cleanse. There are always more words to choose from and rearrange as you wish, and you can produce more and more new combinations until you're too old to remember how to do it, if you live that long.

Make choices when you use words. Don't think you "have to" say certain things, or that you "have no choice" but to say "no," or "wrong," or "stupid." Speak from your heart and your thoughts, not from your hurts or your fears. Use your words for good, for nurturing. Use your words to protect the peace of your home. Keep your words to yourself sometimes, but other times be so courageous that you put some words out there as a warning and a fence between you and those who wish to harm you with their own outflow of dangerous words.

Don't waste your words.

Build gifts from words.

SandraDodd.com/words/words

No more bad days

Years ago someone in the AOL homeschooling discussions said she never liked to think of "a bad day," but only a bad moment. The next moment might always be better. That idea changed my life.

Last weekend, I was thinking a lot and talking a bit with some others about moments, about the value of moments, and hobbies, and work and activities. Moments have different value to different people, certainly.

I'm heating my hot tub, which uses wood. It's right at 100 and I'm aiming for 105 degrees F, and the moon's coming into view through some trees and I was reminded of part of a Robert Louis Stevenson poem:

> *...and the pail by the wall / Would be half full of water and stars.*

Today I was reading a book called *Your Brain on Music*, and yesterday I was reading some very cool reviews of the top 200 songs of the 1960's, because I went to see what others might think about the residual value of "I Want You Back" by the Jackson 5, which has a really great bass line and chord progression. It was #2 on that list I found. #1 was "God Only Knows" by the Beach Boys, which is the closing theme in "Love Actually," a sweet and funny movie with a parody of "Love is All Around You" by the Troggs.

Recently I was thinking about moments, about how many hours of preparation or travel or build-up precede every magic moment in a life, and what makes a thing "worth it."

When, standing stirring my hot tub, I saw the moon this evening, with the past few days' thoughts shuffling and settling in my head, I understood something about haiku for the first time ever. The good ones describe a moment, a perception—one point in time, and the breathtaking thought of an instant.

My next-door neighbor's name is Harry. He was in the Navy in WWII, on a submarine in the Pacific. He was young, and far from Pinos Altos, New Mexico, his boyhood home. He said the officer on watch invited him up to look out at the surface of the ocean, and he saw the rising moon's reflection like a silver road to the horizon. The day he described it to me I got a shiver.   *(Harry Hickel died in the summer of 2009.)*

SandraDodd.com/badmoment

Mindfulness

I live without religion, but not without morals. I know that being good is better than "being bad" (harmful, thoughtless, irresponsible), and I know that optimism is better than negativity. That doesn't mean I think there is magic at work in the fact that stepping out into the day joyfully will make the day better. People don't need to have a construct of "manifestations" or wishes or visualizations to make good better than bad. It just is, in ways linguistic and logical and biochemical.

Mindfulness is about making choices for reasons that are in keeping with a person's values and beliefs. "Mind" is an ancient word, which has relatives in Germanic languages, and Latin, and Sanskrit. It has to do with knowing, and memory, and an awareness involving emotion.

Do you mind?

Who's minding the store?

Mind your manners

Have you lost your mind!?

Once upon a time on the unschooling discussion list, someone seemed unhappy with the way I used "mindful." For years, some of the regular writers here tried to find a good word for what we were trying to convey—a kind of mothering that involved making infinitesimal decisions all the time, day and night, and basing those decisions on our evolving beliefs about living respectfully with our children, and giving *them* room to make their own decisions of the moment.

We finally settled on "mindful," in the sense of being fully in the moment. Though "mindfulness" is used as a term in western Buddhism, the word they chose when they were translating from Japanese, Chinese, Hindu, Vietnamese and whatever all hodgepodge of ideas were eventually described in English–"mindfulness"– is an English word over 800 years old. It's a simple English compound, and has to do with the state of one's mind while performing an action. It creates a state of "if/then" in one. And *if* a parent intends to be a good unschooling parent, a generous freedom-nurturing parent, a parent providing a peaceful nest, a parent wanting to be her child's partner, then the best way she can live in that goal and come ever closer to her ideals is to make all her decisions in that light. The more mindful she is of where she intends to go, the easier her decisions are.

When you come to an intersection, how do you decide which way to go? It helps, before operating a motor vehicle with all its attendant expenses and inherent dangers, to know where you want to go. When you *do* have a destination, then each intersection has some wrong ways, and some better and worse ways. It's the same with unschooling. If that's where you're headed, there are some wrong ways you can avoid simply by being mindful of your intent.

On July 28, 2006 I wrote:

> Today is the last day I can say "I have three teenagers," because tomorrow Kirby turns 20.
>
> When he was four months old, I went to La Leche League. I wish I had gone sooner! I wish I had gone four months before he was born. I had been reading helpful books, and I knew I wanted to be a gentle mom, but being around others who were doing it consciously and thoughtfully helped me greatly.
>
> I had been going to Adult Children of Alcoholics meetings for a year by the time I started La Leche League, and they didn't conflict with each other philosophically at all. They were wholly complementary, in fact, and they bolstered me and Kirby both into a strong relationship.
>
> There are things I would love to go back and redo, but though I'm not completely satisfied, I'm not ashamed either. When I said "okay" to Kirby I was saying okay to the little Sandra inside me who might otherwise have built up some jealous resentment about this new kid getting to do things I never got to do. It was healing to imagine that if my mom had been fortunate enough to have other influences and better circumstances maybe she would have said yes to me more often too.
>
> SandraDodd.com/mindfulness

Being

"Being" is a tricky word in English. It means too many things, and all difficult to consider, fathom or discuss. "I am" ranges from momentary feelings to the essence of existence.

Other languages have it easier.

Someone can say "I am an unschooler" because at that moment she's sure she intends to be an unschooler. Someone can say "I am an unschooler" and discover a year or two later she was never sure what "unschooling" meant.

A parent, at every moment, is being somewhere, some way, somehow. The child is somewhere physically, emotionally, and intellectually. It's best when their being is together, when they are *being* together.

Even though a parent is physically present a child might still be by himself emotionally, or be by himself intellectually, or socially.

"Being there for and with the family" seems so simple and yet many parents miss out on it without even leaving the house. Maybe it's because of English. Maybe we think we're "being there with our family" just because we can hear them in the other room. There is a special kind of "being" and a thoughtful kind of "with" that are necessary for unschooling and mindful parenting to work.

SandraDodd.com/being

Being an Unschooling Parent

This entire book is about being an unschooling parent. This section is about being aware of what that means.

On my site there is a page of other parents' summaries of what they've learned about being unschooling parents, and you might find inspiration there to focus on the *being* part of being an unschooling parent.

Children's being is purer and less damaged and confused than that of most adults. We can help them be. We can "leave them be," in nurturing and mindful ways.

SandraDodd.com/beginning

Being respectful

"Modeling respect" is misunderstood by some parents. It seems they think that if they are courteous to other adults in public and their children see it, their children will be courteous to adults, including the parents. That's useful and important, but it has to do with etiquette and courtesy, generally, more than with a depth of respect.

Probably a better way to explain it then, is to be a model of respectfulness and of respectability. That's confusing too, I know, but parents need to find ways to respect their children—their interests and ideas and preferences of color and texture and temperature and their tastes in music and humor and their need for privacy and for attention.

When a child feels what respect feels like, he will know what others mean when they say "You should respect [whatever]."

"Respect" is not a light thing. It's not easy to respect your child, when it's new to you. There will be people encouraging you to see your child as "just a kid," and "only a child." Think of adults you respect, and think of them as ten years old, four years old, two, newborn. They were those people from birth. There was a newborn Mohandas Gandhi; a four-year-old Abraham Lincoln; an eight-year-old Oprah Winfrey; a twelve-year-old Winston Churchill.

Would my mother have treated me differently if she had known I would grow up to write this book? How should I treat my children?

SandraDodd.com/respect

Being fun

Live a light and playful life. Be patient and sweet. Be generous.

Play with your children, and gently.

Play with your friends, and kindly.

Be glad when things are fun. Help them be so.

SandraDodd.com/playing

Being at peace

No life is peaceful at every moment, but the more peaceful moments you have, the more peaceful are the lives of all concerned. The lives of those indirectly affected are also closer to peace.

On discussing the value of peace, in an online discussion, I wrote, "Some mom reading here might look up and smile at her child, or touch his head softly, or turn off the computer and go watch him build with Lego, or go with him to the park to throw a Frisbee for the dog. Maybe without this list she would've told him to just go do something else because she had to fix dinner."

In the smallest of decisions and actions, if you can choose what will promote calm and avoid tears, you will be moving toward a more peaceful way of being.

SandraDodd.com/parentingpeacefully

Being aware

Don't scoot through your day without using your senses. What is happening around you? What is new and different? How could you easily make others safer and more comfortable?

When you know what you want to find, it's easier to see it. If you know you want learning and peace and joy in your life, removing the smallest of obstacles or distractions will let those things shine forth.

There's a story about Michelangelo saying that to make his marble sculpture of King David, he just chipped away everything that didn't look like David. It might not be true in way of a quote. It's said of horses and elephants, too (to make a sculpture of an elephant, chip away everything that doesn't look like an elephant).

If you want a peaceful life, smooth off the rough parts. Take away the dangerous and irritating things. Spend a moment appreciating peace when you see it or feel it. It's not something you can do once and for all. It's a way of living.

SandraDodd.com/seeingit

Breathing

When people hear "stop and smell the roses" they think of thorns, and ownership, and the cost of the roses, and whether they require more water than xeriscaping would. That's why deep breathing helps. It makes brains slow down. Although it's usually dolled up as formal meditation or chanting or yoga (which has other benefits, certainly, but for my current argument, the breathing...)... what it immediately does is slow the heart, which stills the brain. And then thoughts can step gently and slowly around, instead of trying to jump on the speeding train of brains going the speed of people who are thinking of cost and future and past and promotion and danger and they're breathing fast, fast, fast. And shallow, shallow, shallow.

Deep breaths change everything, for a few moments.

Shallow breathing maintains a state. If you're angry or afraid and you breathe shallowly (or pant, or hold your breath), you stay that way. If you're calm (as in a meditative state) then breathing shallowly maintains it, once you've gotten there.

SandraDodd.com/breathing

Breathe in Self-Defense

To protect from fears and insecurities, breathe.

A baby Kirby once expressed frustration that the world was full of "tiny monsters"—small, unforeseen dangers.

I have something of a monster antidote: breathing. Breathe deeply and calmly. Get oxygen into that part of you that fears the tiny monsters. Once you master calming your hurts and fears (or at least calming the adrenaline that would make you lash out), you'll have time to think about how to deal with them rationally and sweetly and compassionately.

SandraDodd.com/TinyMonsters

Breathe to be Compassionate

If you're feeling anger or resentment or frustration with the annoying stupidity of others, or the incompetence or disorganization of people you usually like, breathe. If you are disappointed in the failure of a loved one to remember to do something, breathe. Remember that people aren't perfect. If you want them to allow you your own failures and imperfections, it will help if you have accepted and forgiven theirs. Calm yourself with the awareness of what's important.

SandraDodd.com/affirmations

Breathe to forestall anger

When a parent learns to calm herself, or himself, many things happen. The home becomes safer. The parent becomes more reliable and more trustworthy. The children can make more choices without fear.

When a parent can learn to take one deep, calming breath while deciding what to do, the parent becomes wiser and more patient.

When a person knows how to calm herself, she can help others.

When children learn how to calm themselves, because the parents have helped them, because the parents understood how to do it, the children have more personal range and power, because they will be more reliable and trustworthy and able to maintain their calm, thoughtful, rational minds.

Probably half the people in prison would not have been there had they known how to take one long deep breath and hold it a bit before letting it all out completely and then huffing out the last bit and waiting a second before filling up with all new, cleansing, oxygen-rich air. They could then have decided not to break or stab or shoot or strike. Then they would be home with their parents or wives or husbands or children.

Don't underestimate the value of the knowledge of how to calm yourself down.

SandraDodd.com/peace/anger

Flow

Flow is learning to go fast in a calm way. Flow is clarity while in motion. The opposite of flow might be "stuckness"—being immobilized while thoughts and fears swoop and swirl inside you.

Flow is a state of being that unschoolers can reach, in which they are no longer laboring to make conscious decisions about how to encourage learning and to maintain peace and joy. It might only last a few moments at a time, but it will be enough.

The term "flow" used in this sense is to the credit of Dr. Mihaly Csikszentmihalyi, a psychologist, researcher, professor and author of the book *Flow: The Psychology of Optimal Experience*. (1991)

You don't need to read his book, though, to think of times when your mind was so lightly intent on something that you forgot where you were or how much time might be passing. You might have been painting, or writing, or reading or building something. You might have been involved in a physical activity such as bicycling or mountain climbing or surfing. Maybe you were sitting and watching a fire, or looking at a mountain stream, or walking in the snow to see someone you really love. It might be something difficult like a solo musical performance, or being at bat during an important game. It might be something monotonous but also somehow soothing, with a rhythm or a physical sensation of wind or sound or smell.

People who practice meditation, yoga, prayer or cross-country running might be more likely to be able to induce flow when they want to. Some might never have felt it yet, but still could.

This book is filled with clues and jewels to lead you toward *flow*. And here's a humorous note:

> I had to email and tell you about what I did today. I was listening to your CD on Flow while driving in the car. There is a part of the speech where you ask people to stop their breath half way and keep doing that. I did it a few times and you mentioned we could feel lightheaded and dizzy and I was like OMG, I'm driving! LOL. I did get a little light headed, but, you kept talking as I was still doing it, so, I heard what you said about getting dizzy. I was able to stop and take a few deeper breaths before I got more lightheaded. Then, I laughed at myself for doing that while driving! —Jen V.

SandraDodd.com/flow

Remember that your children will also experience flow.

If you interrupt them while they're playing Rock Band or drawing or spinning on a tire swing, you might be disturbing a profound experience. So interrupt gently, when you must. Treat them with the respect you would treat anyone who might be in the midst of a transcendental moment.

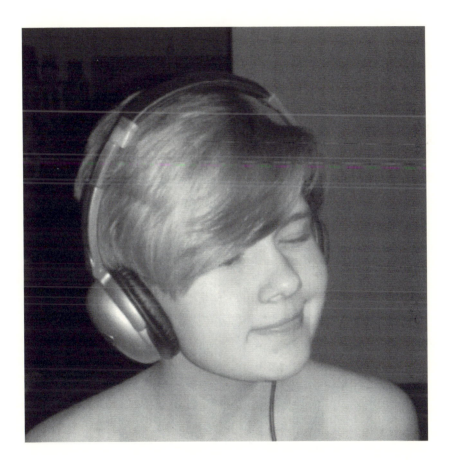

Tone

Sometimes parents advise their children to go with just the words someone said, and not the tone. That is asking them to go against their instincts, though. There is much more to communication than just the words themselves. If you don't believe it, watch some great actors, or some bad ones, or practice saying the same thing several different ways for different meaning and effect, and then add in physical stance to make it more exciting. But even if I were lying in a spa wrapped shoulders to feet like a mummy in steamy sheets (thinking of one time at Ojo Caliente, in the 1970's, when I had no idea what to expect and my dad was over in the men's side), I would be able to speak to you in ways that conveyed much more than the words themselves.

When you say something to your child, remember to feel it and believe it, or you'll be sending mixed messages, and the tone might be louder than the words. And with babies and toddlers, the tone might be the entirety of the communication.

If you hear one of your children scream or yell or cry from the back yard, you probably don't need to know what words he said (if any) to know whether he needs help or is angry or just playing.

Arguments between parents and adults that involve someone defending the words in the absence of the tone, volume, inflection and body language should be halted. The person who's saying "That's not what I said," or "I *said* I didn't mind," or "I *said* I was sorry," is communicating something else on top of that, and it is that somehow, between those two people, words have become more important than compassion and honesty. So rather than argue about it, see it as a little "caution" marker and the next time you're in that area, drive around it. Whether you're the interpreter or the 'interpretee', be honest and accept that there are layers to communication. Don't make people beg you to leave them alone, or to hug them, or to ask them what's wrong, if they're indicating needs in non-verbal ways.

I'm about to repeat myself a little in the next section, because it was written earlier. Repetition can be valuable. Or it can be skipped over.

Also to be avoided: speaking to any human over the age of two as though he were a miniature poodle with a jeweled collar doing tricks on a white carpet. Don't use "the poodle voice" on people.

SandraDodd.com/tone

Parenting Peacefully

We make choices all the time. Learning to make better ones in small little ways, immediate ways, makes life bigger and better. Choosing to be gentle with a child, and patient with ourselves, and generous in ways we think might not even show makes our children more gentle, patient and generous.

One mom had written that she was worried that she wasn't really being consciously present with her child, and was intellectualizing too much. They had a disconnect, and I made this recommendation: " Instead of saying 'Come on, let's go!' maybe you could have picked him up and twirled him around and said something sweet and by the time he knows it he's fifty yards from there, but happy to be with his happy mom."

Peace, in an exchange, has to do with tone of voice, eyes, posture, attitude, intention, compassion—all the non-verbal communications that go with words and actions. Don't underestimate your child's ability to read beneath and around and beyond your statements. You would do well to try to read behind his words, too.

SandraDodd.com/parentingpeacefully

The next section is a transcript in article-form of a presentation given at the 2006 Live and Learn conference. It has been published twice before this; notes are at the link a few pages from here.

Noisy peace

A Loud Peaceful Home

Peace is necessary for learning. Abraham Maslow, who studied learning and human development in the 1930's and 1940's, in his work on the "hierarchy of needs," said that learning just isn't going to happen until some other things are in place.

First level, humans need food, water, air and sleep. Without those, they just can't concern themselves with anything else.

The second level of human needs, according to Maslow, is safety and security. If they don't feel safe and trusting, they can't concern themselves with other things.

Third level is the need for love and belonging—friends, supportive family, some kind of feeling of being part of a social unit.

So for learning to happen in ANY situation, safety and some peace are required.

Can there be too much peace? For learning, yes. Learning requires mental arousal. If an environment is so still and barren that one's curiosity isn't sparked, then people might be closer to a state of sleep than of excited curiosity. Life can be too dull and quiet for learning to spontaneously happen.

Can there be too little peace? Yes, and in many ways. There can be too much noise, stimulation and chaos. So finding the balance place and the comfort level is part of creating a peaceful home.

Peace is a prerequisite to natural, curious, intellectual exploration.

What is peace, then, in a home with children? Contentment is peace.

Is a child happy to be where he is? That is a kind of peace. If he wakes up disappointed, that is not peace, no matter how quiet the house is or how clean and "feng shuid" his room is.

Peace, like learning, is largely internal.

Mother Teresa could have found a more peaceful place than Calcutta, but she was helping people find peace in non-peaceful surroundings.

Back to Maslow for just a minute, though—if my focus is helping my children learn, Maslow's ideas can help. If a hungry child can't learn, I should feed him. He can learn better. If a child can't learn if he's thirsty, I need to make sure there's always water or juice or something for him to drink. If a child needs to feel safe, he won't learn by someone yelling, "Learn now, or I'll hit you."

Children's needs must be met for natural learning to blossom. Part of that learning can be learning about how to keep their own needs fulfilled. Helping children consider whether they're comfortable, hungry, thirsty, sleepy or restless helps them be whole and healthy people.

In English there's a phrase, an idiom, a lump of words: *"peace and quiet."* People speak wistfully of "peace and quiet" as though one requires the other, but I haven't found that to be true in practice.

Is quiet always peace? I can think of lots of times I held my breath to be quiet, out of fear. I've seen families where people passed through the house quietly, out of nervous avoidance. Sometimes "Quiet!" can be very scary and dangerous. Some families live in fear and quiet, not peace and quiet. Quiet anxiety is not peace at all!

Some parents wear their compassion on the outside and say we need peace in the whole world first. That's a little like saying the ocean should be drained before we take the water out of the basement. Does every war have to stop before we can stop hitting our kids? Does every bit of urban violence need to end before we can stop yelling at our kids? Do lions have to stop eating gazelles before we stop harassing our kids? To think in those terms is to justify our own lack of peace. It seems to me that a child who has known strife at home won't blink at it outside.

The more local and personal peace there is, the more peace there will be in the world. That doesn't mean that if Holly's sleeping quietly there will be less violence in the Sudan, but it does mean that there is more peace in the world. And it means that when she's grown, she will be more unhappy to see or hear of neglect and abuse than she would be if she herself had been neglected and abused, and thought it was normal.

If we raise the level of peace our children expect, they will know what peace feels like.

Adults need to know what peace feels like too, though, and some feel it for the first time when they really start to understand unschooling.

What Progress Looks Like

How did I come to make progress on peace in my own life? After I was grown and married, friends persuaded me to attend meetings of Adult Children of Alcoholics, an al-Anon group, which involved itself with healing the inner child. From them, I learned ideas like

HALT (hungry? angry? lonely? tired?)

"How Important Is It?"

"If you have one foot in the past and one foot in the future, you're pissing all over today"—an indelicate but memorable way of saying "live now" and "pay attention to today."

During the time I was active in those meetings, I had Kirby, and then Marty.

When Kirby was a baby, I started going to La Leche League meetings. I wish I had gone before he was born. From LLL, I learned that a mother and baby should be partners, not adversaries. I read, heard about and saw attachment parenting, child-led weaning and separation from babies when the babies indicate a desire to get down and go.

From my teen years, I had learned meditation and breathing exercises and knew how to calm and center myself quickly. More than that, though, I knew what it felt like to be calm.

How might others make progress now? Inner child work was common when I was a new mother, but now cognitive therapy tends to replace that. If we avoid thoughts that are negative or non-productive or illogical, we move toward a better, lighter place. People can work on thinking and on being.

How will you be, as a parent, and why? What's keeping you from being the way you want to be?

Inventory your own tools. What do you already know that can make you a more peaceful parent? What tricks and skills can you bring into your relationships with members of your family?

Below are several things that can help you move toward peace, and each will help the others develop: breathing, understanding, choices, awareness and principles.

Breathing

There are physiological and emotional advantages of breathing. One way to learn this is with meditation. The "meditation" most think of in this country came from Hindu practices. The Buddhist style meditation is referred to often as "breathing" or "sitting." Christian meditation is sitting or kneeling or walking. It involves contemplation while the Eastern versions generally involve trying to avoid contemplation in favor of blankness.

Moms with little children cannot easily do these things.

Other ways to work on breath and breathing might be yoga, maybe running, bicycling, walks or swimming laps.

Moms with little children cannot easily do these things.

What those moms can do is find other things involving breathing and rhythm. They can sing, walk, rock or bounce babies, go to the park and push a swing. How and why they do those things will make a difference. If they're done sweetly and patiently and mindfully, both mother and child will benefit. Done merrily and generously, they will create peace.

Peace is not an element "that can neither be created nor destroyed." Peace is entirely a condition and a mood. It's very, very fragile. It has to be created and maintained and protected.

Counting to ten only works if you're breathing slowly and deeply and looking at (or thinking of) the sky or something else airy and big and peaceful. The purpose of counting to ten is to let the adrenaline pass and to think of some good options from which you can choose. If you count to ten holding your breath, holding your frustration, with a roaring anger in your ears, the adrenaline isn't dissipating—it's just being focused into a beam of extraordinarily dangerous power.

While you're breathing, you might want to think, "I love these people," or "whatever I say could last forever." Think of what you want to be and what you want to create. See what you want, and what you don't want.

As you move toward peace, remember you can't have all of anything in one move. Each thought or action can move you nearer, though (or further).

You know the game of finding something in which other players will say, "You're getting warm," or "You're getting cold"? You need to get warmer and nearer and closer. You don't need absolute peace; you need more peace. You don't need to live in perpetual peace; you need to live with more peace.

You can't be absolutely safe from strife, but you can be saf**er**.

Understanding

Nothing has ever made me feel better about me than the feeling that I was being a good mom.

If you work on understanding what you want, you will have more peace within yourself. Understanding takes inquiry, observation, reading and a lot of thought. These will help to understand yourself as well as you can too, but that can come gradually. Online unschooling sites and discussions are excellent opportunities to increase one's understanding of natural learning and peaceful parenting.

Choices

Unless you considered two or three courses of action, you didn't really make a choice at all. Consciously think of two choices before you act—then make the better choice. Your range of choices will get better as you do this. While you're helping your child learn to choose, you can also learn to choose.

Awareness

Look directly at your child. Practice watching your child without expectations. Try to see what he is really doing, rather than seeing what he's *not* doing. Just look.

Smell your child's hair. They say dogs can smell fear, but moms can smell love, or something, when they smell the top of a young child's head. Something biochemical happens, and something intellectual can happen.

Be aware of who this child is and of your potential to help or to harm.

What is the opposite of peace here? Lack of awareness. In cases of violent crime or crazed fit what do people often cite? "I was unaware; I forgot where I was; I didn't think..." If you can choose to be more aware over less aware, that will help.

One aspect of awareness is working on your ability to be quietly alert, like a mother hawk, aware of the location of your child, her mood and your surroundings.

Principles

So what's the "rule" about peace? There's not a rule about peace.

There will never be perfect peace. We can't even define "peace." There can be a closer approximation to ideal peace. People can come nearer to the way they would like to be, but only incrementally, choice by choice.

If you want to live peacefully, make the more peaceful choice.

Peace is all about choices.

- Choose to breathe consciously sometimes.
- Choose understanding over ignoring and ignorance.
- Choose to make choices.
- Choose awareness over oblivion, when you can.
- Make choices based on your principles.

To have peace in your house, be more peaceful.

SandraDodd.com/peace/noisy

Boredom

Don't punish boredom. If your children were in school or in a music class or at a karate school and there was absolutely nothing happening, and the teacher was on the phone or sitting in his office with his feet up while the children had nothing to do, how would you feel?

If your children are home and they have nothing to do and you're on the phone in your office or with your feet up, I feel you should be providing or suggesting things for them to do, or better yet doing something with them.

An expression of boredom is a request for connection, for input, for assistance in the world. If you ignore or punish that, whatever trust and relationship you have with your child will be weakened.

Sometimes children new to unschooling will say "bored" out of habit, from before unschooling days. Perhaps they need ideas for other ways to see their alleged "boredom." You could help. Maybe they need a whole different kind of input. If they've been playing in the yard and got restless for a change, maybe they need a glass of cold water in a darkish room with a picture book or a video or some music. If one has been reading for hours and comes out and says "bored," maybe she needs to discuss the book, or do something physical, or get a snack, or hear about something she missed while she was reading.

Sometimes rephrasing the statement can help. If I say "I'm bored" today, it might mean I'm frustrated with the writing I'm doing, or that I need to stretch my legs and move the water in the yard or pet the cats and then come back to it. "Bored" might mean disappointed, or impatient or angsty. "Find something to do" isn't a good response to someone attempting to communicate news of the soul.

Based on experiences with many families, I predict that the longer you unschool, the less often you will hear any form of the word "bored." But it will certainly help if the parents consciously avoid using the word themselves. Don't say things are boring. Don't look for boredom nor condemn it when you find it. Try to make the world in and around you more interesting.

SandraDodd.com/BoredNoMore

Bribery

People come to unschooling from all kinds of other upbringings and philosophies, ranging from unexamined blocked out memories to advanced degrees in some form of what children need. Some are steeped in the philosophy or theories of a favorite author or blogger. Some of them use blatant bribery without even thinking. Others condemn any form of enticement as evil *bribery* and begin backing away in fear.

As with other "it depends" and "find a balance" topics, bribery is neither a great all-purpose tool nor a trapdoor to hell.

My husband goes to work because they pay him money. He made a deal long ago to show up there in exchange for some things. Bank deposits. Medical and dental insurance. Paid vacations. Sometimes they bribe him for special occasions, with overtime or parties or shirts commemorating some project or other, if he'll come to a special team-building activity.

When I'm going on errands, I might or might not want to persuade someone else to go with me. It depends on what I need to do, what they're willing to do, and what they might need to be offered to sweeten the deal. Those negotiations are called "bribery" by some people. I disagree.

Now that my children drive, sometimes I'm the one who asks for the extra stop, on an outing. If Holly wants me to go shopping with her, or to go with her to a medical appointment, I might ask if we can stop by the post office on the way, or stop for lunch. I like to eat out more than Holly does.

Bribes are used to get people to do things that they should not be morally or ethically or legally doing. Politicians might take bribes, or border patrolmen, or traffic cops. Three-year-olds being offered ice cream if they'll play quietly for five more minutes are not becoming party to a crime. They are practicing interpersonal relationships and preparing themselves to make wise choices in the job market.

SandraDodd.com/bribery

Coercion

Coercion is another term that is sometimes twisted to the point of abuse in unschooling discussions. Some families go so far as to say that if a parent puts something interesting out on the table (strewing), that it is coercion. Some will say that if their children are limited in their choices of what to wear outside (choosing from clothes the parent thinks are appropriate for snow, or a wedding, or the swimming pool) that the child is being coerced.

In discussions with such people I will use two hundred words sometimes to say, "Are you crazy?" They're not here now, though.

Persuasion in a sweet way (as discussed on the last page) is just persuasion, or negotiation or request. Persuasion in a forceful way can be guilt, or wheedling. But until there is fear or a serious loss of freedom, it's not "coercion."

Using words in ways other than they are intended and then shaming people who disagree is about the most coercive thing I've seen around unschooling discussions. I recommend seeking clarity of thought, and using English words plainly.

I don't have a page on coercion on my site.
Use any old dictionary.

Freedom

A discussion came up in which someone asked about "True Freedom" as though it were a concept central to unschooling. I'd never come across the phrase, and discussion ensued.

It's just musing and analysis of the ideas of freedom, which unschoolers *do* tend toward in lots of things, but in ALL things? Maybe, maybe not.

I think what some families call "freedom," I call "choices." In the discussion referred to above, I wrote:

> Just like getting lots of gifts instead of one big one, if you say "sure," "okay," "yes" to lots of requests for watching a movie late or having cake for breakfast or them playing another half hour on the swings and you can just read a book in the car nearby, then they get TONS of yes, and permission, and approval. If you throw your hands up and say "Whatever," that's a disturbing moment of mom seeming not to care instead of mom seeming the provider of an assortment of joyous approvals.

The bold face print in the quote below came from something Danielle Conger wrote. My responses are indented. It's at the link below.

After reading Sandra's words, I realize that my kids come to me, not because I say they have to, but because they use me as a sounding board.

> Maybe they're coming to you as a font of "yes!"
>
> That's a cool thing, if every time they want something loving and positive, they run to mom, huh?

Asking permission becomes a way of gauging their own sense of right and wrong because they know that I will explain a no and help them come up with better alternatives.

> My big guys still ask little things, like "Can I have this last soda?" What that means is "had you dibsed it?" or "Is this perhaps NOT the last soda, so I'll feel better about taking it?"
>
> If I say "Sure," they're drinking a soda I gave them, and I bet it tastes better than one they snagged knowing they had "the right" to drink it, but they wanted the blessing.

SandraDodd.com/freedom

Respect

Respect was discussed in the section on "being," earlier in the book, but in light of "freedom," respect can take another whirl. If I "give my children freedom" in a situation, it's because I had some leeway or rights myself. I cannot "give them freedom" that I don't have.

Some unschoolers become confused on that, and they begin to frolic in the "freedom" that they are pretty sure some stranger online granted them, and that unschoolers have inalienably from God, bypassing all forms of government and the limitations of wallboard. And so if an unschooling family is up at 3:00 a.m. playing Guitar Hero, they seem mystified that the neighbors have called the landlord.

I'm exaggerating. I hope I'm exaggerating.

If a storeowner says not to touch the crystal figures, a parent cannot "give her child the freedom" to touch them anyway. She could buy one and take it out of the store and let her kid touch the heck out of it, but she can't tell a store owner, "You don't understand; we're unschoolers."

So although I might seem to be wandering aimlessly here, freedom should involve a respect for others, and a respect for logic. And a family might not feel they "respect the law," but the laws still do apply to them, no matter how twinkly-eyed they have become in their newfound "freedom."

So if someone is selling you "True Freedom" (or snake oil, or the elixir of the fountain of life), have respect for yourself and your family and take a pass on it.

Meanwhile, parents with a realistic and considered awareness of what their own freedoms are within the laws of the apartment building, housing development, city, county/parish/township, state/province or nation are free to share some of those with their children. We let Holly choose carpet once, but we couldn't have legally required her to pay for it, as she was only eight or nine at the time. We have surprised waiters in many restaurants by turning to our children questioningly when the waiter asks the adults "Would you like to see the dessert menu?" They're even more surprised when the kids say, "No thanks," or "I'm full," while making friendly eye contact with the waiter.

SandraDodd.com/respect

Myths too many Parents Believe

Sugar causes hyperactivity.

False, but repeated OFTEN in sitcoms and comedies, and by moms who want to limit and shame their kids.

Children can spoil

That's not exactly the way they word it, but the idea of "spoiled" children is interesting and dangerous.

Children who can't read by the time they're eight will never catch up.

Schools operate to make that true, but in the real world (where so many children unfortunately are prevented from being), it's not a bit true.

With dyslexia you HAVE to be trained in how to get past it.

Each child learns to read and write in his own way.

If my son had his way he would play video games all day long.

Unschooling parents who have spent years giving their children freedom and choices have learned that limitations create need while freedom creates intelligent choices.

If children or teens aren't made to write reports, they'll never be able to write.

"Report writing" is one of the holy icons of the Church of School. People don't even think about what it means to "write a report" in the real world when they think of school science reports and history reports and book reports.

If children are allowed sleep as late as they want, they'll never be able to get up and go to work.

SandraDodd.com/sleeping has a fair amount of information, but I have three children (at this writing 16, 19 and 21), all of whom have had jobs, none of whom has failed to learn to use an alarm clock and good judgment, none of whom has ever been let go from a job, all of whom have been free to sleep or get up for 16 years or more (depending). If there were no other refutation of the myth above than this, it would be sufficient.

It's also worth noting that none of those jobs have been "regular hours." Shifts have started as early as 6:30 a.m. and ended as late as 3:00 a.m. Good thing they were well prepared by years of irregular sleep!

Children have to be taught to self-regulate.

"Children have to be taught" is dealt with here:
    SandraDodd.com/unschooling
Self regulation is discussed here:
    SandraDodd.com/control

Wait a half hour before swimming

Snopes.com gently debunks the whole deal, but who needs Snopes? It never made sense. What *did* seem apparent to me when I was a kid, and is confirmed by my experiences as a parent hanging out with other parents, is that adults take longer to eat than kids, and the adults want to lounge around and eat and then smoke (especially in the 50's and 60's when the warning was so widespread) and they did *not* want to heave themselves up off their butts to go and play with the kids, or even to watch the kids. So they made up a deadly boogey-man to make the kids stay out of the water until the adults could take their leisurely conversational long lunch (often followed by cigarettes and liquor).

I categorize it with good chocolate is bad for little kids and coffee will stunt your growth. The best way not to share something expensive with kids is to tell them it's bad for them. There's a long tradition of lying to children, for the convenience of adults.

There are links to references and documentation at:
    SandraDodd.com/myths

Empowerment

"Power" is an odd thing to talk about until one considers the reality or fear of being "powerless." Traditionally, children are made powerless. It has been the tradition among unschoolers (for good reasons involving how learning works) to "empower" those children—for the parents to find ways to give the children many options and choices.

The results in the area of "academics" and learning are easy to see. Some children will base their early knowledge of geography and history on where dinosaurs live, and where and when bones have been found. Those kids also get a head start on English vocabulary with Latin roots (from words such as "heterodontosaurus" and "velociraptor"), and they're gathering biology and geology. Others might know when and how guitars developed and what's been done with them when and where, or the history of flower arranging or religions.

The benefits of empowering young children to begin helping to make decisions that affect them and their families have led many times to teens and adults who make better choices than their parents predicted they might. This paragraph might mean very little to those whose children are four or five, but check back in ten or twelve years and if you have any good stories, please share them with other unschoolers.

Part of the empowerment of children can involve the simple decision to let them say no to foods that smell or look unappealing, or to clothes that are scratchy, or to sleeping alone or between parents or in the dark. Responses to and respect for the input of toddlers improves the quality of input of those children when they're older. The freedom to make choices about small amounts of money and time gives them practice to make careful, thoughtful decisions when the money and time are no longer small.

Power has to do with responsibility (watch Spiderman if you had forgotten that). While parents are sharing their power and freedom with their children, they can't fully share the responsibility. Parents are still the more experienced partners on these teams, so assist your child in keeping within the bounds of what he can handle emotionally and physically—not to disempower him, but to empower him to succeed.

Below is one of my oldest published works on unschooling. I used to distribute individually-signed certificates, sometimes printed on fancy paper, whenever I spoke at a conference. It's a little dated, but it can still be helpful. At the time it was written, I had others help me tweak and polish it, and I wish I had saved all their names. They were in the unschooling discussions on the AOL.com forum in the early- and mid-1990's.

CERTIFICATE OF EMPOWERMENT

As bearer of this certificate you are no longer required to depend on the advice of experts. You may step back and view the entire world—not just your home, neighborhood or town, but the whole Earth—as a learning experience, a laboratory containing languages (and native speakers thereof), plants, animals, history, geology, weather (real live weather, in the sky, not in a book), music, art, mathematics, physics, engineering, foods, human dynamics, and ideas without end. Although collections of these treasures have been located in museums for your convenience, they are to be found everywhere else, too.

This authorizes you to experiment; to trust and enjoy your kids; to rejoice when your children surpass you in skill, knowledge or wisdom; to make mistakes, and to say "I don't know." Furthermore, you may allow your children to experience boredom without taking full responsibility for finding them something to do.

Henceforth you shall neither be required nor expected to finish everything you start. Projects, books, experiments and plans may be discontinued as soon as something more interesting comes along (or for any other reason) without penalty, and picked up again at any time in the future (or never).

You may reclaim control of your family's daily life, and take what steps you feel necessary to protect your children from physical, emotional or social harm.

You have leave to think your own thoughts, and to encourage your children to think theirs.

Each person who reads and understands this is authorized to extend these privileges to others, by reproducing and distributing this certificate or by creating another of his/her own design. Those who don't feel the need to obtain approval to experiment, to think, or to do things they've never seen others do are exempt, as they didn't need permission in the first place.

SandraDodd.com/empowerment

Online Safety

A dad wrote that he only allowed his children and the exchange students who lived with them to IM people they knew, because there were "determined predators" out there. ("IM" stands for "instant message.")

I responded:
> Confident kids who communicate well with parents and wouldn't be tempted to sneak out or to lie wouldn't be in danger of meeting someone who says he'll marry her if she meets him at the train station. That doesn't happen randomly.
>
> There can be something wrong with being cautious. Disallowing instant messages altogether because of imagined dangers is like locking a kid up. Not letting a teen have a webpage because of imagined or rumored dangers is like saying "Here's a big library—don't touch the books," or "Here's a telephone; don't call anyone," or "Here's a TV; don't turn it on."
>
> That's what teens do with computers—chat with other kids and make webpages. What it's good for is practice using computers and programs (some easier than others) and encoding and artistic decisions (Kirby will end up getting help from Holly on his webpage because she knows things about how to make it easier to read), and social exchanges.
>
> Or a family can say "There's nothing wrong with being cautious" and just say no. It's legal, and millions would say "Good; good parents do that," but it's not a good unschooling move.

Most of the unschoolers who know other unschoolers personally have "met" on the internet, or at least found a place to meet by looking at internet announcements or invitations, or by joining local mailing lists.

Assuming the worst of children isn't in keeping with respecting and empowering them. I've read a few detailed accounts by young adults or older teens who did fall for the bunk of some online predator. One of them makes her living (or did for a while) telling parents not to let their kids on the internet. In no case did the internet cause the problem; it was deep unhappiness in the teen. Playing Halo online isn't as dangerous as hanging around outside a convenience store.

SandraDodd.com/onlinesafety

When Siblings Fight

Here is most of a webpage, because it makes the most sense in the context of it being remembered and retrieved. Whatever is not indented is my writing.

> Sandra, I remember reading a post of yours a year or so ago where you described how you handled it when your kids were fighting. Seems like it was mostly Marty and Kirby you were talking about. You had a way of helping the underdog not feel so much the underdog and a way to help the big dog not feel outnumbered either. A good friend of mine is really bothered by how much her kids fight and I wanted to send her the post but can't find it. Could you possibly describe how you referee your kids' fights? A section on this topic on your website would be wonderful some day. Many thanks.
>
> —Priss

First, I must say that I hate it when parents say "They need to learn to work it out for themselves." I never smile or nod when a parent says that.

The post Priss had remembered was found by Joyce Fetteroll, who is a whiz at finding things, and I'm grateful that she has that skill and talent.

Here, from 2/2/03, is what I responded to someone having written of her children fighting:

> I can't just let it go because there seems to be no natural consequence for hitting.

I've told kids from time to time when it was fast and severe that if they do *not* learn to control their tempers they could end up in prison or dead. Because just in brief, the natural consequences of being a violent adult are often retaliatory violence or conviction of a crime.

For little kids at home, I separate them. A trick I learned as a Jr. High teacher has served well. To break up a fight, grab the loser and remove him. He *wants* to be saved. If you grab the winning participant, you might get hurt. If you remove the underdog, they both save face. He can think he wouldn't necessarily have lost. The winner still thinks he won.

I talk to the apparent victim first. Sometimes it turns out he wasn't such a victim. But in our case at home, with my boys, that has usually been Marty, who's younger by two and a half years. At the moment they're 16 and 14 and physical problems might be over. Kirby's learned enough karate that he's developed the self-control that ideally comes with being able to seriously hurt someone. And they're both verbal, so physical isn't their first thought. So what I'm going to tell is a summary of various things over the years when they were younger, in various stages.

What has worked best is taking the one away and letting him tell me what happened. While he's calming down and stating his case, I'm asking him what he did to try to make things better. "Did you think of doing this?" "No," or "Yes, but it didn't work."

So partly it's a session in possibilities. Then that kid's calmer. But I remind them that I'm responsible for seeing that BOTH of them are safe in their own homes, and happy.

Then I go to the other kid (usually Kirby) who's calm by then too, and ask for his side. He tells me the whole thing, and I ask him at the end (since I'm wanting his whole story to compare to the other whole version) whether he doesn't think he could have prevented it by this or that.

(Unfortunately in many of the scenarios, Marty had sneaked up close enough to hear and jumped in with "I DID NOT!" so I have to go and deposit Marty elsewhere and say later "That really didn't help me convince him, y'know.")

Then I say to Kirby, "Marty says you said/did this."

So Kirby tells me his version of the evils Marty contributed to the argument.

I remind Kirby he's older and has a responsibility to show some maturity and set an example (as appropriate, if appropriate). And I tell him yada yada, Marty needs to be safe in his own home, and not feel like his life is ruined because he has an older brother who's bullying him (if appropriate...)

Finally I'd go back to Marty and say "Why didn't you tell me this part?" or "Kirby says you threw this/said this..." And I go through it again with Marty.

I know lots of people say to let kids work out their own stuff but I think that's lazy at best and sadistic at worst. My parents raised two cousins of mine and one was mean and violent and frustrated and hurt both me and my sister. There should have been more active supervision and peacemaking and advisement.

I know some people believe each soul chose their family and they need to learn to work out their own interactions. I think it's random, personally. I don't think any one of my kids needs to be the material on which another kid works out his karma unchecked anyway.

So in the interest of helping them develop a set of alternative responses and social skills, and keeping them safe, I let each tell his story in private instead of in front of the other. It cuts out arguments instead of turning a little argument into a big one (Jerry Springer show style, in worst cases). And it lets each kid vent to me about his frustrations about the other one. They *need* to express that. Better to me than to friends outside the family, I think. Because in this case they have a lot of mutual friends. It's to the benefit of lots of people for them to be sociably at peace. And it lets me commiserate with them about the flaws of the sibling and to tell them how hard it is to be a parent and to love both kids but to see when one is being hurt without me saying in front of one "Yeah, I know it can be a drag" in front of the other one.

That might not be clear. It's not that I'll say to Marty "Yeah, Kirby sucks, doesn't he?" It's more like "Marty, I really did want to have you. I LOVE you. And things would be different if you were the oldest. I'm sorry it frustrates you. But I was an oldest and there are disadvantages to that, too." It helps the relationship between me and each child for me to be able to discuss the emotions and reactions in some depth with them.

On verbal abuse, one thing that has worked here is to remind them that it's their own reputation and self/soul that they're hurting when they're mean. If someone is cruel, it makes him a cruel person. It might hurt the other kid too, but it immediately hurts the one who was mean for meanness' sake. And it disturbs the peace of the others around them. If two kids are fighting, the third kid isn't having peace either.

(end of the long quote)

I have seen my kids use that same method to help their friends sort through disagreements. I guess they don't know it doesn't happen at every house. It does happen at lots of unschoolers' houses, though, thanks to Priss and Joyce finding that writing.

SandraDodd.com/peace/fighting

Guns

When kids are forbidden to play with toy guns, they use sticks and fingers and Lego for guns. They play ashamedly, and in secret, while their mothers assure friends smugly that their children never play with guns.

No doubt stone-age children played with toy spears and bows and arrows and atlatls and slings. Surely bronze- and iron-age children played with toy swords. Part of learning about culture and tools and technology, for children, is playing.

So to the present: Children play with toy guns. Sometimes those guns squirt water, or fire little start-trek phaser disks, or they shoot light. Some of them make noise.

There is no young-child gun play so violent as a mother saying "NO. I said **NO!**" to a young child who has dared to pick up a friend's toy gun.

At the site below are photos of children in various parts of the world dressed in costumes and holding toy guns, or posing with water guns in parks, or otherwise amusing themselves with pieces of plastic or wood. I defy anyone to find the slightest trace of hurt or violence in those photos.

Anyone who wants to try to persuade unschoolers that toy guns are bad for their children should join the AlwaysLearning list and fire away.

SandraDodd.com/peace/guns

groups.yahoo.com/group/AlwaysLearning

Violence

Most violence in homes is inflicted on children by adults.

It's natural and healthy for children to play rough and to pretend all sorts of things.

I'm going to quote a bit of an article by a comic-book author named Gerard Jones. There is a link to it on my page, and to a back-up version in case the first link disappears:

> One of my mother's students convinced her that Marvel Comics, despite their apparent juvenility and violence, were in fact devoted to lofty messages of pacifism and tolerance. My mother borrowed some, thinking they'd be good for me. And so they were. But not because they preached lofty messages of benevolence. They were good for me because they were juvenile. And violent.
>
> The character who caught me, and freed me, was the Hulk: overgendered and undersocialized, half-naked and half-witted, raging against a frightened world that misunderstood and persecuted him. Suddenly I had a fantasy self to carry my stifled rage and buried desire for power. I had a fantasy self who was a self: unafraid of his desires and the world's disapproval, unhesitating and effective in action. "Puny boy follow Hulk!" roared my fantasy self, and I followed.
>
> I followed him to new friends—other sensitive geeks chasing their own inner brutes—and I followed him to the arrogant, self-exposing, self-assertive, superheroic decision to become a writer....
>
> (the link is here: SandraDodd.com/t/violence)

The most common scapegoat for the crime-itself of violence is the TV. Parents believe that somehow, magically, depriving their children of television will make them ignorant of the existence of violence. At that same link above t/violence, Deb Lewis has provided a list of dramatic crimes to challenge the idea that TV causes violence. One example:

> In Bath, Michigan in May, 1927 Andrew Kehoe who was fifty (five?—don't remember) committed the worst case of school violence in American history. First he killed his wife, locked his animals in the barn and blew them up, blew up the school where he was a handyman and blew up his truck full of shrapnel. More explosives were set to go off to kill rescue workers but were found

by the police. In all, thirty-eight children were killed and seven teachers. Sixty some others were injured. Mr. Kehoe never saw a TV set.

I think it would have been much, much better if Mr. Kehoe had been home watching TV but alas; it wasn't yet invented. Many people would've wished he had stayed in to read trashy dime novels or to listen to the play-by-play of a boxing match on the crystal-set radio.

And then there are video games. When it comes to television and video games, some adults seem unable to distinguish between fantasy and reality. The kids understand it, but sometimes they just can't manage to explain it to their mothers.

When a child of mine is sitting on the couch at my house fiddling with an electronic game controller, that is not violent. If I were to yell and insult him and wound his soul and our relationship, that would be much closer to violence.

But yelling isn't "violence." Hitting is violence. And who, in families, can be legally hit?

SandraDodd.com/violence

Spanking

It is not legal for a 200 lb man to hit a 100 lb woman. Increase or change the numbers and genders around however you wish to, but it is not legal. Where I live, if there is a domestic violence call, someone is taken to jail, for the safety of the other partner.

It is, however, legal for the 200 lb man to hit a 60 lb child, or even a ten lb. child. Imagine that. And for the woman to hit the children too. They can hit them hard, and often. And the police won't take anyone to jail at all. They can hit them with things that might even be called "deadly weapon" in some other circumstances, but it's just not a crime.

Because learning can't happen when a child feels unsafe, spanking isn't any good for unschooling families. It's not "good" for any families, but if the child can leave the dangerous home and go to a relatively safe school, at least he has a chance of learning.

Because unschooling needs trust and affection and peace, spanking isn't going to move a family toward unschooling, but will move them away from it.

Because learning about the world in a homeschooling environment of any sort needs children who aren't afraid to ask real questions, and parents who are willing to answer them as truly and honestly as they can, spanking will inhibit communication and learning in those families.

If anyone reading here is already planning to write and tell me spanking is illegal where you live, don't write; I know. I'm in the United States of America, though, and we have something in common with Somalia. The U.S. and Somalia are the only two nations, as I'm writing, not to have signed off on the United Nations Treaty from the Convention on the Rights of the Child. The Sudan People's Liberation Army signed it, and they're not even a nation. Many of this book's readers will live in a more enlightened part of the world than I do.

SandraDodd.com/spanking

The Effects of Spanking

Anyone who is waffling about whether spanking is really so bad is invited (by me) to read *For Your Own Good: Hidden Cruelty in Child-Rearing and the Roots of Violence* (by Alice Miller). One of her special areas of knowledge is Adolf Hitler and other Nazi leaders, and the ways in which they were punished as children, both at home and in school.

Even the effects of people talking about spanking are embarrassing. You might want to ask your friends and relatives whether this is in the Bible:

Spare the rod and spoil the child.

They'll probably tell you it is. Ask them to find it. They'll probably say it's not exactly the right words in the translation or concordance they have, but that it's in there.

Some Christians can't tell God from Samuel Butler. Apparently lots don't care. They just take someone else's word for what the literal word of God is.

If you think all that spanking advice is nineteenth-century trivia, you are wrong. In 2003, Kelly Lovejoy wrote this:

> Cameron went to a friend's 8th grade commencement yesterday (here in the Christian South). The *old* headmistress spoke to the crowd. Cameron said that she said the "S" word no less than 7-8 times (he said it could have been much more—he was so stunned!). She kept telling the parents that DISCIPLINE was so important. That they shouldn't be afraid to spank. That spanking was good. That to spank was to show their children that they love them. That the world needs more spanking. This went on and on. I was appalled that someone could get away with this in public—in a public address!

There are still, sadly, conventions at which spanking implements are sold. Many Christian homeschoolers attend them. There are still radio shows that talk enthusiastically about spanking. Unashamedly advise grown men to strike young children. Twenty-first century. On the radio. In church. At conventions.

There are many stories and links on my site. They might make you cry. Not as much as spankings have made children cry, though.

SandraDodd.com/s/rod

Other punishments?

Well what about "natural consequences" then? Unfortunately, the English phrase "natural consequences" was commandeered by punishing parents decades ago. A natural consequence of lying in the real natural world would be that someone might get caught and lose friends and not gain faith or integrity. But when parenting manuals recommend "natural consequences," they usually mean a punishment. They have punishments; kids break rules, so "naturally," there are "consequences." It's embarrassing. Don't think about it too hard.

When children's allowance is withheld, it gives them the incentive to find or steal money, or to lie in the future not to get caught.

When kids are grounded, they are cut off from others who could comfort or distract them or cheer them up, and many will sneak a phone call or go out the window.

It probably won't take many questions to find stories of crazy, too-huge punishments inflicted on people you know, or stories you remember because you witnessed them or because you were inconvenienced or blamed in part when your friend's privileges were taken away.

Recently someone said that cellular phones were the greatest invention in modern times, because teens would do whatever parents said to keep their phones. I honestly don't remember who said it. I was stunned at the casual cruelty and short-sightedness of it. I have a teenage daughter with a cell phone that we pay for. If she feels unsafe or afraid, she can call for help. I want her to have that ability at all times, day and night. But in some families, the child's fears are not of the outside world, but of the parents on the other side of the door. And so we're back to violence, and internet danger.

What happens when children are not spanked? Turns out they are shocked and offended when they discover other children have been and still are.

SandraDodd.com/s/backstage
SandraDodd.com/spanking

Clarity

Clarity is one of my favorite topics and the thing I value most in others, after honesty. I think clarity is being honest with oneself, in part, but it also involves seeing the difference between language that is repetition of other people's phrases, and words that describe their actual thoughts.

Even when people move from parroting and clichés and idioms to using their own words, they might not have thought yet about the meanings of the words.

If Howard Gardner is right, maybe some people won't be able to do this any better than I could swim the Mississippi and play soccer on the other side. But just as some people value athletes, I value people's careful use of language.

Online discussions of natural learning and parenting give people a serious opportunity to practice communicating clearly and carefully. For some people, an unschooling discussion will be their first "real writing"—the first time they've written real things for real people, rather than practice things for teachers. Those who stick with it or who have a native talent for it will find themselves getting direct and immediate feedback from other parents who have taken the ideas or examples or stories and used them to change their own real children's lives, and that is bigtime.

So, clearly, we're all onto something touching on people's souls and psyches, on their beliefs and philosophies. You don't see that every day!

SandraDodd.com/clarity

If I let him...

A collection of fallacies!

These are statements actual parents made in writing, and in public. I wish I had saved all I'd ever seen, but twelve years ago I had no idea there would be *so many*. So this is a collection begun in 2003, for the edification of those who are trying to move from authoritarian parenting to mindful partnerships. The names have not been saved because many of them changed their minds before long after reading what the unschoolers online had to say. Others, unwilling to defend their beliefs, went away grumpy that anyone would give children choices and freedom.

If this were a big bug museum, I might put a giant jungle beetle right in the entryway, so here it is:

If I didn't place some kind of restrictions on these immature souls, they would try EVERYTHING. Are you saying that I should tell them "Forget everything I ever said about drugs. Do what you want and make your own decisions?" Where the heck do you people draw the line? And if you don't, may God Protect your children!!!

I have a son who'd eat flour and sugar all the time.

If I were to allow it all they would do is play video games, watch cartoons, and play.

My children LOVE video and computer games. If left to them they would play them ALL DAY LONG.

I do struggle with the fact that he could sit and play computer games all day - literally form morning until bed - if I let him.

if there is junk in the house my 3 yo will eat that and nothing else if i let him

I do know that my son would eat trash and dead birds if I let him, so in that way I am not permissive. (the mother of a 22 month old wrote that in 2007)

If my boys were allowed to self-direct, they'd spend all day reading Hardy Boy books, blowing up the house with science experiments, and not much else.

If I left him to do what he wanted, he would eat junk food and play video games all day long...

She mentioned at that point that if her daughter is left to herself to be inspired she will sit down and read all day.

If my son had his way he would play video games all day long.

My son is one of those who would spend 24 hours a day playing video and computer games, if nobody dragged his nose away from them

I can tell you that if my children could do WHATEVER they wanted they would be wild. My 3 yr old would eat until he pukes and my 4 yr old would get into so much trouble...

He would play games all day if I let him...

Also, he LOVES to play Final Fantasy Online. If I let him, he'd play ALL day!

They would spend all day, every day, in front of the TV, computer or Playstation if they were allowed to.

If I I left him to his own plans, he would be playing the Gameboy or watching TV all day long.

Left to himself he would play Gamecube and torment his sister.

My Mitchell (5) would watch it all day if I didn't say that's enough...get outside and play, now.

I know if I let my son do ONLY what he wanted to do that is what he would choose. *[of video games]*

If I let him do exactly what he wants he will just watch tv constantly.

I'm telling you, he would NEVER stop playing if we didn't make him once in a while...

My boys are lazy and it seems like if left to their own devices they'd just watch TV and play with toys or computer games all day.

If I let them they would sit in front of the TV ALL day.

I have one that would sit in front of the TV all day everyday.

No matter how tired she is, she would *never* just doze off in front of a video. *[That one is a version of "would never go to sleep."]*

If left to his own devices, my son would eat sugar all day.

If left on their own, they will see nothing wrong with eating junk food all day.

He will choose to go without food and just eat sweets if allowed.

My son would subsist on sweets if I didn't occasionally intervene and tell him that he's free to graze on "junk food" after he eats nutritious foods (fruits, veggies, etc.).

[I]f I answered every question my kids asked, my son would ask questions all day.

If he had his choice he would want me to just play with him all day. *(of a nine-year-old boy)*

If he had his way, he'd have me playing video games with him, watching T.V. with him, doing something with him ALL DAY LONG!

I'm telling you, he would NEVER stop playing [video games] if we didn't make him once in a while...

We have to have rules about when bedtime is or she would never stop moving long enough to fall asleep.

She can't leave them totally alone or they would do nothing productive.

Left to her own devices, she would choose nothing.

If allowed, she will do NOTHING but watch television all day.

It would be my son's choice to spend all day on the computer playing games, or playing Playstation.

If I let them, they would decide that they are big enough and capable of deciding to hop in the car and drive to their gran's house.

He'll talk your ear off if you'll let him.

Not to mention my son would sit and play Playstation for hours at a time if I didn't limit it.

I do restrict his computer access - otherwise he would just play all the time - he loves strategy games.

I am mainly concerned about the littles- because they would choose to eat chocolate chip cookies all day every day if they were allowed to.

If I let him go and say you can do whatever (or even tell him we are going to try unschooling) he knows what it is we have friends who unschool. I am so afraid to have a couch potato kid that would never come out to the light of the day, and he would be brain dead from games.

Two about chores:

If I just let my kids hang out without doing any housework or having any responsibilities, my house would be condemned.

[I]f we tried that nothing would ever get done and the house would be full of garbage and cockroaches!

Three statements pulled from the same long paragraph:

I wish my daughter could just stop eating the sweets after just a few bites like someone else's does.....she would eat sweets non-stop.

If she was given a choice, she would choose the sweets anytime!

She'll eat whatever I put in front of her for dinner, but would otherwise eat candy/junk food all day long, constantly, if I let her.

Here are some with addenda or follow-ups:

Left on his own he would play War Craft all day (or at least a lot) that would include breaks for drum playing. *[That one was in private e-mail, not in public, and the next e-mail said "I must admit that this game is probably responsible for some of the reading ability that he currently has. And he pretty brilliant in the game. His drumming is pretty amazing too."]*

This one is just almost too big for the page, so brace yourself:

If my kids had their way, they'd go barefoot outside of their own yard, run in the street between cars, never take baths, never eat their veggies and instead opt for chocolate cake every meal, mistreat animals, burn down the house playing with matches, never go to bed, never brush their teeth, etc.

Holly was twelve years old when that was written. I shared it with her and noted her response:

I read that to Holly and she was speechless. Seriously mouth-open disbelief. Then she asked "WHY would they burn the house down with matches?"

Me: "The only reason her house is not burned down is because she has a rule against playing with matches."

Holly: "So she can't even say 'You can play with matches but only in the front driveway'?"

Me: "Nope."

Holly: "So they'll never go to bed because they'll never get tired unless she tells them they're tired?"

She asked me to read it to her again. I did. She looked at it and looked at me and said with more feeling, "Why the hell would they run between cars in the street!?"

Notes I posted with that at the time:

ABOUT HOLLY:

Holly Dodd is twelve years old, and has gone barefoot AND decided to wear shoes on thousands of occasions, depending on the circumstances.

Holly has never run in the street between cars.

She takes lots of baths and always has.

Holly loves lots of vegetables (especially spinach, carrots, artichokes, avocados which she says are actually a fruit, but they're green), but there are no veggies that are "her veggies." We don't assign her veggies or require veggie-eating of her. Never have. Holly doesn't really like chocolate cake much at all.

She has never mistreated an animal in her life.

She has played with matches but has never burned anything that she shouldn't have or that she didn't mean to. She's good at building fires in the fireplace. That's a good life skill.

Holly has gone to bed every night her whole life, except two nights when she took a nap early and then got up at midnight to stay awake with a friend who was supposed to be awake all night for medical tests in the morning.

Holly brushes her teeth, and since she got braces she has been flossing quite a bit, and she wanted to get a Water Pik so we got her one.

Holly is not an exception. LOTS of kids whose parents respect them and allow them to make choices make good choices!

Seven years later, Holly is as sensible as she was then. How is it that mothers can know their children so little and Holly can know so much? 1) because those mothers are not looking at their children,

 and

2) because Holly was unschooled.

Sandra Dodd
Holly's mom

SandraDodd.com/ifilet

Truth/Honesty/Lies

Every person who hopes to have a positive influence on any other person needs to figure out how to find and maintain as much integrity as possible.

Integrity is a strong wholeness. The fabric of the being of a thing can't be broken. A bucket with one hole in it is lacking integrity. It's not a good bucket. A frayed rope lacks integrity. No matter how long or strong the rest of the rope is, that frayed part keeps it from being a good rope.

In people, integrity requires some degree of reliability and honesty (the more the better). Part of the integrity of some of the young adult and teen unschoolers I know comes from their having grown up relatively undamaged. They have a wholeness most young people are never allowed to have, or which is destroyed by the realities of school's grading system and its too-glorified "socialization."

There are families in which these undamaged young people have more integrity than the parents, but that's okay. Sometimes the parents' fears and wounds are such that they might never recover fully.

Anyone reading about or exploring unschooling should remember that there is no certification, no "degree granting," and no credentials. Some people have made up their own, claiming to be and to have done things that are much more fantasy than fact. Some haven't had much success persuading their own relatives that unschooling can work, but they keep that quiet in public.

Look at the ideas and use what will help you. If you get a chance to go to conferences or to meet unschoolers in other ways, don't expect them to be perfect. They're people. Some are fully honest. Some are not. Some are unclear on what "fully honest" would mean.

I hope you find some unschoolers you can trust and respect to help you through the rough spots if you have any, and to share your joys and successes. I know that some of you will become trusted and respected helpers for future unschoolers. Thank you for the honesty and clarity you might bring to the lives of others now and in years to come.

SandraDodd.com/integrity

Fact/Fallacy/Opinion

This is partly for parents who are reading and learning, but it's also worth considering for helping children navigate the world of opinion, advertising, research, and evidence of all sorts.

Rhetorically and logically speaking, things are not divided into truth and lies. Some things cannot be "quantified," meaning they can't be measured or weighed or counted. They are nebulous and vague. They might involve feelings or beliefs or trends or opinions that won't hold still even if someone finds a good way to measure them. Some things can be weighed, but it's hard to build the scales. Some things could be studied or researched, but the odds are high of finding botch-job "reports" and "evidence." Bad research is all around us. Good research can become outdated, or be defined, later, as not-as-good-as-once-believed.

Don't plant your feet solidly in the flow of ideas, or you'll be knocked on your ass. Accept the fact that "truth" flows and changes, so that real life and thought won't upset you. Instead of making absolute statements about what *is*, concerning any field of study, talk about what is currently believed. Plan on things changing and you will be ready to learn happily as they do change.

When you're considering a statement, maybe it's an opinion and can't be proven. Fine. Set those aside for now.

If a statement can be proven or disproven, it could be a fact, or it could be a fallacy, or it could be an outright lie. What would the difference in those last two be? If a "fact" is wrong, then it's not a fact. If it is innocently wrong it's a fallacy right away. If it used to seem right, but the evidence and bases of the beliefs supporting it changed, then it becomes a fallacy—false without the intent to perpetrate a falsehood. Then there are lies. Lies are statements made by people who know that what they're saying is untrue. Or occasionally, I suppose, they are reclassified as fallacies created by people who aren't sure what is true and what is wishful fantasy thinking. (Kind of the "insanity" subgroup of liars.)

I'm sorry people and advertisements and news stories and magazine articles and blog posts don't come with guarantees or certificates of authenticity. What you need to do with and for your children is to practice sorting through and discovering what will help and what will hurt, what is to be trusted and what is just noise.

Without becoming too critical or cynical, maybe consider, with your children sometimes, changes in knowledge (the platypus, Mars, Pluto, leeches, volcanic activity and virgin sacrifice compared to global warming's medicine men; anything smaller than an atom?), or geography ("Four Corners" has been in the wrong place all these years; the U.S.S.R. is still on maps in some public places) or spellings ("plough" or "plow"? wooly or woolly?). Play lightly with these ideas. There's no advantage to getting huffy or angry about it. Just see it as the reality it is. People learn. People change their minds. Knowledge grows. Evidence is reclassified. Language is alive. People who are alive are changing and learning. You can resist that or you can ride it with gusto.

SandraDodd.com/logic

Marty Dodd *(photo by Ashlee Junker)*

Regrets

I have taken the names off the statements below. Some are attached, in the quotes on the website, at the address below. These are sad, but the authors allowed me to leave them in public in hopes that other parents would not wait and stall, as some of them had done.

"If Only I'd Started Sooner..."
a collection of wishes and regrets

I wish things for our family had been different earlier than later, but it is what it is. Unschooling really helped make us better people. I can't even imagine, or rather I can, how different things would be with our relationships with our kids if they'd been in school all these years.

Kids absorb the good and the bad. Unschooling really focuses on the good, and that's, well, GOOD!

I regret that we didn't come to the decision to homeschool the very first time our son had an issue with public school which was when he was in first grade and was very bored and found the days too long. His health issues began gradually that year and grew over the following years to one degree or another. I regret we didn't trust from the very beginning that he would always know what he needed if we just followed his lead.

We discover new things all the time, and haven't done anything schooly in a long time. They are changing so quickly, and all in a positive way. It's weird to see the changes in them, since they haven't been in public school. I can honestly say that I wish I had pulled them out sooner, but I can't change that now. I have only the future to look forward to, and with my kids I know it will be exciting.

I wish I would've *gotten* radical unschooling earlier with [my son] but I'm so glad that I didn't wait any longer than I did for his sake, [my daughter's] and mine. He's really one of the best human beings I know—and I know a lot of good human beings!

I just wish these lists and you had been around when I had my first baby.

I do wish I had known about unschooling from the start.

I am awakened! I thought that my awakening had completely already happened. I WAS this Radical Unschooling mom. Now I know that I was in my dark space (Thanks Mary Gold – Lions & Tigers & Teens, Oh My!) and that I had emerged from being a "school at home mom" years ago, but yet I have just been sitting strengthening my wings. I have so many places to fly and so many journeys to yet take. . .

I am saddened. I know, that is a funny one. I am saddened that I did not get it long ago. I saw all these amazing kids and teens and wish that [my daughter] had what she now has years ago. I know that I cannot go back and change it, but I am dam sure that her world will never be what it was.

Unfortunately, I came to it in the middle of raising my children. We have four grown that went through public school, and I SO wish I would have seen the light much sooner. I never realized the resources available to me.

I have learned so much from you and the unschooling list and feel so confident in living life as unschoolers. I "get it". I only wish I had unschooled years ago. I began unschooling my daughter (8 yr old) only 3 months and 8 days ago, and she has changed so much, she has gone from insecure, sullen, angry, to the child I used to have, she loves to learn, and we really have fun again. I wish I had done this earlier, but she didn't want to!! We are still deschooling (the whole family), but we are on the right track. Welcome to the list and the journey!!! It is amazing.

I am green with envy of all the rest of ya'll who figured this all out really early.

I wish I'd found the family bed, I wish I'd discovered peaceful parenting, I wish I'd not sent my kid...

We waited 'til [our son] was twelve.

Nobody here is going to tell you "I wish I'd found unschooling later."

I could just kick myself for not pursuing it any earlier.

I do want to thank you for your posts on the group and your web site writings as they have really helped our family on our journey (that is still progressing). The only regret I have is we didn't find this path earlier in our life, but better late than never!

I endured eight years of English boarding school. My older daughter aged 19 was in school for two years, tried two alternative schools and then was home educated like school at home but a bit more relaxed.

Only after my younger daughter was born did we move to an eclectic style of home education and she did attend (much to my regret) a year of nursery.

It's only in the last couple of years that we have moved to unschooling, it's been a very long journey. I have found myself talking to my older daughter a lot about how I feel and have told her I regret not knowing about unschooling fully when I was bringing her up.

For some reason most of my friends seem to think that if I truly cared about my kids then I would put them in school and in every extra-curricular activity. They can't fathom what my kids do all day as being learning. They simply think I am wasting their lives away and will regret it later.

My regrets are that I didn't unschool them in all areas of their lives from the beginning. I hate seeing others do what I have done in the past. I feel like I can give them insight if I am painfully honest with the harm I inflicted on my own kids.

We've been unschooling for two years now and our house has become a more peaceful and a happier place to be. I've learned to trust my children and I am a better parent and a better thinker.

In the beginning of our homeschooling I bought a curriculum and our experiment with school at home lasted about day when I realized it was completely offensive to my older daughter (and to me!) [My daughter] (7 years now) wanted nothing to do with school at home but we did enjoy reading some of the books and using up the stuff that came with it. Otherwise it was an expensive ($500) lesson on stuff we don't need. Money we now spend on trips and museums and stuff the kids want or are interested in.

Anyway, this ... is to say how exciting life is when you trust your children and support them—and to say thank you to the experienced unschoolers who post here. I've learned so much but I do get frustrated with newbies who post and then seem to fight every bit of wisdom that is so graciously given.

Hi Sandra. . . . I have been following you. . . since my daughter was three. Ohhh, how I wished I could have handled your advice to others on lists at that time. I was not ready, unfortunately for my child. Now my daughter is 7 and for the past year we have been unschooling. Our new focus is Radical Unschooling. We are definitely getting there. Thank you for all you do for this community and our children. My husband and I are very excited to receive your book and are looking forward to the many more you write.

I'm happy I found unschooling, but I wish I would have found it many, many years ago. The damage to my oldest can't be undone, but hopefully he will be better now, and his kids will be much better for it. (He said if he ever has kids he would love to unschool them.)

[To someone who asked if anyone on a forum had homeschooled and then unschooled:]

I am not sure what you're looking for as far as before and after, but: I wish I had known about unschooling from the start, and never done anything else.

The net effect is (with unschooling), we're all happier. We're less stressed. We have our own schedule - or lack of schedule - not one imposed on us by school, or even homeschooling. The kids' relationship with their dad is better. MY relationship with their dad is better. *grin*

I have so many regrets.

My head knows that I did what I thought was best at the time and that if I had known better I would have done better (and whole-life unschooling is THE best), but my heart still feels so bad.

A friend suggested I needed to grieve for those lost opportunities.

So now, each time I remember something I did, I reflect on it and think about what I would do differently and I cry about it. I cry it all out as long as I need to. I do it often when I read here or on the lists.

It's been better for me since I've allowed myself to do that.

I guess I finally get what people mean when they say they found Jesus and were saved. That's how I'm feeling about unschooling.

I am questioning so many of the old beliefs I carry that block joy.

I feel overwhelmed with grief when I think of the ten years I have been parenting my son from a place of judgment. I think that is a normal reaction because it is a loss. I feel inspired to parent from a place of unconditional love and acceptance (which I actually thought I was doing before). I could cry about the 10 years wasted or say "Thank God he's just turning 10"! There is still time!

I feel grateful to all of you who contribute and share and especially Sandra Dodd whose writings have changed my life.

SandraDodd.com/ifonly

This was hard to place, so I've put it just before the section on teens.

Sex Education

Some families say "Abstain!" and if a pregnancy results, they see it as a punishment from God, the ultimate outing of sneaky, bad behavior.

There are more loving ways to handle teens and sexuality. There are more compassionate and sensible things to think and say and do.

Undoubtedly some of those reading here were the product of unintended pregnancy, and it is not the fashion for people to say "shouldn't have been born" about themselves or anyone else. To be honest, though, with the world population approaching seven billion, helping your children only have babies they really want is good for you, them, and the hypothetical, potentially-unwanted children.

A girl can put a baby up for unseen adoption, and many parents have required teenaged girls to do that. There are risks to physical health and life, and certain effects on emotional health and life.

We can continue the tradition of the ages of punishing and shaming and controlling teenagers, or we can find better ways to help them learn what they need to know to make good decisions and to live a responsible, happy life.

That was all about pregnancy. There are other things to consider. It's easy to lie to kids or to create a cloud of fear and nonsense. What's not as easy is for parents to review and update their own knowledge so that what they're saying is helpful and current and true.

I was talking to Holly about "control," and of a family forbidding a 16-year-old to see her boyfriend (who attended the same school she did), which resulted in the murder of her family, house burned down, all the teens in prison…

I said: "Some families tell their boys never to look at dirty pictures and never to touch their penises."

Holly: "Ed Gein's mother told him that, hardcore."

Sandra: "Never to jack off?"

Holly: "Yes. And he dug his mother's body up, cut off her vagina and painted it silver."

SandraDodd.com/sex

Teenagers

When I had been unschooling for several years, I still dreaded and joked about how different it would be when I had teens. I expected what I thought was "natural" and what was probably inevitable teenaged behavior.

It turns out that much of what is considered "normal teen behavior" is a normal reaction to many years of school, and to being controlled and treated as children and school kids and students rather than as full, thoughtful human beings.

Being wrong doesn't bother me one bit when the truth is so much better than my fears and predictions!

I had fears, but unschooled teens can have fears too. They might fear the unknown, impending responsibilities, being too different or not different enough. Compare those fears to the fears of traditionally-parented high school students, though, and the difference is that unschooled kids aren't afraid of bullies at school, of tests and assignments, of being really hungry an hour before the meager lunch, and a hundred other things that it turns out are not part of "the real world," but part of school world.

The fears that unschoolers have can be dealt with at home, with trusted family members. They're not compounded by the pressures and helplessness so many teens around them live with.

Having had good relationships with my young children made it easy for that to continue through their teen years. Marty will turn 21 in early 2010. Holly will be 18 by the time most people read this.

Pam Sorooshian, whose three children are slightly older than my three, and about the same age spread, wrote:

> As we get older and our kids grow up, we eventually come to realize that all the big things in our lives are really the direct result of how we've handled all the little things.

SandraDodd.com/teen

Saying Yes to Teens

If you had a business partner or a camping buddy or were a member of a musical duet, would you try to ditch the other person or tell him to hush or wait or leave you alone? Would you say, "I'm the real human here, and you're only a partner/musician/camper-in-training"? Would you belittle him or "ground" him or tell him it didn't matter what he thought?

If the answer to any of the above was affirmative, I'm guessing you don't actually have a partner or buddy (not anymore, anyway).

Laws try to keep teenagers at home. Sometimes laws fail. Often teens leave. Sometimes they'll graduate early from high school to get to go to college to leave. I did. Sometimes they'll kill themselves to leave. Charles did. Alice did. I went to their funerals, when we were 14 and 15, respectively. Sometimes teens run away and hide for years, if they live long enough to hide for years.

In families in which parents have considered themselves partners in their children's rich lives, teens don't have the desperate urge to leave. A natural desire to leave the nest does kick in, as it does for many mammals. It might have kicked in sooner if the culture didn't require parents to take care of their children and be responsible for them until they were 18 years old. I know dozens of teens up close, by name, who are loving and patient with their parents even though the parents are getting old and forgetful. Teens can be helpful and generous with parents and siblings when they themselves have been generously helped up to that point.

SandraDodd.com/yes

Driver's education

Because laws are different all over the world, I will say a few general things about teenagers learning to drive. Take what might help and leave the rest.

Some people live in cities with public transportation and teens might already be mobile by sixteen or seventeen using subways and busses and trains as the adults around them are. That's easy.

Most people live where transportation long distances requires an automobile. Sometimes unschooling parents get tired of driving.

One of the greatest responsibilities of any unschooling parent is to find or provide transportation to very many places for a child, and the number of places rarely becomes fewer as the child gets older.

Some families with children in school treat driving as a rite of passage, as a great and ominous privilege. They make the children pay for their driver's ed, and their gasoline, and their insurance, and still they are stingy with their car. I'm not saying children should never pay a cent, or that new drivers should be risking a Porsche. What I'm saying is that transportation is part of life, and few places have a hitching post for the horses anymore, and skateboards have limitations.

Pressing a child to drive before he or she has an interest or confidence is not a great idea. Trying to force a child to learn to drive is as bad as forbidding him to touch a car or a motor vehicles test manual. Somewhere in there, though, is a balance point.

Just as with learning anything, being somewhere between calm and very interested is a good place. Being afraid or resentful is not a good learning mood.

If you don't have a car you feel comfortable with your teens practicing with, consider getting one. Used-but-safe is good. I was impressed when a young friend's mom got a used Volvo wagon because their crash test ratings were the best of what she could afford used.

Some parents get an ugly beater, hoping the child will be ashamed to drive it and that will save gasoline or something. Some parents are sadistic that way. Don't be one of those.

Some parents only let their children drive to the store and back, or to a lesson and back, with no side trips at all. That isn't about trust or learning or choices. Avoid setting up a situation in which you only win when the teen loses. *Be partners.* And be a good partner.

Here's what you gain when your children can drive: You can stay home and start up some of your long-abandoned hobbies. You can sleep later, and not need to stay up so long at night. If you're out of milk and bread, you might ask one of them to go and get some, or if you want a fish sandwich, provided you have gone through many drive-through windows for your children, one might be glad to go through one for you and bring your food back and deliver it right where you're sitting.

Not too many parents of kids in school can order up a burger and fries just any old time!

The downside, of course, is the danger and worry, but now that people tend to have cell phones and to visit homes in which there is internet, it's easier to get a message back home to say plans have changed. The days of sitting up and watching the clock can be a thing of the dated-TV-sitcom past.

SandraDodd.com/driversed
(There is an essay on my children's experiences in
drivers' ed near the end of this book.)

Rebellion

Some people have taken a teenager out of school and begun unschooling at that point in life. Although most of the stories are positive, they can be dealing with a dozen years or so of schooling or parent-support of schooliness. In such cases, this article might not apply.

For those who started a decade or so before the teen years, who conscientiously treated their children with respect and consideration, who gave them choices of all sizes and helped them figure out how to get along well and happily in the world, rebellion does not come.

It's one of those regular "You people are CRAZY" topics, the idea that teens wouldn't rebel. And so people will say, "Well I guess you don't care if they shoot heroin and steal cars."

Just about all children have the potential to choose to shoot heroin and steal cars. I'm pretty sure those who are in juvenile detention (or worse) for having done so are not kids whose parents have paid attention to them and hung out with them every day for ten or fifteen years. I do know that I never told my children not to steal cars, yet they have never even so much as borrowed one of ours without permission. I've never told them "Do not shoot heroin." I do have a nephew who has done that, but my own kids haven't. I don't even think they know anyone who has, not counting the one cousin who is in rehab and will do better or he won't. (And sure enough, he had several years of parents paying insufficient attention to what he might need, or might want to talk about.)

It's not about obedience; it's about good judgment. It's about avoiding an adversarial relationship. If you're partners, the child *and* the parents can win at all times.

When rules are shaken off and principles are in play, it wouldn't make sense for a teen to think and then choose something really horrible. If the parents were saying "Consider all the factors you know and do the best you can," why would someone "rebel" against that?

This is the alternative scenario:

> My daughter, age 16, is going her own way, refusing to believe that she doesn't have to attend public high school to succeed in college. She's been a rebellion factory for years now–this is nothing new. I

know if I wanted her to attend a public school she would be begging for homeschool.

"Refusing to believe"?

That phrase doesn't come up at our house. I think mostly it's because I don't just *tell* my kids that something is or isn't true, I try to find evidence so they can see for themselves and believe it because of proof. There's no "refusal to believe" what is clearly shown.

There are millions of parents with the harsh attitude expressed above, though. Millions of kids are thought of as "rebellion factories," but weren't the "factories" created by those who had the power to set the conditions of those shared lives? I think the "rebellion factories" are the parents who chose to be their children's adversaries rather than their partners. It is not necessary. It is not inevitable.

There are hundreds (maybe thousands by the time you read this, maybe tens of thousands someday) of never-schooled teenagers who have no need for rebellion. Mindful parenting and radical unschooling don't provide an environment for the creation of a rebellion factory.

SandraDodd.com/rebellion

How are they as people?

Keith was at a party with his co-workers. The others started moaning about how lazy and unmotivated teens are, and Keith said something to the effect that Kirby (15 or 16 at the time) had a job he liked and was good at. They didn't say "tell us more." The responses were more to doubt Keith and to treat it like a conversation-killing thing. They weren't really conversing for informational purposes. It was "support." It was a calm frenzy of teen bashing and commiseration. It was "poor us," but Keith felt lucky.

I once wrote: People warned me "Oooh, you'll have three teens, watch out, it will be horrible," but so far, with Holly 12 and Kirby 17, it hasn't been horrible in any way whatsoever.

When I put that on my webpage, I added: *Update with Holly nearly 16, Marty 18, Kirby 21 and moved away, it was never horrible, and has become better and better.*

When this book is finished, they will be 17, 20 and 23, and our lives are the opposite of "horrible."

I've seen enough families function and have enough memories from my own youth that I know for certain how I could have made it horrible. I could have made them unhappy and rebellious and full of rage and hatred and frustration, but I chose instead to help them be happy and full of joy.

What Keith was describing to his co-workers involved choices and contentment, but those things are foreign to most families. Finding happiness and joy in situations they've chosen has been true of all my kids. It was true in driver's ed. It was true when Marty went to the junior police academy. It was true of Kirby at the karate dojo, and of his other jobs. It has been true of Holly in situations large and small.

Their supervisors and co-workers just *gush* about how they are.

One day there was a minor emergency, and I walked up to the grocery store where Marty was working, to tell him about it. He asked if he should go to the hospital, but we were down by one car and I was going to need to go to the airport in a few hours. I told him he might ask to get off early, because the store was pretty quiet, but he looked at me like that was quite unreasonable and said no, he needed to finish his shift.

A side effect of school is that school kids know all kinds of ways to get out of school or work, and my kids don't have those tricks. When they go to the orthodontist they get a slip that has a tear-off note to the school, and it has the time they left. As a longtime former school kid, I look at that and think "darn," and calculate the amount of stall-time that would be acceptable before reporting back to school. I could get there in five minutes, but would twenty minutes be "too long"? I still have those reactions. I still see five minutes till 3:00 on an analog clock and think "almost time!"

There is something *huge* that comes from that non-exposure to school.

Most of the unschooled teens I've met had a calm and maturity that I'm not used to finding even in random adults in their 20's and 30's, who are sometimes awkwardly pretending to be mature, or sometimes still actively reveling in their new-adult freedom.

I've known teens (and am related to some) who are as comfortable with younger children as with older teens and adults and grandparents. They see people as people. They will be drawn to interesting people and will avoid dull or harsh people, but they don't choose by age.

I've also seen a difference in motivation in teens who have been nurtured and whose parents were not adversarial with them. They don't consider food a reward, and so they're less likely to spend all their money on food to self-soothe. They rarely need to "self-soothe" anyway. If they have a success in a project or at work they enjoy it for itself, for the feeling of accomplishment. And if their parents have managed not to use money in lieu of attention and expressions of affection, they're careful with money, too. If money means love, a needy person will want more money. If money is a tool like a hammer, or a substance like bread and toilet paper—necessary for comfort, and it's good to have extra—then it would make no more sense for them to spend all their money than it would make to throw a hammer away because they had already put the nail in the wall, or to unroll all the toilet paper just because it was there.

If the parents have been generous, many other problems are averted.

SandraDodd.com/teen/people

Jobs

Holly has had a few jobs. One was working at a skateboard and clothing store in a mall a few miles away. One was working at a flower shop just a few hundred yards away; she walked. But the shop had another shop on the air base, and sometimes she worked there, so she had a base pass and a key to both shops. When Holly's jobs require driving, we let her use a car. Some of her school-attending friends are told they can't get a job unless they buy a car first. It seems to be a way for the parents to say no and then blame the kids for it.

Some mainstream families press their teenaged children to get jobs, and shame them if they fail, while putting conditions on when and where they can work. The result is that getting a job was just one more "do what the parents make you do" situation, and the jobs aren't fun; they're an extension of school and of parental control.

When teens or young adults have chosen to have a job without desperation for money, and when they are accustomed to learning all the time and living joyfully, they are a different sort of employee.

The question of people new to unschooling is usually "But what kinds of jobs can they get without having graduated from high school?" Here are the jobs my kids have had:

- Retail/game store/clothing store/skateboard shop
- Teaching/karate dojo
- Food/pizza place (Kirby trained others on cash register)
- Making leather boots and pouches
- Grocery store courtesy clerk
- Babysitting
- Housesitting/dogsitting
- Art/web design
- Flower shop (retail and assisting with design)
- Kirby works for Blizzard Entertainment but can't share the particulars of his job.

In every case outside the babysitting and dogsitting, they were working with people who not only had high school diplomas, but college degrees. And I don't mean to say they were working with bosses who were college educated; some of their co-workers were "educated," and working the same jobs as my kids who learned on their own in fun ways. Some of their bosses had no college; some had.

This is touched upon in the section on sleeping, but another common question is whether someone who grew up without a schedule and a bed time and could ever hold "a real job." The assumption, I think, is that "real jobs" require getting up very early and at the same time every day. Marty did that for over a year when he worked at the grocery store near us. He worked Monday through Friday at 6:30 a.m. He had no problem with that schedule.

Looking up through the list of jobs, I will give as many shift-starting-times as I can remember, and you might wonder if someone who had grown up with a bed time and a regular schedule could ever hold a job.

AM	6:30	PM	1:00
	8:00		3:00
	9:00		4:30
	10:00		5:00
	11:00		6:00

SandraDodd.com/teen/jobs

Marty at the Persian restaurant where he worked for a year or so.

College

I think half the unschoolers I know who are grown have gone to college. Some went early; some went "late." Some went at 17 or 18. Some have gone to community college, some to fancy universities, and some to alternative schools such as The New College of Florida, and Antioch College in Ohio.

Several have graduated; some haven't yet, some who haven't gone yet might later. Some thought they would go but got good jobs without college and haven't had time or interest.

These informal counts might seem about like high school graduates' outcomes. Perhaps so. What's very different is that few to none of the unschoolers are going to college against their will, or just to get away from home. Each one I've known who has chosen college did it because it was of interest to them for one reason or another.

When my children were young and people would say "Yes, but can they get into college?" I would tell them of my own experience, at the age of eighteen, getting my fifteen-year-old sister into a state university. She was on her way to drop out of high school, when the principal met her in the hallway and expelled her. My dad asked me to help her out. She couldn't get into the university I was in, but I got her into another one in another city and it must not have been very difficult, because she hadn't finished high school and I was a teen myself.

With that experience, I've never thought it could be difficult for a parent to get an eighteen-year-old into college.

There is a frightful frenzy associated with the supposed be-all/end-all of Ivy League colleges. If people can back up and not have their noses against SAT preparation booklets, they will see how small that is in a very large world.

I don't know about other nations' systems as well as I do the U.S., but I do know that alternatively educated students can and do "succeed" when success is defined as college, and they also very often succeed without it.

A couple of things to remember: Foreign students come to American universities and they catch up even if the language, food, beds, toilets, system of writing and mathematical notation are entirely new and foreign to them. A native English-speaker who knows a cheeseburger from a burrito and can flush will certainly be able to "catch up" too, if necessary. As far as I have seen and heard, unschoolers start off with a newness to the situation that seems quaint and then turns to an advantage, when most of the students doze off or see how little work they can do to pass the course, while the unschooled kids are interested in the subject matter and are accustomed to learning in different ways and for fun. Professors have reported surprise and enjoyment when they encounter unschoolers. Sometimes they offer them special opportunities, and sometimes scholarships.

Wanting to learn, and making the choice to be in a school when one has the choice to leave without shame or punishment is a world apart from "no choice" and "have to."

There are more particular, entertaining
and impressive stories here:
SandraDodd.com/teen/college

Interesting Alternatives to College

One family furnished a teenaged boy with equipment for rock and roll performances. This has happened in families in which the children went to school, too, but for the unschooling family it was considered an investment in a possible career. The parents were supporting an interest that they knew could be not only the means of expression and musical joy, but a potential source of income. And the equipment itself has a value, so if the son had decided to do something altogether different, he could sell the sound system and instruments. His family had provided start-up resources.

Many families have helped their teenagers travel, for various purposes—sometimes to be around other families with home businesses or hobbies in which the teen is interested. Sometimes it's for Not Back to School Camp, or other camps or wilderness experiences.

Some families travel, and so the cost of the RV and add-ons such as bicycles and sports equipment are a part of life and educational supplies, because those have ended up being the same in the family budget.

Conventions about dolls, computers, anime, video games and other interests have been family destinations. Camps to learn about particular skills and sciences are attended sometimes by families, and sometimes by just the teens.

If a child isn't interested in college, the parents shouldn't do the happy "we won't have to pay for college!" dance without considering whether there are other ways a portion of that college savings or loan potential could be applied to helping the child toward learning and experiences they couldn't have partaken in as younger children, and which might also lead to a career.

If your child wants a camera or art supplies, a musical instrument or skis or a better computer, don't see it as a toy, but as a tool and as an entrée into a community of people from whom they can learn more.

SandraDodd.com/peace/newview

Young Adults

I will know more later, but from my vantage point as someone with two "of age" boys and a girl about to turn eighteen, it seems that the adult products of unschooling turn out to be adult humans who were relatively unhampered as they learned and grew. Many things we have been told and assumed were natural human behavior seem now to be natural side effects of schooling.

School promises a child that if he's good, someday he can take his place in the world. They're still making him that promise when he's a young adult: "Someday…"

Unschooled children are in the world from an early age. When they reach adulthood they have a carriage and calm that I believe came from having being respected as people for many years. It's hard to describe, but impossible to ignore.

SandraDodd.com/youngadults

Partners

Your child might have been your partner and companion for years, but it's very likely that he will want a companion of his very own, a "significant other."

I don't know as much about this as I will in a few years. Many of those unschoolers I've watched grow up are in their early 20s now, and most are unmarried. I've seen some choices made and some relationships ended, so I have ideas and I see some patterns emerging, but I might decide in ten years that there's not a significant pattern, and it might also be that the stories would involve so many adults that have nothing directly to do with unschooling that it will be none of my business and I won't be able to write about it.

For now, though, I can say I have seen teens and young adults turn down opportunities for quick and easy relationships for reasons I would never have considered when I was young. Other families have seen similar effects of decision-making skills.

Keith and I joked years ago that someone would need to make quite an impressive offer to lure our children away from home. Years have passed and it's not a joke anymore.

During my childhood when parents said to find someone of the same race or religion, it seemed offensive. Few people my age were willing to trust that the advice had much to do with our own futures, but with the comfort of parents who lived through the Great Depression or WWII or both, who hadn't seemed to care very much about our feelings or our concerns or ideas. And now they were telling us who to date, and sending suitors away for what seemed to be spurious and unfair reasons. Long hair. Hot car. Parents' income. Religion or lack thereof. Skin too dark; skin too light.

Some of our first opportunities to make our own choices were fueled by the desire to *finally* get to do what *we* wanted to do, to prove that we were independent people.

When a young adult has been making real decisions for years, and what their parents want is to help them think clearly and to make careful decisions based on the preferences and beliefs of the young person himself, the same old world looks very different.

When my children have had love interests, the decisions have not been made to please the parents nor to spite them. It turns out not to be about me at all, which is wonderful.

From my communications with other unschooling parents, I know that many grown children ask parents for relationship advice. Sometimes the significant others have approached an unschooling parent to discuss the relationship, too. I didn't foresee that, but I like it.

Left to make their own decisions in a supportive atmosphere, I've seen my children consider the genetic background of potential partners, for issues like mental health and addiction. Loving a partner isn't the same for them as choosing someone with whom to reproduce. They're not desperate to get out of the house. They like people who are interesting and cheery and energetic. Dishonesty and irresponsibility aren't accepted without objection. I shouldn't be surprised, but I am.

*I don't have a web link for this,
because it's not about unschooling
when it becomes about their relationships
with people who might not have been unschooled.*

Saying Yes to Grown Children

When Kirby was offered a job in another state, including an allowance for his moving expenses, I wanted to be encouraging without seeming to push him out and shut the door. So we promised to leave his room available for a year, in case he wanted to move back. He had taken the furniture and much of his belongings. The room became a video games room for the rest of the family, but it was still "Kirby's room."

I felt better knowing he was only tentatively gone. It might have helped him to know that it wasn't "do or die" there, in Austin. He was able to decide whether he liked it enough to stay there, knowing he did have the option to return to his own room at home.

A choice is always better than "no choice." We were able to cushion his leaving with a real fallback plan.

Before the year was up, he told Holly she could have that room because he liked his job and apartment and roommate enough that he was sure he would stay there.

When Marty wanted a jeep, we took the loan in our names and he pays his dad monthly for the car payment and insurance. We could have "made him" pay on his own, but this way it's safer for him. If he can't make a payment one month, we can keep him legal and he can catch up later. I have relatives who have refused to do any such thing for their children, and even laughed at their children for asking.

Marty hasn't missed a payment and he takes excellent care of the jeep.

Holly wants to live somewhere else, and we've helped her find places and contacts with other unschooling families.

You will be able to find stories of other families having done similar things to help their children get out and about in the world, while still being ready to welcome them back home.

SandraDodd.com/yes

Changes in the Parents

Earlier in the book, personal change has been a topic, but some people will skip around, and I think there are some changes that come with having had teenagers, so here's one more page on change. And really, the whole book is about personal change and a growing awareness of living with our children.

I think the most common changes parents have reported are that they are happier and calmer, and have become clearer in their thought processes. The "reports" I hear are often in online discussions, so that might explain the latter. When people help each other work through confusions in thinking, writing becomes clearer.

As to being happier, I see many contributing aspects of unschooling. The big one is that feeling like a good parent is huge. The opportunity to be successful every day at something with immediate feedback (hugs and smiles and the little-kid happy dance) is rare in the world. But giving children more slack and choices creates more slack and choice for the parent, too. If it's okay for a child not to finish everything on his plate, might it be okay if the mom only cooks what he likes next time? Or makes the best parts in new ways? Not every meal has to look like the centerfold of a cookbook. If children can sleep late, maybe the mom can too. If children can watch a silly movie twice, maybe the mom gets to be in on that. If a child (or a seventeen-year-old) wants to watch a butterfly for a long time, perhaps the parent will have the priceless experience of watching her own child watch a butterfly.

Questions such as "How important is this, really?" and "What's the worst that can happen?" change people's perspectives in several directions. They might decide the project really is pressing and urgent, but the difference will be that they considered the circumstances, the consequences, a range of choices, and made that decision.

SandraDodd.com/change

Unexpected Outcomes

When my children were young I knew their lives would be different, the differences were greater than any of my expectations. I hadn't known then, either, to predict how different my own life would be, and my husband's.

I didn't expect this to change my children's ability to make eye contact with people.

It surprises me that they have friends of such a range of ages.

I didn't expect them to learn so much without me.

I didn't expect Kirby and Marty to be offered jobs they didn't even apply for.

I didn't know that our relationships could stay so good even when they were teenagers.

I didn't know they would be so compassionate.

I'm impressed at their real-world courage and principles.

I didn't expect to like to lose arguments.

I didn't know I would be so accepting of kids saying "no."

I didn't expect it to make things so sweet between me and Keith.

I didn't expect unschooling to make the grocery store so fun.

I didn't expect to see school so differently.

I didn't expect this to improve my relationships with pets.

I didn't know how much people could learn without reading.

I didn't know we would have friends all over the country, and later all over the world.

SandraDodd.com/unexpected

Spouses

When spouses have common interests or hobbies, before they have children, sometimes their projects and successes there form the basis of their relationship. Maybe they're in theatrical productions together, or they ski or hike, or race go-karts, or volunteer to help people file their taxes, or they're both interested in the same period of history.

When responsibilities and children come along, it's easy for that early relationship to falter, and for the mom to know more about the kids, and for the dad to have work stories she's too exhausted to keep straight.

Sometimes unschooling becomes a new common interest, and their successes there can make them a successful team again. When I saw it the first couple of times, I thought it was nice, but partly coincidental. When I saw it over a dozen times I looked again.

Being a good parent makes a person more attractive to the other parent, and makes the other parent grateful and respectful. Gratitude and respect make it easier to have compassion and patience.

Just as being kinder and gentler with a child makes one a kinder, gentler parent, being more attentive and concerned about a spouse or partner makes that person, in turn, more attentive and concerned.

It doesn't happen all at once, and you can't send them the bill. You can't count or measure it. It has to be selfless and generous. Your kindness needs to be given because it makes you kinder, not because you want any further reward.

Being patient and compassionate with a child who is sad or hungry or tired or maybe teething or frustrated with his friends is good. Feeling good makes you calmer and more confident. It will give you stores of calm and clarity so that you can remember that your spouse might be sad or hungry or tired, maybe aging, aching, or frustrated with his co-workers and friends.

If you have come to feel adversarial in any way toward your partner, remember "partnership." Help him or her follow interests or hobbies or to take care of collections, or to see a favorite TV show. Support his interests. Being nicer makes you a nicer person.

Photos and mushy accounts:
SandraDodd.com/spouses

Healing

Just as the adult a child will be already lives in him, so the child you were still lives in you as an adult. If you have memories of childhood, examine them objectively sometimes when you're considering how to be with your own children.

There might be things from your past that you would do just as your parents did, and by doing that you would honor the happiness you remember from childhood. That's a way to show gratitude to your parents even if they're not living anymore.

There might be things you remember that you would not want to pass on to your children. For me, being put to bed alone in a dark room is not something healing for me or for my children. When I let them have a light, or let them sleep with me and their dad or wherever they want to, I imagine peacefully how nice that would have been for me, as a child, and that soothes and heals my soul. I still have the memories, but they're not as scary. They don't trigger resentment now, but nicer emotions, because now they're about my own children.

The list of things that marred your childhood can be your checklist of things to avoid or change or undo. The things that brought joy to you as a child can be things for you to do for and with your children, too, if you can.

Knowing some of my husband's childhood hurts helped too. Those also went on the "don't do this" list in my heart. Sometimes I was able to find little ways to see and comfort the little boy still living in that big strong man who works so hard to take care of us.

For me, the most healing thing of all was feeling that I was being a good mother. That didn't happen because of unschooling, it happened because of breastfeeding my first baby. I was doing something profoundly right, and it was deeply bonding for us. I had nursed the second baby and was pregnant with the third when we started unschooling. It seemed the logical extension of the attachment parenting that had made me feel so confident as a parent, and so good about myself from that present day back to my earliest memories.

When I soothe my child, I soothe myself.

SandraDodd.com/parentingpeacefully

Patience

Patience is a problem. The idea of it is a problem. Patience is associated with virtue and sainthood—with silent endurance of something painful. By some it is seen as waiting someone else out, being the last to blink or to speak. That's not very useful for unschoolers.

The patience that parents need is more like compassion and understanding. To be "impatient" with a person is a cocktail of frustration and resentment, often involving bad planning on the part of the impatient person.

What will look like patience will probably involve learning about your own child's needs and preferences and finding ways to meet and consider those, along with gaining the decision-making skills to be consciously breathing and considering your best options for a few seconds. That will appear to be, and will eventually become, patience.

When someone else has declared that something must be finished by a certain date or time, and it's an employment or contract situation and the tools and competence are present, it's doable, but can still involve stress. It happens all the time with construction and printing and party planning and a thousand other jobs.

Applying deadlines to learning is not the same thing. It would be like applying deadlines to physical growth. If you're told dramatically that a child's feet need to be size 4 by a certain age, ask yourself *why*? What would that be about? I've never heard of such a requirement, ever. But I have heard people say similarly arbitrary and unreasonable things about arithmetic and reading and writing. Will stress help?

When parents move off the assembly line model of building children and start to see it as helping an individual human grow in peace, those ages and charts will not seem a part of the child, but of a system of measures and comparisons that are guaranteed to create fears and failures in some percentage of children.

If you start living with your child at his or her pace, it will be easier to be patient.

A classic moment for impatience is getting in the car to go somewhere. Even with adults that can be difficult, because one will go back to turn off the light or say goodbye, and another will go back to get something, and another will remember to put down extra cat food, or to check that appliances are off. When that happens, they all calmly know they should've planned better or left sooner.

With children, it seems simpler sometimes for the adult to yell at the kids and become a model of impatience. It's likely the adult should have planned better *and* left sooner.

If a parent forgets that he or she is the only adult in a situation and that the responsibility for seeing all the factors falls on her, and that yelling at children for being children is not good for anyone involved, the lessons learned there can apply to situations other than getting in the car to go somewhere.

Planning for snacks and having them handy can seem like patience.

Planning for clothing and having extra with you can seem like patience.

Having a map and directions and having the phone charged up and a flashlight and an umbrella can seem like patience.

Impatience is often the beacon of unpreparedness and the resulting embarrassment. Be prepared!

With "academics," or bicycle riding, or swimming, impatience can cause things to stall out or go backwards. What a child doesn't need when he's trying something new is for someone to yell at him or to be gruff and cranky. And pressing a child to do something before he has an interest can ruin all future curiosity about that activity or food or topic.

Being patient can mean not being so controlling. Being patient can mean thinking to yourself "How important is it?" and relaxing, while others figure out their next moves.

Sometimes there IS an emergency. Then patience can be collecting your own emotions with a couple of deep breaths and not flipping out. Your family needs you to be present and helpful, not going off the deep end and making a difficult situation worse.

Some internal dialog that might help with patience:

- Breathe.
- He's still a baby.
- When she can do better, she will.
- He's tired
- She's nervous; I should hold her.
- We don't need to stay the whole time.

- We can come back to this later.
- Music might help.
- More quiet might help.
- Smile and be soothing.
- I love my family.

Reassure yourself in mental words and calm yourself with breathing slowly and deeply so that your stress dissipates a bit, and then you will probably make a better decision than you would have two seconds before that.

Patience can look like two seconds of calm.

SandraDodd.com/choice

Sandra and baby Marty (our most patient child)

Joy

Is the cup half empty, half full, defective or overflowing?

One mindful step in a better direction can be joyous. You don't need to reach a destination to have joy.

Some of the things that help people be confidently in the moment, feeling satisfied and content are:

- Breathing
- Gratitude
- Happy thoughts
- Fondness
- Acceptance

At first it might be relief and not joy, but as relief is a step away from fear, more relief will be progress toward joy.

Did you do something to make a child's life better and richer? Be grateful that you thought to do that, or know how to do that. Did your child look at you with affection? Can you tweak your life enough that those affectionate looks come even more often?

"Enjoyment." Something can put joy into something else. You can put joy into your child's life, and your child's contentment can put joy into yours. You can created a joyous feedback loop, or you can prevent one.

You can learn to induce and nurture joy. You can relax into letting joy arise from the smallest of stimuli. I saw a hummingbird outside the window while I was writing this. I'm glad I saw that. It was better than not seeing it. I didn't create the hummingbird, I simply enjoyed watching and thinking about it. The hummingbird gave my flowers more importance.

Practice finding and feeling joy. It won't be with you every moment, but the moments will increase.

SandraDodd.com/joy

Values

It's possible for a childless person or couple to live a long life without ever thinking about values. It's possible to go along with the crowd and get a nice place to live and a car and watch TV every night and pay the bills and not think about what might have been better or different.

With children, though, a new aspect comes into place. It's possible for a couple with children to live a long life doing what they think the neighbors and the relatives and the school want them to do, "valuing" discipline and good grades, valuing college and getting the house empty and the children married and into jobs.

What if a family wants to step off the path and look around on their own? What if a family wants to take a different path to the future that's quicker, or more dangerous, or more leisurely, or funnier? Will their values then involve excitement or peace or humor?

Our family values helping others and being honest. Keith and I were that way together before we had children, and whether by nature or nurture or both, we see our children being honest and helpful. I remember being a child in school and getting in trouble for being honest and helpful, in various situations. It wasn't always valued in school.

We value curiosity, at our house, and no one here would scoff at an off-the-wall question, or the examination of a plant or bug. At school, kids will be told, "That's not going to be on the test." Even if the question could have been answered in fewer than those eight words, curiosity isn't always valued in school.

It will help unschooling for a family to accept the value of learning and of living peacefully. One family might value industry over music; one might value art over organization. But if they value their relationships and the comfort and safety of others in their family, they can thrive. As unschooling grows, you will find your priorities.

SandraDodd.com/priorities

Pets

This was written a while back. When I re-read it I was surprised that I used to hiss at cats.

> I noticed one morning I was really patient with my irritating cat. That was cool, and announced to one of the discussion lists that I was going to work it into my talk about things that surprised me. We've long been sweeter with our current dog than we ever were with a dog before, and somewhat the cats too, but usually I hiss at the cat to get away from me when he gets in my face early in the morning and this morning I told myself that the cat can't open a can, and he's excited that I'm awake, and the dog probably ate their canned food, so I just very calmly followed him in there and fed him and he was very happy. I doubt it's my last frontier, it's just my current frontier.
>
> We leave food down for our dog. Sometimes the neighbor dog comes in and eats it. We have a friend who's house sitting for us. She was surprised that our dog and cats didn't mind her dog eating from their dishes. Her dog is fed separately, and finishes it all. Ours know there will be some more later if that gets eaten, so they only eat when they're hungry.

The time might come when you don't even remember having been so unreasonable, and that's pretty wonderful.

For all the "be gentle" that parents give their babies about how to touch cats and dogs, the parents themselves aren't always so gentle. Over the years of having children grow up around our dogs and cats I became more compassionate toward the pets. Having learned to communicate with and to understand non-verbal babies, I was better at understanding "non-human-speaking" animal companions.

SandraDodd.com/unexpected

Trees and Plants

I even garden differently than I used to. I certainly didn't expect that. I have let trees grow their own way without frustration on my part, and appealed to my husband not to prune so much. I have found things for vines to grow on that aren't fancy or store-bought. The vines are going to cover it up anyway. I've let native plants go ahead and grow, if they don't have stickers. Some of them are really pretty, and they *want* to grow there. If I destroy them and put in some foreign plants, will the neighbors be impressed?

Considering what is natural in my children, and what I can't control and shouldn't even try to control, has made it easier for me to look for what's "natural" in nature. That seems pretty obvious, written down that way, but many people want to control trees, and grass, and flowers. I don't mind influencing them and encouraging them, and nurturing them, but "to control" them? I don't even "control" tumbleweeds. I pull up any I find and put their little carcasses in the compost pile. That's tumbleweed euthanasia, maybe, but not "control."

If I plant something and it's dying, I'm more likely to let it die without calculating the cost or feeling bad inside about the lost potential of its produce or shade. I don't feel as much pressure or angst about the yard, and both the yard and I are happier.

I had cousins who were made to pull every weed out of their large lawn. If there was ever a weed or sticker, the kids were in trouble. The parents were openly critical and disdainful and belittling about the whole thing. The kids weren't thanked; the parents weren't thankful. It wasn't relationship building. Things weren't always good with that family.

I pull my own weeds, and the children tell me the yard looks nice, and when they have yards I hope they will not make their children pull any weeds against their will.

SandraDodd.com/unexpected

Wonder

The most common use of the word "wonder" these days is to express a question in a way that isn't likely to be answered, as in "I wonder when this tree will blossom?" It's also used to play with very young children with peek-a-boo games. "I wonder where Holly is? Where could she be? There she is!"

The deeper meaning of the word is what makes things wonderful. Full of wonder. Some adults are afraid of "wonder," though, because it involves relaxing into not understanding. It requires acceptance that one does not know. At its core, it is acceptance of and admiration for the mysterious and the hidden. It is taking joy in the revelation of simple things for which there are no words.

"Wonder" is part of the idiomatic phrase "childlike wonder," and that is the very wonder that unschooling parents should foster in themselves. Children have it already, if it's not extinguished with negativity and shame. If yours has been snuffed out by years of people saying "grow up" or "act your age" or "who cares" or "it doesn't matter," try to find it again. Look at clouds and the sunset—not for weather predictions, but for their form and color. Listen to birds. Smell flowers and fresh baked foods with focus and stillness. Hold a baby's hand; touch his soft skin. Don't even talk about it. Just smell. Listen. Look. Touch. Taste honey in silence.

Nurture your own curiosity and amazement. Let life be marvelous. Let nature and music be bigger than you are, and find gratitude in being able to be in the presence of the lyrical magic of the everyday world.

What will help wonder return to you? Pay closer attention to young children. See what they're seeing. Think about what they're asking. Wonder at what they wonder.

Many examples, quotes, photos and a playlist
of songs with the word "wonder" in them at
SandraDodd.com/wonder

Honoring Other Voices

While hundreds of people have written over the years in ways that helped others, some have gone beyond casual help, and have proven to be trustworthy and reliable helpers of other unschoolers. Here are some of my favorites.

Joyce Fetteroll

Joyce was an engineer until she decided to stay home with her daughter, an only child who is an artist, athlete and musician. Joyce lives in Massachusetts with her husband, who teaches at Western New England College.

"Joyfully Rejoycing" is Joyce's unschooling and parenting website. It is perfect for those who find my own website confusing. Joyce's writing is clear and encouraging and logical at all times.

SandraDodd.com/joycefetteroll
JoyfullyRejoycing.com

Pam Sorooshian

Pam and her husband live in southern California where they once worked doing data analysis for the power company. Cyrus works there still, but Pam teaches economics at Cypress College. Their three daughters are all past school age now, and the tales of their interests and accomplishments are easy to find and read.

The oldest has a degree in recreation and leisure, and is employed by a company that provides outings and activities for mentally handicapped adults.

The middle daughter has a deep, longtime interest in musical theatre, has performed many times, and recently directed.

The youngest teaches Kung Fu and studies American Sign Language.

Looking up at those summaries, I see them as the lightest sketches of very rich lives.

Pam has a great interest in how people make the transition from traditional parenting to unschooling.

SandraDodd.com/pamsorooshian

Schuyler Waynforth

Schuyler Waynforth sees the world as an anthropologist, and as an unschooling mother of two children. She usually sees it from England, where she lives with her husband David, a professor of Darwinian biology at the Medical School of the University of East Anglia.

Schuyler grew up American and has a view of the cultural differences that affect people's ability to relax into new ways of being. The family has lived in the U.S., Japan and the U.K.

In discussions, Schuyler can cut through people's expressions of wishful thinking to the scientific causes and evidence.

SandraDodd.com/schuylerwaynforth

Deb Lewis

When I see a post from Deb, I perk right up. They're always interesting and often hilarious. Deb is never wrong. I like that in a person.

Deb has read more of John Holt than most people, and she's great at making interesting lists of things to do with children.

At the end of telling about one of her typical days, Deb wrote, "My real and happy kid says a lot more about unschooling than I could ever convey by analyzing human nature. If I'm afraid to talk about my real unschooling life, how will I single-handedly change the world for the better? I've printed out my super hero license and I've sewn my Tick suit. Now, Evildoers, Eat My Justice!"

When someone asked how long unschooling had been around, Deb documented it back to the Neanderthals.

Her writings always inspire me. She lives with her husband and son in the Wild West. I live in New Mexico, so she lives in the wilder west than I do!

SandraDodd.com/deblewis
SandraDodd.com/day/debl

Ren Allen

Ren grew up in Alaska in a fundamentalist sect that didn't allow makeup. Now she lives in Tennessee with her husband Markus and their four children, and does makeup for a living. Her artistry and imagination are a marvel. Ren organizes get-togethers for unschoolers and speaks at conferences.

To understand what Ren does requires photos, so if you're interested go to this link:

SandraDodd.com/renallen

Robyn Coburn

Robyn writes, makes costumes, props and dolls, and lives in southern California with her husband James and their daughter, who is also involved in doll collecting and artistry. James works on movies in technical ways mysterious to me.

Robyn's mother was a singer. Her father was a famous juggler and circus performer named Elimar Clemens Buschmann. There is a video of him linked from my page on Robyn. Her father-in-law was the actor James Coburn, and so her daughter has talented genes. Her parents are nurturing nature.

Robyn is very good at helping people see how they can make their children feel whole and good, and that is a great gift she offers freely to any parents who can use it!

SandraDodd.com/robyncoburn

Jenny Cyphers

Jenny is a newer voice than some of the others, but no less powerful. She read quietly for years and then started sharing confidently and beautifully. She has two daughters, and her accounts of interactions with her teenager fascinate me. I'm looking forward to meeting her family someday. Jenny is an artist.

SandraDodd.com/jennycyphers

Kelly Lovejoy

Kelly writes tirades sometimes, and they're wonderful. She lives in South Carolina with her husband, Ben. They're both native locals with great accents. (They can't hear it but the rest of us can.)

Kelly went to exclusive private schools, and Ben went to The Citadel, and yet they became model unschooling parents!

They have one son who went to school for several years and then left when he was twelve, and another son who missed out on all that school experience completely.

Kelly organized and ran a series of conferences called "Live and Learn," which will live in legend and on t-shirts and bumper stickers forever. Many unschooling friendships were formed internationally from those seven conferences.

Both Kelly's and Ben's writings have inspired many people, and can be found online, some linked from my site.

SandraDodd.com/kellylovejoy

Mary Gold

Mary Gold was the first to write about video games, in all this batch of unschoolers, and that article is frequently read, years later. Mary and her husband, Jon, own Sunnyside Up, a breakfast café and coffee shop in Corvallis, Oregon. Mary coordinates and inspires a local unschooling group, and the family runs the annual "Life is Good" conference.

SandraDodd.com/marygold

Danielle Conger

Danielle Conger lives where the expectation is that very young children will be in school, but she resisted that and has been helping others with younger children implement unschooling in their own lives. Danielle lives with her husband and their three children on an organic farm in Maryland.

SandraDodd.com/danielleconger

Criticisms of Unschooling

The most common criticisms from the outside about unschooling are that unschooling parents are lazy, their children will be undisciplined criminals or unemployed bums living at home the rest of their lives, that the kids won't be able to read or write or get into college, and that the parents can't possibly teach algebra if they aren't college algebra professors, or something vague about algebra (always "algebra").

The most common criticisms of unschoolers by other homeschoolers are that we're making them look bad by not doing school at home, or that our children might bring down the average test scores of homeschoolers, which might endanger their right to homeschool (in places where test scores are an issue). A few say we're lazy and that our children never learn anything, but any of them who have actually been around unschoolers shush up about those things pretty quickly.

Criticisms of radical unschoolers by other unschoolers are that we are taking things too far, and that it doesn't hurt anything for parents to tell kids what to do, that bedtimes and food and TV restrictions have nothing to do with academics, and that there are as many ways to unschool as there are unschoolers.

I say just because there's no single right way doesn't mean there aren't some wrong ways. There are some practices, conditions and beliefs that can make unschooling impossible. Some think that if there isn't one single way to unschool, then it means everything in the whole wide world is unschooling. They won't be able to unschool because their thinking is rudimentary and stuck in "everything or nothing," black or white.

Some particular charges and criticisms follow.

Humanism

The idea that people have instincts that are healthy, good and right goes against some other people's religious beliefs. I don't consider myself "a humanist," I don't go to humanist meetings or have a humanist bumper sticker, but I have sometimes been assured that I am one of those, and that it's not good to be so.

I did grow up Baptist, and so I was once steeped in the "you're either with us or against us" feeling that divides the world into Christ's influence and Satan's, into the church and the heathen sinners, into the chosen and the cast out, into the saved and the damned.

Just because I understand it doesn't mean I agree with it. But from the point of view of those who do believe that they must live and think and act in certain ways so that they will live in paradise after death, then anything that looks like humanism has insufficient respect for the fear of eternal damnation.

These arguments don't make sense in all of the home educating world, so anyone baffled at this point should be grateful.

One factor that helps with deciding how to treat children, even infants, is knowing how one feels about "sin nature," whether a newborn baby is innocent and intelligent, or whether he's a stinky wad of proof of the Fall of Man in the Garden of Eden. Those latter might have the hardest time of any considering letting him choose his own foods.*

SandraDodd.com/feedback/humanism

*that was an apple joke

Anarchy

Because when rules are removed suddenly people can tend to behave wildly, families with rules assume that it's their rules and bedtimes and meal schedules that keep their children from breaking out all the neighbors' windows.

Rules should never be removed suddenly. If a family or a nation is going to change their socio-political operations, they should first really understand the new plan, and then they should step toward it in an orderly fashion.

My children have had few rules in their lives, but they've never broken a single neighbor's window, nor stolen a TV or stereo, nor even pissed in a fountain. *How can that be!?*

Unschooling isn't anarchy. Being kind to a baby isn't anarchy; it's tender protection of one's young. Being sweet with a toddler isn't anarchy; it's opening up the world to a human being seeing it with new eyes.

When freedom and choices are given to children, they are given by a parent who has the power to withhold them. The parents are still the authorities and the responsible parties in the group. They don't need to abuse authority to prove they have it. They don't have to have a steep hierarchy; they can have a closer, cooperative hierarchy, but there is still a hierarchy. If parents earn their children's respect by being kind and helpful and truthful and protective, then there will be a natural hierarchical relationship, not something the parents claimed out of tradition or the air.

Anarchy is the reaction to too much control. Without too much control in the first place, anarchy doesn't make sense.

SandraDodd.com/anarchy

(This is a quote from a longer tirade,
preserved, with the response, at the link below.)

"It's hedonism gone berserk!!"

".... Allowing children—who are not just little adults—free rein over absolutely everything that affects their lives is doing them a great disservice. It's hedonism gone berserk!!

"You say you're giving your children "freedom" to choose their own paths, but are you really? Isn't this whole "unschooling" concept just another form of brainwashing, of manipulation? Whatever happened to children needing boundaries? How can anyone, in good conscience, allow children to choose their own boundaries to the extent that you all seem to be doing? You all just seem to be feeding off of each other with no clear direction. It's some type of dysfunction disguised as good parenting. Bullshit!! There are some things you just shouldn't mess with, one of them being human nature. Children seek and need limitations in their lives. They don't need to be wholly left to their own devices—that's why they are children and we are adults! And this whole thing about letting the child choose what he/she is interested in. Okay, that's good—to a point. If I hadn't insisted when my kids were younger on their participating in certain events, taking up certain activities, etc., they never would have discovered their true interest in those activities. This extreme position I'm seeing here, which you define as "unschooling" is looking more and more like laziness to me. Let the kid play video games all day, what the hell—I'll just read this book I've wanted to read, or watch my soaps, blah, blah. Give me a break! What you're doing is inviting criticism and, ultimately, disgust. It's a form of covert child abuse. You've got a cult thing going on here, and you're convinced you're doing the right thing. I shudder to think of a future world populated by unschooled automatons."

SandraDodd.com/lazyhedonists

Arrogance

One of the charges about unschoolers in general (and me in particular) is "arrogance." "Unschoolers are arrogant," say those who are flitting from one curriculum to another (or maybe worse, sticking with the first one they ever heard of, because they want to teach their children to finish what they start).

I spend VERY little time and energy listening patiently while people tell me that the public schools are really pretty good. I attended public school (zipped through more quickly and happily than some, and kindergarten hadn't become required, so I was there for "only" 11 years). I taught in public school for six years (7th and 9th grade English). I've had custody of three kids who attended public schools (when I was younger, not in the past 20 years). School apologists won't say anything I haven't heard (or experienced, or done, or said myself).

I've sought out writings about all kinds of homeschooling. I read some of the most conservative Christian homeschooling magazines for a while: Home School Digest (scary) and The Old Schoolhouse (where I read that Pat Farenga's three daughters have all gone to school; I don't think he's always said that when he speaks at unschooling conferences; very nice man, but unschooling wasn't their priority, which is fine).

Some people just want to learn as little as is necessary for them to go and do what they think they need to do to homeschool or unschool. I think it's a "Will this be on the test?" mentality—a souvenir of school.

I've researched methods I knew I wouldn't pursue in a thousand years, because I didn't want to be ignorant when the subject came up. In the early days of online unschooling discussions there was no such thing as unschooling being discussed off in a corner by itself. It was always in and among the others, many of whom believed that there was no reason to homeschool other than God had called Christians to set their children apart, and they "knew" that secular homeschoolers were riding the coattails of Christian homeschoolers.

Their history of homeschooling started with Christian homeschoolers in the 1980's. I knew that wasn't true, but THEY didn't know it wasn't true. When I defended my stance I really wanted to know what I was talking about.

It wasn't too many years before unschoolers had our own corner on the AOL boards, and online chats (and the edited files of those available for download). People were paying $3 an hour for online access. There is more available to new unschoolers now, online sitting and waiting to be read for free, than existed in the whole world twenty years ago.

I'm confident. I'm not guessing unschooling can work, I know. I've also seen how it can fail, through my correspondence and discussions with so many other homeschooling families. I'm not hoping that kids can still get a job without fifteen years of practice bedtimes; I know they can. (And they would've been "practicing" for the wrong shift anyway.) I don't conjecture that kids can learn to read without being taught, I know. It's happened at my house, in three people's lives.

There have been people come by over the years who said "We should all learn from each other," meaning I should compromise with them, "meet them half way," admit that their ways were just as valid and useful as what I was doing. But none of them have brought any ideas or practice I had never seen and that seemed better than what was happening at my house, or that could do anything to improve the flow we already had going.

On the other hand, the years of discussions of how to put principles into practice have expanded lots of people's understanding of this subset of unschooling. Mine, definitely! I learned from others about how well it can work to make housework fun and peaceful and kids would eventually volunteer to do things, in surprisingly cool ways. That has happened at my house, but I wouldn't have thought it up on my own. I learned that the idea of "a bad day" is much inferior to "a bad moment," from which one can recover immediately. From me sharing my experiences, some families have loosened up about bedtimes and wake-up times. From Robyn's and other people's success with being patient and kind with explosive kids, many fewer children are punished or shamed for having sudden outbursts of pure neediness. And interestingly, both Pam Sorooshian and I have been accused of not knowing anything about having such children, because our two explosive kids learned ways to deal YEARS ago with what some families punish or ignore or exacerbate. Those who know our kids probably wouldn't be able to guess which in each set of three was the scary-go-nuts kid when they were younger, because we figured out loving ways to help them recognize and deal with the emotions. And it's a physical thing with some people, that their emotional biochemicals come on QUICKLY, and hard. But they can learn to deal with it cognitively and physically, for the good of their own health and relationships, and for the good of others around them.

I'm not thinking that's true, I KNOW that's true. This is confidence and experience.

My confidence as a parent has come from seeing the growth and the robust emotional health of my children. Some of their confidence seems to come from knowing that they have confident parents taking care of them. We grew in our confidence together, as partners, and as a team.

SandraDodd.com/confidence

Kirby, Holly and Marty, in Albuquerque, June 2009

Karma

I was cursed by someone who was angry about having been asked (for the fourth time) to take the advertising off her postings to an unschooling discussion list. At the end of various insults, she wrote, "I truly hope karma smites you and yours."

I did warn my family that we had been cosmically threatened in that way, but I believe my detractor misunderstood karma (or at best was trying to control both karma and me).

If karma works the way I think it does, for the time and work my husband has put into supporting our family so that I could spend my days with our children, may karma strike him.

To my children for their willingness to have their "experimental" lives lived in the open so that other families could find happier ways of learning and being, may karma rain down on them.

To every unschooling parent, young adult, teen or child who has written or spoken of the benefits of unschooling to their lives, may karma bring them peace and joy for the foreseeable future and beyond.

I share credit for the positive notes and feedback I receive with my family, and with those other unschooling parents who have dedicated so much of their time to answering questions and explaining, again, how unschooling works.

SandraDodd.com/feedback

Part Two

Essays and Bonus Materials

Essays

Precisely How to Unschool

Occasionally it comes up and recently did again—the question of exactly how to unschool. No philosophical nattering, some folks say; just tell us what we have to do. Of all the things in the world that don't work like that, unschooling must be in the top ten. Unschooling and I both are all about philosophical nattering. One of the truest and clearest answers I can give is often "It depends," after which much "if/then" ensues.

Explaining unschooling is kind of like "Let's play knock-knock. You go first."

I did ask, on one discussion list recently, for people to give me their best practical advice. Guess how many responses I got! Zero. None. So I thought about the answers I didn't get, and thought the best two answers are "Take your child out of school" and "Don't buy a curriculum." But that's not enough. There's much more, but I can't tell you exactly what it is.

Then I thought about another periodic "it depends" question, which is "How much time will this take?" or more specifically, "How many hours should I spend with my child?" And the answer came to me.

I have kept it secret until now.

I thought and thought and have even made a graph of a quantifiable recommendation for which people can set their clocks and calendars. A mom can calculate today, right now, how much time she will need to spend with her child ten years from now.

It's not entirely an unschooling answer, but it's a parenting answer, and here it is:

When a baby is born, before he's a year old, spend 23 hours a day with him, or thinking about him, or sleeping with him, or carrying, or feeding him.

When he turns one, spend 22 hours a day with him (and gradually less). For two hours you might be in the shower or sleeping without even knowing you're asleep. Let that time slide at a steady pace until he's ten or eleven, and you're spending half of it, twelve hours, with him, on him, in his presence, doing things for or with him. Steadily slide that back until he's twenty, as my oldest, Kirby is, and then one hour a day is plenty.

No cheating. If you aren't diligent in the early years, the 20-year-old will be gone in a huff or might have slunk away sadly. If you want to complete your goal, spend lots of time with the young ones. When Kirby turns 21, my obligation will have been fulfilled.

Pretty simple, huh?

I did it with a ruler and a felt tip pen. Now I'll have it, when people ask in the future.

You didn't count the squares on that, did you, or spend much time wondering whether a ten-year-old should get ten or twelve hours, or maybe 14? Because that's not a real graph, it's just a sketch of a graph. Mine's just an illustration of a graph, to help you think. (Y'think?)

I suppose some of you will have questions, such as what if you have twins, or what if you have three children. The answer is simple. You find things that three people can do together, or you talk to one person while you make lunch or do laundry or repair the favorite jeans of another. You play at the park with one while another is in a dance class. You take everyone to the movies and sleep like a baby at night (if your youngest is at least six or seven, that is). Whatever you do, make it fun, interesting, comforting, memorable, unusual, familiar, nourishing, productive, or restful. If it can be three or four of those things at the same time, good job!

I myself, for instance, spent an hour with Kirby yesterday, in little bits over three hours. I met two of his friends I hadn't met, gave him a Weird Al CD, and watched him listen to a couple of tracks I knew he would like. I ate a brownie that he made! We joked. For every bit of that time, Holly was also in the room, so I scored a two-for-one deal on the time.

Because Holly is 14, I still need to be in mom-mode at least six hours a day, but that's pretty easy with three kids home. Wednesday I worked overtime, because Holly and I spent the day together, mostly on the road, driving nearly to Taos to visit relatives. After eight solid hours together, she declared it magical. That was cool.

If you want to measure, measure generously. If you want to give, give generously. If you want to unschool, or be a mindful parent, give, give, give. You'll find after a few years that you still have everything you thought you had given away, and more.

SandraDodd.com/howto/precisely
(with links)

Originally appeared in *Connections* e-zine in 2006

To Get More Jokes

or "Thinking and Learning and Bears"

I remember being in school and asking, "Why do we need to know this?" I asked it, other kids asked it, and one answer I remember was when I asked my Algebra II teacher, when I was 15, why we needed to know how to figure out square roots. He said in was in case we wanted to figure out how far away stars were. I said, "Don't we have people to do that?"

I didn't care how far away stars were. I thought it should be left to those who really are curious or have a need to know. That need to know the distance of stars has never been good for anything at all yet, as far as I know.

It wasn't long after that (six years) that I myself was a teacher in that same school. Luckily for me and for all the world, I wasn't teaching algebra or astronomy. But still I would be asked "Why do we have to learn this?" Sometimes I gave a serious answer, and sometimes a philosophical answer. Sometimes I made light of it. Sometimes the honest answer was "You don't have to learn this, but I have to try to teach it so I can get paid." Or "Only some of you will need to know it, but they don't know which ones yet, so I have to say it to everybody."

Then one day, the question came phrased a new and better way: "What is this GOOD for?" The answer I gave then changed my life and thinking. I said quickly "So you can get more jokes." I think we were reading a simplified Romeo and Juliet at the time. I could've gone into literature and history and fine arts, but the truth is that the best and most immediate use of most random learning is that it illuminates the world. The more we know, the more jokes we will get.

Humor is all around us, in art, hats, billboards, t-shirts, magazines, toys, songs, stories, friendly banter, cereal boxes and wordplay. What can make or break a day, or a moment, is whether people see it and smile, or see it and make a face of disgust. The direction parents take with humor can make the difference between a joyful shared moment or an uncomfortable, embarrassing stuckness. And each of those leads to the next moment.

Did the subtitle "Thinking and Learning and Bears" remind you of anything? Forestry and conservation? Animal behavior studies? The Three Bears? The Wizard of Oz? All of those and other things?

What if it had been

>Wishing and Hoping and Bears?

>Lions and Tigers and Learning?

>Lions and Tigers and Jokes?

Different connections conjure different ideas.

The way jokes usually work is that they cause you to connect two things in your mind that you hadn't connected before, and if it happens quickly and surprisingly, you laugh. Humor induces thought. Those without the information inside won't "get the joke." No one gets all jokes, but the more we know the more we'll get.

Over the next few days when something funny happens you might want to take a moment to think about why it amused you, and what you needed to know to understand that joke. (There are many studies and analyses of humor, but they're never funny. Some are written in such stilted jargon that *that* is funny!) I do not recommend discussing this with young children. They don't need to know how humor works. They need to have parents who appreciate their laughter and who can find even more things to amuse them and help them do the mental gymnastics necessary for that happy laughter to arise.

Sometimes it's even easier if the humor comes first and the "real" information later. Someone who has seen *Rosencrantz and Guildenstern are Dead*, the Simpsons episode about Hamlet, and the Reduced Shakespeare Company's little Hamlet will have many hooks to hang the real *Hamlet* on, if and when they see it.

Parents new to unschooling tend to worry that some activities are good preparation for life, but others are frivolous and should be forbidden or discouraged. Life and thought and learning, though, depend on connections being made. And the more points of information about anything at all being made inside an individual, the more points there will be to connect.

The term "The Chewbacca Defense" from a South Park episode has already moved into common usage, generalized to other situations. If you want to avoid watching South Park, you might at least look on Google for "Chewbacca Defense." You will need to know more about Star Wars than about South Park to fully appreciate it, but people who know nothing about either one will be hearing the term "Chewbacca Defense" in regard to legal proceedings and political debates for many years.

Part of the strength of certain abiding cartoon comedy is that there are several levels of humor. There are visual surprises and word play that little kids would enjoy, and references that go right over their heads. Bugs Bunny, Bullwinkle or Homer Simpson are likely to say things that can be taken literally by young viewers, but that have a whole different overlay of meaning for those who know more.

Parents who get jokes about video games their kids are playing wouldn't need to be tested to show that they, as parents, are learning as they should be. If you can watch Red vs Blue and laugh, you're doing well as a parent. (If you have no Halo-playing kids, never mind that, but if you're an artist you might want to know that the style is being called "machinima." Something new to learn!) If you can watch the "Japanese Cartoon" installment of Strongbad's e-mail and understand why it's funny, you're giving your mind a workout and can be grateful to your children for expanding your world. (If you've never watched any Japanese animation, maybe try "My Neighbor Totoro," especially if you have little girls.)

Humor is a great warm-up for any thinking. If one's mind can jump to get a joke, it will be easier for it to jump to synthesize any ideas, to make a complex plan, to use a tool in an unexpected way, to understand history and the complexities of politics. If a child can connect something about a food with a place name or an article of clothing, parents shouldn't worry that he hasn't memorized political boundaries or the multiplication table.

The more that fun, divergent thought is discouraged, the more quiet and dark those minds will be. The more that sparkly, happy, random thoughts are encouraged, the brighter that home will be.

With links & photos: SandraDodd.com/connections/jokes
Originally appeared in *Connections* e-zine (also linked there)
in 2007.

To Be Fascinating at Cocktail Parties

In a discussion on why children should learn things, I suggested that it would make them more interesting at cocktail parties. Someone objected, saying children shouldn't be pushed to learn things just to make them interesting. She had missed my point, but that only made the discussion more vibrant.

The cocktail party goal might be more worthy than pushing them to learn things so that they can get into college, but I was really enjoying the discussion because it was so different. For one thing, it's quite a figure of speech now, so many years after the heyday of "cocktail parties." And wouldn't an admissions officer prefer fascinating over non-fascinating? But the stated objection was this: "To push kids in all kinds of directions in order for them to be fluent at cocktail parties is a waste of time, in my humble opinion." It amused me and I responded.

Depends whether the goal is for them to be fascinating and interesting to the brightest people there, or just not to embarrass themselves in front of the other safe, quiet, dull folks. Some people really, truly *want* to only discuss the weather, current local (yet safe) politics, current events (just the innocuous stuff) and the decor of the house. That way they can make some soft noise for a couple of hours and not really *say* anything. That's cocktail party stuff for you. There seem to be whole friendships, organizations and marriages based on this very surface, calm, don't-rock-the-boat behavior.

Public school discourages kids from coming up with off-the-wall responses. No bank shots, please. Just go directly from the question to the first sufficient answer—nothing tricky or dramatic, and nothing that makes you think, or makes the teacher think. If your answer isn't what's in the teacher's manual your answer is wrong. If you did extra thinking you wasted your time.

If you want your kids to be *really* interesting at cocktail parties, leave their passions alone. I would pay money to be at parties with *really* interesting people because I don't give a rat's patootie what the scores of yesterday's sports games were, or whether a new government contract is coming to town, or how the weather was in southern California if I wasn't even there. But if those people want to talk about their own new job or a sport they were involved in or their response to seeing a tornado or a hurricane for the first time, that's something I would like to hear. If they saw the Lion King stage show and have read everything there is to find about the designer, *that* I want to hear. If they got to touch the brigandine plate armor that was found near Four Corners, YES!! TELL ME!!! That stuff didn't come from school, or Newsweek, or the local paper.

Life. People can live lives, even little kids live lives, without preparation, learning on the job, as they go. They can learn while doing real things with real happiness and real success.

There's a story in which people are "created equal" by government handicaps. It's the democratic way. Smart people hear a frightening/alarming sound every minute or two from the headphones they're required to wear. Strong people have to wear weights. Good-looking people have to wear masks.

School tries to do that. Even in the gifted programs, kids are often stuck in a chair and asked to complete checklists of tasks, not to go off on their own at maximum speed and change directions when they feel the urge. Homeschoolers can do that, unless they're careful not to. We're taught to sublimate urges, to prove we're mature by ignoring our desire and by doing what we're told.

Creativity doesn't come from reading the chapter and answering the questions.

When I was a new unschooler, I sought out reports of college success and social ease. As the years passed, the social ease seemed so central to my children's lives that the college thoughts receded. As they reached the teen years, and their friends (schooled or not) went to the university (or not), they saw college "education" (and partying, and class skipping) as just another part of the infinite fabric of life. They haven't been channeled toward it in the dark, as so many millions have been.

It has been a long time since I worried about whether they would grow up whole and functional. They were whole, functional, bright and conversant all along. They surprise and impress older friends, co-workers and classmates (when those temporary relationships do arise) with their energy and joy.

As it turns out, they're interesting everywhere and they continue to learn. Fascinating.

With links & photos: SandraDodd.com/connections/cocktail
Originally appeared in *Connections* e-zine (also linked there)
in 2006.

Originally written in 2006.

A Mom's-Eye View of Driver's Ed

The third of my three children has a learner's permit now, and so that puts me in a new category of motherhood—Moms whose nearly-grown children all drive. Looking back at how this all happened, I see that they've been learning about cars, roads and driving since they rode in car seats, and I've also seen each one experience the newness and formality of a thirty-classroom-hour course.

My first exposure to an unschooler in driver's ed involved Brett Henry, who had left public school partway through third grade and has been in and around our house and family quite a bit since then. Brett researched and chose a driver's ed school near our house. He was living nearly 50 miles away and couldn't be delivered back and forth, so he stayed with us and we took him to class and picked him up.

Brett's time in driver's ed was a learning experience for our family, too. Every day he told us what they'd done in class, and he critiqued my driving during the transports, which amused my own kids greatly. It was useful for all of them too, though, because I would explain why I had chosen to do what I had done, sometimes to great humorous effect.

Kirby started driver's ed classes late, for his age. Partly, he was worried he couldn't write fast or legibly enough to take notes. Partly, he had older friends driving him anywhere his heart desired, day and night. Partly, he worked four or five days a week and went to karate twice and didn't have time to schedule a class.

Finally, when he went, he was nearly seventeen. That was his first day of school, ever. He took an apple and gave it to the teacher saying, "I've never been to school before; I understand this is what people do."

On that first day there was a pre-test with a question booklet and a separate answer sheet. Kirby was circling the letter and then writing out the right answer.

When the teacher asked if everyone was through, Kirby had three more left and said he was still writing. The teacher said "writing?" So his only problem with driver's ed was his total unfamiliarity with the traditions involved with test-taking. He got seven out of ten. He missed one about hydroplaning, which he said wasn't worded well to get the answer they wanted. I doubt that many of the other kids were analyzing the construction of the test questions.

Marty started driver's ed as soon as I could get him in when he was fifteen. A weeklong intensive Junior Police Academy, in which he had taken notes, kept this from being his first classroom experience, but he'd never taken a test. He knew from hearing Kirby's stories that he shouldn't write the answer out, but he didn't realize that those kinds of multiple choice tests would have only one answer. He misread a question about what one should carry in the car and marked three things that should be there, instead of the one that shouldn't. All those years of no preparation, and that was the worst problem he had.

Marty, like Kirby, was good at asking questions in class and caring about the answers. They were better than most at participating when there was something interesting to do (such as get into the cab of a semi for a demonstration, which Kirby did without hesitation, but the other kids were too cool to want to do).

In that season, someone who didn't know better wrote on a discussion list and assured us that unschooled kids would be totally unprepared to go to classes—they wouldn't be able to wake up and get to a class on time, to take notes, to take a test or to write an essay. I knew from my experience with Brett, Kirby and Marty that they had no problem showing up early and well-prepared, taking notes, participating in class or driving.

As I write this, Holly is fifteen and in the midst of her second week of the classroom portion of driver's education. The first day she was a little intimidated about notetaking. She came home and asked Kirby if he still had the notebook he and Marty had used. He knew exactly where it was on the shelf in his room, and so she has taken that every day since. She finds where Kirby or Marty took notes for that chapter, follows along, and writes down anything they missed that she'd like to remember. Now the notebook will have the notes of the three of them combined.

Holly could have been finished by now, had she been willing to go to class on Halloween, but she's always loved dressing up and going trick or treating and had already made arrangements with friends, so she opted to wait until the first session after Halloween. Her desire to dress up and frolic outweighs her hurry to drive.

As was also true with her brothers, she's not the only homeschooler in the class. It's not as homogeneous a group as she had expected. Besides another homeschooler, there is also a girl in Palestinian dress and two exchange students from Germany.

Holly likes the class and is always eager to go. She enjoys the different styles of the two teachers she's had, and the movies, and the other kids.

She has fun taking notes. When we're on practice drives, she tells me the stories she's heard in class about freak accidents. She got to sit in a semi, as Kirby did years ago, and heard stories of runaway truck ramps and about some dangerous and safer ways to park on the side of the highway.

Just a few hours into her required fifty hours of practice, Holly is already a confident driver. Her time with Brett, Kirby and Marty, as they went through this process, was clearly a time of learning for her. She refers often to things they said or did.

The car seats are long gone. Soon the requests for rides will be gone too. The learning is thick, and rich, and fast, and because of Holly's unschooling life, she doesn't consider stories from the certified driver's ed teachers to be more valuable than those of the guest truck driver, or her dad, or her brothers, or their friend Brett.

It's not only the notebook that bound these experiences together. Even though they didn't attend the school at the same time, my three and Brett have a sense of sharing and camaraderie about their learning to drive. They've watched and helped each other for years. Each of them had fun with the course, had great stories about the teachers and the practice driving, and they've left good impressions about homeschooled kids at the school, too.

One day while Holly was in class, Marty got a call to come and rescue Brett, who had been in an accident across town. It was someone else's fault entirely, and he was uninjured, but his truck had to be towed. Their shared learning continues.

Kirby

305

Those who were once my three little babies are about to be my three driver's ed graduates. Marty was talking about the possibility of driving to the Live and Learn conference in North Carolina next fall, just he and Holly, because she'll be able to drive by then. I think they'll fly to Florida and ride with another family, but just discussing it with him changed my perspective as a mother. Everyone is happy, but there's a little sorrow in the mom whose last child is about to drive away.

Notes from the time of that writing:
Kirby is 20 and has a new Wii (Nintendo thing), so he can take breaks from World of Warcraft (when he's not at work). Marty is 17, reads comic books, and just became a squire to a king (medieval parallel life and all, when he's not at work or running around with friends). Holly is 15 and is driving when the traffic's not too heavy.

With links & photos: SandraDodd.com/driversed
Originally appeared in *Connections* e-zine (also linked there) in 2006.

Marty and Holly in Silver City

I wrote this in October, 2007, when Holly was still fifteen.

Magic Window

I don't believe in magic, but I find joy in wonderful coincidences and confluences. I like looking at a digital clock right at 11:11, for its pattern and symmetry. When planets line up I'm happy, even though I believe it to have no effect whatsoever on humans on earth outside the happiness they might have if they know about it.

Our family is experiencing a sort of magic window. As of November 2, our children (who are no longer children) have attained a set of momentous ages: 21, 18 and 16. This alignment ends on January 14, when Marty turns 19, but for a couple of months we have the only and last set of landmark years we'll ever have.

Our two boys are at the traditional ages of majority in different ways, in different places and times. Kirby is a man. Marty is a junior man. Our baby and only girl is "sweet sixteen."

I remember vividly when they were five, and three, and a newborn. Now they are, as a group, entering adulthood. I am moved to reflect and review.

There was some talk recently of the "end results" of the sort of parenting and unschooling our family has lived and shared. It seems this would be a good time to discuss end results, with two of ours past "school age."

Kirby was nearly twenty-one when he was offered a job in Austin, working for Blizzard, a video game company. He had been twenty-one for less than a month when he moved 600 miles away. Marty has been to visit him, and Holly plans to go next year. Thanks to cell phones and instant messaging, one of us usually has some Kirby news. He seems extremely happy to be where he is, doing what he's doing. He's had one small promotion and although I helped him with a resume, he decided not to apply for a senior position quite yet. His reasons were thoughtful and sound, and he is only twenty-one years old.

Marty worked a full-time job the whole time he was seventeen, and for the past six months he has been traveling, mostly at his own expense. I had never known a teenager before to save over $5,000 and use it mostly for airline tickets. He's been to Washington state, Colorado, Oregon, Texas, Florida and North Carolina, mostly by air.

Much of Holly's time is spent on MySpace, out and about in the cyber world while safe at home. She plays with words, formatting, music and image manipulation. She keeps in touch with friends on two continents. Holly earned money babysitting, and paid her own airfare for a trip to Rhode Island to visit Quinn Trainor and her family last summer. In the fall she went with Marty to Florida to visit the Higgins-McBroom family and to go with them to the Live and Learn Conference in North Carolina.

Although it seems time for a status report, their lives aren't static. The excitement for me, as a mom, of having three children at special ages doesn't slow them down. I've thought of it as an alignment of planets, but it's more like a Triforce. Together they have power. They have friendship. They've experienced something out of the ordinary. Their lives have been shared for the benefit of other families, and they've always agreed to and helped out with that, by answering questions and being available at gatherings of unschoolers whenever possible, and by graciously allowing me to continue sharing details of their changes and adventures.

I can't really speak to any "end results," because they're still growing and experiencing the newness of many firsts in their lives. If there is ever an "end," the results won't matter anymore. But as long as life continues, the results unfold.

Are my children better friends and better employees because of the freedom they had? It seems so. What kind of managers will they be when they're in positions to make decisions about other people's employment?

When they marry will they be good partners? Would that be an "end result"? What kind of parents will they be?

What kind of neighbors will they be? How will their long-term health be affected by their early freedom to make their own choices? Will they be more or less likely to be binge eaters, substance abusers, or hypochondriacs? When they're old, will they still be active and interesting? Will their early freedoms affect their geriatric physical and mental health? I don't know, and probably won't be around to see.

In this window of time, though, I am satisfied. The peace and joy with which they live attests to the success of our attachment parenting and unschooling. Our lives are entwined and growing. The end result of twenty-one years of parenting as mindfully and as peacefully as I could is that I am content with the outcome. Someday I might report on the end result of twenty-five or thirty years of parenting, as life burgeons on.

The magic of the window is all mine, though, and Keith's. Looking out at our offspring, they are aligned in a certain way from our perspective, but they're not paused and gazing back. They are in the full motion of their own harmonic and intersecting spheres, spinning ever further away from us, and we marvel to see the celestial show.

With links & photos: SandraDodd.com/magicwindow
Originally appeared in *Connections* e-zine (also linked there)
in 2007.

Quotes

Most of these appear in the random quotes generator at SandraDodd.com/unschooling. They have been collected over a dozen years. Some were saved and re-supplied by Ren Allen, Jin Burton, Lee Roversi, Lauren Stranahan, Heather (Crazyzeus1) and Gil from RUN, and some I had or have added later.

Some people love quotes by Benjamin Franklin or John Holt; I do too. But for helping people unschool, I love the words of unschoolers, written about unschooling for other unschoolers.

If you calligraph or embroider any of these I'd love to put an image of that on my site.

It only takes a second to do better.

—Sandra Dodd

It helps unschooling and mindful parenting to be aware of *your* kids and *their* unique needs rather than treating them as generic kids with all the worst possible traits.

— Joyce Fetteroll

Unschooling is *much* harder than school at home because it takes a great deal of self examination and change in ourselves to help our kids and not get in their way!

—Joyce Fetteroll

A joyful attitude is your best tool.

—Sandra Dodd

As we get older and our kids grow up, we eventually come to realize that all the big things in our lives are really the direct result of how we've handled all the little things.

—Pam Sorooshian

One of the first effects of school is to break the bond between parents and children, when the children are five or younger. It breaks bonds between siblings, and replaces them with prejudices about age and grade, with rules against playing with kids of other ages, and with social pressure to be hateful and secretive.

—Sandra Dodd

Nobody here is going to tell you 'I wish I'd found unschooling later.' I could just kick myself for not pursuing it any earlier.

—Kelly Lovejoy

We wanted our children to become thoughtful intelligent, undamaged adults.

—Keith Dodd

How you live in the moment affects how you live in the hour, and the day, and the lifetime.

—Sandra Dodd

People who look at what they have and how they can work with it find the ways quicker (and are happier) than those who look at what they don't have.

—Joyce Fetteroll

A different approach to life yields a very different set of results.

—Sandra Dodd

School calls a small sliver of the world "all", and we call all of life's learning "some".

—Sandra Dodd

The goal of unschooling is not education. It is to help a child be who she is and blossom into who she will become. Education happens as side effect.

—Joyce Fetteroll

Kids who are in school just visit life sometimes, and then they have to stop to do homework or go to sleep early or get to school on time. They're constantly reminded they are preparing "for real life," while being isolated from it.

—Sandra Dodd

I think unschooling works better when parents get over their prejudices about relative value of the media.

—Sandra Dodd

Halfway between the past we can't change and the future we can only imagine, we find ourselves in the present. Not just the present year, but the present day; not just the present day, but the present moment.

—Sandra Dodd

Try to learn to be, and to see learning in all kinds of things.

—Sandra Dodd

See if you have a dial in your mind that says "everything" at one extreme and "nothing" at the other. It's impossible for anyone to do everything or nothing. Maybe label it "too much" and "not enough" instead, and try for the midpoint. Replace any on/off switches in your mind with slide bars or dimmers!

—Sandra Dodd

If you're following any curriculum at all, you'll be missing the happy unfolding of real life. If you schedule so carefully that you can't change your schedule when something really cool happens or you pass by a folk festival or you get invited last-minute to see a magician, that schedule could be detrimental.

—Sandra Dodd

A child does not have to be motivated to learn; in fact, learning cannot be stopped. A child will focus on the world around him and long to understand it. He will want to know why things are the way they are. He won't have to be told to be curious; he will just be curious. He has no desire to be ignorant; rather he wants to know everything.

—Valerie Fitzenreiter, in *The Unprocessed Child: Living Without School*

I've never known a single unschooled teen (and by now I've known pretty many) who was anxious and eager to leave home.

—Sandra Dodd

My world's pretty cool. It has become gradually cooler since I had kids and have tried to figure out how to make THEIR worlds cooler. Mine got the side benefit of what I learned about how to help keep them happy.

—Sandra Dodd

The point that I am trying to make here is that I feel that I am more keeper of the flame than flame-maker. I feel that my kids have these interesting lives that I have the honor to not just watch unfold but guide in any way they need. As I told a friend, I sometimes look at them and feel like I have nothing to do with who they are. Not that I have no influence, because I do, but that the whole idea of parenting as authorship of children, as if they where things to be molded and not human beings living life, has been blown away by my kids' greatness.

—Sandra Dodd

I think it's been the changes in my parenting that have really made our unschooling lifestyle so positive."

—Gail Higgins

Unschooling didn't blossom until I stepped away from traditional parenting.

—Mercedes/mulwiler

Only listen to your mom if your mom is worth listening to. If your own childhood was screwed up, there's a good chance that she doesn't know better than you.

—Lyle Perry

PLAY with your kids. Playing can be the single best way to really get to know your kids. Get down on the floor, follow their lead, and *play* with them.

—Lyle Perry

Let your kids be *who they are*, not who someone thinks they should be. Throw away the mold and let your kids *live*.

—Lyle Perry

Respect your kids. Too many adults DEMAND respect from kids without showing any respect in return. Doesn't work.

—Lyle Perry

"Unschooling has had an incredibly positive impact on our lives, and not only in an educational aspect, but in everything we do. It's changed the way we live, the way we think, and the way we look at the world in general."

—Lyle Perry

Jon and I do not see housework as a chore. We do it cheerfully, in order to make our home a place we all enjoy.

—Rue Kream

Unschooling, in a very real sense, *is* a mindfulness practice. Being in the moment with our children, trusting the flow of life, seeing our connections to them and to all of the universe etc...

—Ren Allen

One interaction at a time. Just make the next interaction a relationship-building one. Don't worry about the one *after* that, until *it* becomes "the next one."

—Pam Sorooshian

The more you strew, the more you do!

—Cinnamon [C.K.]

My real and happy kid says a lot more about unschooling than I could ever convey by analyzing human nature.

—Deb Lewis

"The thing that works with unschooling is to follow delight - and scatter it like a flower girl in front of the bride - not every petal will be crushed to release fragrance - but enough will. ...of course to follow delight, you have to admit to yourself that you feel delight."

—Nora Cannon

[The] curiosity to learn new things is VITAL in my opinion, to helping our children be life-long learners and seekers.

—Ren Allen

Unschooling should and can be bigger and better than school. If it's smaller and quieter than school, the mom should do more to make life sparkly.

—Sandra Dodd

Kids blossom and get bigger from doing adult things because they want to, instead of kid-things they have to do because they're small.

—Sandra Dodd

We make choices ALL the time. Learning to make better ones in small little ways, immediate ways, makes life bigger and better. Choosing to be gentle with a child, and patient with ourselves, and generous in ways we think might not even show makes our children more gentle, patient and generous.

—Sandra Dodd

Unschooling really is a mutually rewarding lifestyle! My family has never been happier.

—dragonfly (Ronnie Maier)

There's always something to do, someone to talk to, some road leading somewhere.

—Deb Lewis

A bed isn't the only place to sleep though. The idea that sleeping must equal a bed is the same thing as saying that eating equals a fork.

—Brandie

When our children were babies and others would ask 'When does he go to bed?' Keith used to say 'About half an hour after he goes to sleep.'

—Sandra Dodd

For a lot of people, thinking too deeply about what they believe is too painful. It's just easier to do what was done to them.

—Deb Lewis

Rules in the absence of principle are often found to be irrelevant by children. Principles lived fully make rules unnecessary.

—Karen Tucker

[On Negativity:] It's a hole. A dark hole. Hop out into the happy light!

—Sandra Dodd

Maybe because I kept playing I had an advantage, but I don't think it is beyond more serious adults to regain their playfulness.

—Sandra Dodd

The more we practice these principles, the more peaceful our house becomes.

—Amy

Confident kids who communicate well with parents and wouldn't be tempted to sneak out or to lie wouldn't be in danger of meeting someone who says he'll marry her if she meets him at the train station. That doesn't happen randomly.

—Sandra Dodd

Predators are looking for vulnerable, needy kids. They know there isn't a reason to waste time on confident secure kids.

—Joyce Fetteroll, on Online Safety

Every time you feel the urge to control a choice, you can ask yourself "why?" and begin to question the assumptions (or fears) about children, parenting, learning and living joyfully that you are holding on to.

—Robyn Coburn

'You can't give what you don't have,' some people say, and if you want your children to give generosity and kindness and patience to others, you should give them so much they're overflowing with it.

—Sandra Dodd

Once the power struggle stopped, the learning could begin.

—Amy

It is about saying "yes" through my actions, as well as my words.

—Robyn Coburn

Unschooling works well when parents are interesting, positive, thoughtful, considerate, generous, passionate, honest, respectful individuals.

—Deb Lewis

All this talkin'—what is it good for? Everything in the whole wide world.

—Sandra Dodd

Unschoolers don't "just live." They live large. They live expansively, and richly and joyfully. Those are the things that make it work.

—Sandra Dodd

People learn by playing, thinking and amazing themselves. They learn while they're laughing at some–thing surprising, and they learn while they're wondering 'What the heck is this?

—Sandra Dodd

Until a person stops doing the things that keep unschooling from working, unschooling cannot begin to work. It seems simple to me. If you're trying to listen for a sound, you have to stop talking and be still.

—Sandra Dodd

What you're dealing with is a very well meaning person who is convinced the world is flat and is worried that you're so clueless that you want to head off across the horizon. It's a lot healthier and more useful to listen to the people who've been across the horizon than to the person who fears it.

—Joyce Fetteroll

Our culture lies. They say they want to encourage and reward individuality and creativity, but in practice they try to hammer down the pointy parts, and shame off the different parts.

—Sandra Dodd

I was asked in public once, 'Are you willing to risk your children's future on your *theories*?' 'Yes. Aren't you?' was my answer then and still is.

—SandraDodd

'Self discipline' is like 'self regulation.' It's still about discipline and rules. How and why should one discipline and regulate oneself, when decision making in the light of compassion and goodness will work much better?

—Sandra Dodd

They're not embarrassed about their interests or hobbies, they're not afraid to wear used clothes, or to play with younger children, or to hang around with adults. Because they are respected, they are respectful.

—Sandra Dodd

Make it happy and funny and comfortable and exciting so that they want to be with you. Be sparkly.

—Sandra Dodd

The way to know the right direction is to identify the wrong direction.

—Sandra Dodd

For me it's as if I have a spontaneous and totally unpredictable tutor jumping out from nowhere asking questions on any topic under the sun.

—Sarah Maitland Parks (of her son)

Scientifically speaking, my children are not a control group. They're not isolated and kept purely away from school methods and messages. But what is unquestionable is that there are now thousands of children who are learning without formal teaching.

—Sandra Dodd

Once you start looking for connections and welcoming them, it creates a kind of flow that builds and grows.

—Sandra Dodd

Given a rich environment, learning becomes like the air—it's in and around us.

— Sandra Dodd

That all 'just happened,' but it happened because we've been building up to it with our whole lives and our whole style of communicating and living together in a constant state of open curiosity.

—Sandra Dodd

The way to learn math naturally is to let it be a natural part of everything, like it is, and not make such a point of it all the time.

—Linda Wyatt

Don't pass your fears and prejudices on to your children!

— Sandra Dodd

Mindfulness is about remembering that what I'm doing right now is going to have an effect on what will happen next, not just in my own life, but in other people's lives.

— Sandra Dodd

Patience is about trying to endure the present moment until a better one comes. Unschooling is about enjoying the present moment for what it is.

— Melissa Wiley

It sounds too good to be true, but it isn't. Being connected is better than being controlling. Being interested is better than being bored. Being fun is more fun than not being fun!

— Melissa Wiley

How will you be, as a parent, and why? What's keeping you from being the way you want to be?

— Sandra Dodd

It has more to do with why people are doing what they are doing and what they believe about it than what they are doing.

— Sandra Dodd

If you're trapped by have-to's then there are no other solutions. If you recognize that there are other solutions then you can free up your thinking to allow them to come.

—Joyce Fetteroll

When I started rethinking how to handle conflicts, a shocking thing was how immediately and drastically the number of conflicts dropped.

— Melissa Wiley

It helps to think of the solutions instead of the obstacles.

—Schuyler Waynforth

When I stopped seeing my daughter as adversarial it changed the world for us.

—Joanna Murphy

On the whole, the spirit of the home has changed. And the spirit now prevalent is consideration.

—Julie B

If you want to measure, measure generously. If you want to give, give generously. If you want to unschool, or be a mindful parent, give, give, give. You'll find after a few years that you still have everything you thought you had given away, and more.

— Sandra Dodd

Practice being accepting of whatever cool things come along, and providing more opportunities for coolness to unfold.

— Sandra Dodd

What will help to create an environment in which unschooling can flourish? For children to learn from the world around them, the world around them should be merrily available, musically and colorfully accessible, it should feel good and taste good. They should have safety and choices and smiles and laughter.

— Sandra Dodd

Any time a mom thinks there's nothing to know, I don't think she knows nearly enough. When a mom thinks unschooling is doing nothing, she's not doing nearly enough.

— Sandra Dodd

It's much better to be their partner than their roadblock. If you become an obstacle they'll find a way around you. Is that what you want for your relationship with your kids?

—Joyce Fetteroll

Instead of being my mother's child, I am my children's mother.

—Sandra Dodd

It still amazes me how a few words on a page-sometimes entirely (seemingly) unrelated-can trigger a massive door that I didn't know was there to open in my brain. It lets in the light and the fresh breeze of new thoughts.

— De (Denise R. Smith)

Funny how parents say 'It's your home too and your responsibility,' when it comes to chores, but 'It's my home,' when it comes to setting standards or how money is spent or how to decorate it or ...

—Joyce Fetteroll

...it is the place where the relationship exists that everyone fantasizes that they will have with their children before they are born, but then you don't because you are caught up in power struggles!

—Joanna Murphy

Unfortunately most people are convinced that when control fails it's because they didn't control enough.

—Joyce Fetteroll

When we can we should always do more, offer more, think more, and make our bit of the world as big and full as we can for our kids. Our kid's lives get bigger and better when our thinking gets bigger and better.

—Deb Lewis

Being happy has never diminished my partnership, and being miserable has never enhanced it.

—Beth Fuller

Get the world swirling around you (first) and your children (second) so there are sounds, sights, smells, tastes and textures...

—Sandra Dodd

School kids don't know the world is a million times bigger than school's version of it.

—Sandra Dodd

Who can argue with joy, healthy relationships, and learning??

—Susan (DaBreeze21)

If your child is more important than your vision of your child, life becomes easier.

—Sandra Dodd

If the goal is to know everything, and if each person's internal "universe" is unique, then the order in which the information is acquired isn't as important as the ease and joy with which it is absorbed.

—Sandra Dodd

Parents who do make meeting their children's needs a higher priority will find that life is good and they, often unexpectedly, find that they are, themselves, less needy when they feel like really good parents.

—Pam Sorooshian

Every morning is good here. We wake when we feel rested and we eat as we will each morning. It's a good feeling.

—Hema A. Bharadwaj

We don't clean up messes to have a clean house. We clean up messes so there is room for more mess!

—Dawn Adams

Children's questions are answered and an atmosphere of learning is created so that questions are constant and answers are never far away.

—Sandra Dodd

I want my kids to feel empowered, so I empower them.

—Jenny Cyphers

When learning is recognized in the fabric of life and encouraged, when families make their decisions based on what leads to more interesting and educational ends, children learn without effort, often without even knowing it, and parents learn along with them.

—Sandra Dodd

Unschooling works best with more choices, not less, and TV should count as a choice.

—Jenny Cyphers

So how do you choose? You decide where you want to go before you decide to turn left or right, don't you? Just like that.

—Sandra Dodd

"Self regulate" means to make a rule and then follow it yourself. They're not self regulating. They're making choices. It's different. It's better!

—Sandra Dodd

It's amazing to see doing for others as a gift. It takes the whole angst about servitude away.

—Schuyler Waynforth

LIVE LOVE LAUGH LEARN—That's the best thing about unschooling, having all of those L-words bundled up into one lovely lifestyle.

—Ronnie Maier

Other Resources

Some people love books, and I'm certainly one of them, but for learning about something new there are tools with other advantages.

As this book is based on a website, I can't help but recommend websites for their ability to be updated and corrected. I would be shocked if this book had no typos. If there's a typo on a web page, it can be fixed. If a link or phone number or reference is old on a website, it can be updated.

People do learn in different ways, and adults are people too! Some need to hear, or see, rather than just read. Some want to watch other unschoolers in person, or see color photos of their children and houses. Some want quick and personal answers to immediate questions.

All these resources are available, and most are available with just a computer. High-speed internet access helps, for seeing video and photos, and conferences can cost money, but much of this is freely and easily available.

Thinking Sticks

Because I couldn't find blank dice once for a conference presentation on thinking, I used popsicle sticks (long called "craft sticks"). I thought of that because of split-stick dice, which I learned about from a Senet game I got for Keith long before we had children. I had intended to write, on the blank dice, the names of school subjects: math, science, history, English, music, art, sports, home economics... and whatever might have made twelve subjects. Then, I thought, I would roll the dice and have people in the workshop talk about how those topics were connected.

I made a better set for Pam Sorooshian, and kept the ratty first set. Other people wanted some. I made a few sets for a conference, with colored sticks, to sell. More people wanted some. I started using colored pens, and when I couldn't get colored sticks I liked, I started painting some of them.

In the packet with the 30-or-more sticks there are instructions and ideas and comments, and a special set of safety warnings.

From the directions:

Sandra Dodd's Thought Manipulatives

an intro to learning through play

One of the worst legacies of school is that graduates have learned to totally separate math from history, and music from science. Even if we can occasionally make a crossover (Roman numerals, or the physics of how a violin string works), we don't HAVE to if we don't want to, because we've already taken the tests and graduated.

Unschooling's challenge is to combine and recombine and cross-pollinate everything. When a person's mind is neatly organized, though, that can be hard to do.

This is a game to mess up your mind a little bit.

On the theory that once a connection has been made in your brain the trail will remain for future short-cutting, messing up your mind can be a good thing. If you have interstates and boulevards, they'll still be there if you add a lot of small streets and side paths. And the level-ground analogy is insufficient. You can travel up, down, past and future.

Basic Use of Thinking Sticks

Choose two sticks.

Throw them down.

Discuss.

. . . .

Flaws in the Coupling

Some people have picked up a single stick, looked at both sides, and said, "This is too bad—since they're on the same stick we can't think of them at the same time." By that point it's too late, though, they already HAVE thought of them at the same time and thought of a connection. So if you wish your set hadn't had "hats" on the back side of "history," go with that thought! Maybe play a whole game with the two sides of single sticks. That's no flaw; that's opportunity.

. . . .

How to Win

If you throw two and can't think of anything, throw two more, or turn those two over. There's no scorekeeping, and the biggest win you can have is that the game doesn't end, but that the questions stay in your mind to continue to gather "answers" (connections) forever. Thinking is winning.

How to Lose

Don't make this a pressure situation, especially for a young person. If anyone's not having fun, that's the end of the game. (You can play solitaire, though!)

SandraDodd.com/thinkingsticks

Chats

What one might read in a book about chats might be outdated, but as I'm writing I do have some thoughts.

Naturally, in-person chats are wonderful if you can find them. Some people live where there are other unschoolers, and get together a few times a month and can exchange thoughts in person.

Another way is to join an online chat, or to have regular buddies on an instant message program of some sort.

There is a chat room on my site with scheduled chats at least twice a week (although if you're reading this much past 2010 it might not be there anymore). Those chats involve reading quickly and typing, so some can't do it, but it's a format others just love. In the best moments, it's a brainstorming session in a format you can save. Sometimes they're edited and made available with links.

Although other formats can provide some of the same benefits as chats, they can't do it as immediately. The bad thing about a chat is that sometimes people, well... chat! It might not be as thoughtful as some discussions, but some of the most wonderful and intense moments I can remember were in chats in the days of the AOL homeschooling forum.

Chats are good for brainstorming. They look like this:

Shannon: sandra...LOVE Holly's cover...fingers are itching for the book!
RVB: How old are they again?
JillP: Me too! I love that cover.
kcbhsu: and he's also very much wanting to win, which she doesn't appreciate. my son is five and my daughter is three
Shannon: KCBHSU - we had that trouble, too....with chess,
SandraDodd: Thanks, about the cover. Kirby was a play to win guy.
RVB: Michelle, too.
SandraDodd: He would get mad if he didn't win, and get mad if I let him win. And get mad if I didn't let him win.

SandraDodd.com/chats

Sound Files

While not nearly as fun as a conference, conference presentations in a sound file are way less expensive, even if you end up paying full price for them from a conference website.

Thanks to friends and technology, though, there are many things to hear free on my website, many with accompanying notes:

Introduction to Unschooling, from 1997

Peaceful Parenting, with Richard Prystowsky, from 2002

Mindful Parenting, with Ren Allen, from 2005

Improving Unschooling (Strewing and Spirituality), 2005

Relaxed Unschooler Podcast, 2008

Video

With Transcripts:

Sandra Dodd Pt 1 : Path To Unschooling

Sandra Dodd Pt 2: Unschooling & Real Learning

Sandra Dodd Pt 3 : The Universe Inside Your Head

Unschooled Teenager Holly Dodd

Those will link to others, mostly without transcripts.

SandraDodd.com/listen

Blogs

My biggest collection of unschoolers' blogs is in the lefthand column at

ThinkingSticks.blogspot.com

and if you go to any of those there will be links to that writer's favorite other writers.

"Blog" is short for "web log" (for the way it sounds when it's spoken). At first they were just words on sites like Live Journal, but they've evolved into pages with photos and videos and music and links.

Many unschoolers keep accounts of fun things their families have done, partly in case they need evidence that their children are being intellectually inspired and having opportunities to learn and experience the world. Sometimes it's evidence for the educational jurisdiction. Sometimes it's for relatives, or just for the mom's own edification and inspiration.

Friends who move can keep up with friends through reading and commenting on blog posts. Unschoolers who have no local friends with children the same age as their own might have online friends with similar children, and they'll be able to keep up with each other's learning experiences.

If the stories in this book have not been enough to help you get a picture of unschooling, and if you've gone to the links at the bottoms of the past many pages but you want more input, go to blogs! You could start with mine:

SandraDodd.blogspot.com

Conferences

Every year there are a dozen unschooling get-togethers, and the number is increasing. Some are expensive and some are not. Some involve camping or are one-day conferences. Some are in hotels. Usually the greatest expenses are travel and lodging. If there were college courses on unschooling, many parents would (ironically) take them. What we have instead are conferences.

At a homeschooling conference, one can see curriculum sales tables, and other businesses thriving on sales to homeschoolers.

At an unschooling conference, one can see families who have not spent money on a curriculum at all, but who are living in the real world, doing things they might not have had the opportunity to do if their children were in school. There are speakers and discussions.

When deciding whether it's worth the money to go to an unschooling conference, factor in the money you saved by not buying a curriculum for each child. Count it as research for the parents, a learning experience for the children and a vacation for the family.

If your children are younger, you might gain a great deal of confidence from seeing the interactions of families with older children and teens, and perhaps from speaking with some of those older unschoolers yourself, or watching them in social interactions.

Knowing you're not the only ones can take you a long way toward peace and confidence. Seeing evidence of the peace and happiness that can come of living in this way might be worth the cost of attending a conference at least once, fairly early in your unschooling years.

Meeting other unschoolers, hearing their voices and seeing their eyes will give you a connection that books and websites cannot provide.

SandraDodd.com/speaking

Justifications for Being Online to Learn About Unschooling

- Message boards stay there. Lists flow by like a little brook or a raging, flooding, logjammed river.

- If you keep posting, your typing speed will become faster. That's good. (Unless you're already around 95 wpm, then... at least you're not spending unnecessary hunt'n'peck energy.)

- If time spent there keeps you from poking and prodding and pushing your kids, that's good.

- If time spent there gives you confidence to unschool, that will save you TONS of money and energy and worry and heartache and interpersonal repair. That's good.

- If you took a course on unschooling and had to go to class a time or two a week, with commuting time, and reading and paper-writing time, and if it cost what a college class costs in tuition, but you could just do THIS instead, that would be good. (And hey! It's true!)

- If this satisfies your urge for adult company sometimes, it keeps you from having to leave the kids or from having to pay for expensive coffee and snacks at some hoity-toity bakery/magazine stand.

- It keeps you from biting your nails, picking at your scabs, twirling your hair... (if you have no such vices, you can't count that one).

SandraDodd.com/lists/justification

Always Learning

Over fifteen years I have had "jobs," some lightly compensated and most voluntary, moderating discussion lists, chats, and publishing e-mail newsletters about one aspect or another of homeschooling. Since November 2001, though, I have had a discussion list of my very own called Always Learning. It's on yahoogroups and has over 2000 members, but I say "over 1000" because some of those 2000 are undoubtedly people who've changed e-mail and forgotten they joined, or were once interested in unschooling but they've wandered off.

The way an online discussion list works is that people can read all the messages that come to any list of which they're a member. It's free to sign up, and easy to leave the list if you're tired of it or too busy to keep up. You can opt to always go to the website online, or to have all the messages come to you by e-mail. You can respond to the entire group by answering one of those e-mails, or you can respond to the group from the webpage.

With hundreds of posts per month, sometimes over a thousand, Always Learning is the go-to place for serious discussion of radical unschooling. From the main page:

> This is a list for the examination of the philosophy of unschooling and attentive parenting and a place for sharing examined lives based on the principles underlying unschooling.

Some feedback on that discussion list:

> I can honestly say that I've grown more as a person, parent and unschooler due to the discussions on this list than on any other list I've been on.

* * * * * * * *

> I was just reading the list over at Always Learning, and there was a discussion about TV-watching that I just loved reading, not just because it espouses the value of TV, but because the voices of the unschooling moms are so full of respect, love, and connection with their families. I often visit this list to read the voices of Sandra Dodd, Pam Sorooshian, Joyce Fetteroll, and others, because they inspire me and remind me about why we have chosen to unschool our kids. And they help me get better at it.

* * * * * * * *

I have gleaned a plethora of wonderful ideas and insights from this group. So first I want to say thank you. Thank you for helping me change my perspective. Thank you for enlightening me. Thank you for helping me want to be a better mother.

* * * * * * * *

I just wanted to say that this list group has to be by far the most loving and encouraging one out there!!!

* * * * * * * *

Thanks so much for the encouragement and friendship and for the love of unschooling. You guys rock.

* * * * * * * *

I am new to this journey and I am happy to say THANKS for helping me on my way to learning what feel right for my kids!!

If this book has sparked your thinking and you would like to discuss these ideas with others, you can read more about the Always Learning list and find a link to it here:

SandraDodd.com/alwayslearning

There are over 45,000 posts in the archives.
Most of them are on topic and well considered.

Websites

The two largest and best-maintained unschooling websites are mine and Joyce Fetteroll's. We link to others from there, too. Those "web" and "net" names exist for good reason. You can get to more about unschooling than you could ever read just by clicking along.

JoyfullyRejoycing.com

Joyce's site is "Joyfully Rejoycing," and is extremely well organized. From her intro page:

This site is about unschooling. And it's about parenting more peacefully. But overall it's about living more joyful family lives. If I had to summarize it the message would be "Put the relationship first and then figure out how to fit everything else around that."

As you're reading the parenting answers, probably the most useful piece of advice is:

Don't drop all your parenting rules at once. Just say "Yes!" more.

SandraDodd.com/unschooling

Compared to Joyce's, my site is more like a "Choose Your Own Adventure in the Prairie Dog Village." In a way, that means mine is a better model of unschooling. I think you should use them both as much as you need to. They're both still growing.

Mine is a little like this book, only with photos, art, colored fonts sometimes, music upon occasions, videos of unschoolers being and doing, and hundreds of firsthand reports of unschooling as it unfolded, and accounts of the feelings parents had as they realized how wonderful their lives were becoming by making just a few small changes to attitude and behaviors.

My site also has dozens of lists of things to do, consider, eat, watch, find and hear.

The text and photos below were my answers to a set of questions several unschoolers have answered about their families. I wrote in May, 2009. The project lives at doliferight.com, and can be accessed by going down the lefthand column to the word cloud and clicking "20 Questions." (I didn't answer all twenty.)

About the Dodd Family's Unschooling

DoLifeRight: Tell me a bit about yourself and your family (name, children's ages, where you live, etc.).

Sandra: I'm Sandra Dodd and I live with my husband, Keith, who's an engineer at Honeywell, and with two of our three children. Kirby (22) lives in Austin and works for a video game company. Marty (20) works at a Persian restaurant and is buying a jeep of his own. Holly (17) has two jobs. She works at Zumiez, at Coronado Mall (a skateboard/snowboard shop with clothing and shoes) and also for a florist who has two shops.

Marty, Holly, Sandra and Keith Dodd
(Kirby's on the next page)

DoLifeRight: How long have you homeschooled your children? Do you consider your family an unschooling family? What does this mean for your family?

Sandra: My children have been unschooled always. Kirby was five when we first tried it out, knowing he could go back to school if he wanted to. He didn't. As the others came along we asked if they'd rather go to school or stay home, and each year we used to ask, at first. They all chose to be at home.

We knew two other unschooling families through La Leche League, so it was an easy choice.

I started writing online when Holly was a baby, and I first spoke at a local conference when Kirby was nine years old. What it has meant to our family over the years is that my children's learning has been fairly public. We've discussed it at various times over the years, and they knew that their stories being out there could make other children's lives easier. They understood that from La Leche League and from the park day, too. Being the organizing family has more responsibilities even for the kids than other families have. They've grown up that way.

DoLifeRight: Did you plan to homeschool your children before you actually had children? What is your own educational background?

Sandra: I was good in school and enjoyed it. I went from first grade to 11th and graduated early, and finished college in four years, so when I was 20 I graduated from the University of New Mexico, turned 21 in the summer, and was teaching in the fall. I had been trained by school reformers, and part of our required reading was John Holt (this was before he advocated home schooling, and was still working on school reform). My degree was in English with a minor in psychology, another minor (finished the year after I graduated) in anthropology, and a teaching certificate. I made very good use of college!

I took various and assorted graduate courses over the years, but didn't finish a master's degree, partly because of hobbies, a seriously broken leg, and the birth of Kirby in 1986.

I was pregnant for the third time before Kirby would have started school. We figured they would be in school, but attachment parenting changed things for the better!

DoLifeRight: Why did you decide to not send your children to school? What research did you do to make this decision? Were there any books, magazines, or websites you would recommend for new parents (or parents who are new to homeschooling) to read?

Sandra: Kirby took an art class when he was four, and he was TOO enthusiastic and quick and didn't have the patience to wait for others to catch up, or to do things slowly as the teacher wanted. The teacher loved him, though, and did some one-on-one projects with him other times. Then he took a dance class he had been looking forward to, and (long story) it didn't go well, but in a whole different way. He was sad in ways I couldn't fix, and he wasn't doing the groups any good either.

Because his birthday is in the late summer, we had the option to wait a year for kindergarten. We signed him up for homeschooling, figuring it was a totally risk-free year. The next year he could either go into kindergarten, or first grade, or stay home again. It was quite a luxury, to have two other unschooling families in our babysitting co-op and have a one-year free trial time.

In those days, the only thing available was Growing Without Schooling Magazine. I subscribed, bought some back issues, and read every word, some of it twice. Each time an issue came, I read it cover to cover, every word.

When *Prodigy (an early e-mail program) came along, I participated in a bulletin board group—a rudimentary sort of message board. There were about 80 families represented, mostly fundamentalist Christian homeschoolers.

When AOL was new, they had message forums and chat rooms. That was a huge improvement. People were able to put collections of ideas and experiences in public. Later came web pages, and blogs.

Several of the homeschooling magazines are defunct now; online information is less expensive and quicker to come by, and takes less storage. I think any web search for "unschooling" will yield more information in one day than someone could have found in a year, in the early 1990s.

DoLifeRight: Did you consider yourself an "Attachment Parent" when your children were infants? How did this (or didn't this) affect your choice to unschool/homeschool your children?

Sandra: We were active in La Leche League, and Keith and I both fell in love with being parents, and with the ideas we were learning there. We were active in a group that had many late-night parties and meetings, and campouts, so our kids were used to sleeping in different places, and falling asleep in our laps, or in a frame backpack either indoors or in the mountains under the stars. That helped us know without a doubt that children will sleep when they're tired, and that it's more important for them to be with their parents doing interesting things than to be home in bed simply because it's 8:00 or 9:00.

"Child-led weaning" and all the food awareness that went with that did a world of good for us, too. We never had fights over food with our children. They wanted to try what grownups were eating, and they were never pressed to eat anything they didn't like the look or smell or taste of. They were free to spit it in my hand if they wanted to.

I'm sure the common La Leche League phrase "child-led weaning" resulted in the phrase "child-led learning" which many apply to unschooling, but after nearly 20 years of unschooling, I think "child-led learning" is a detrimental concept that keeps parents from creating and maintaining busy, rich lives with lots of choices.

DoLifeRight: What specific benefits to your children (or family as a whole) have you actually seen since you became unschoolers?

Sandra: They are courteous, courageous and whole. They smile and laugh. They're not mean. They have rarely ever cried. People trust them, confide in them, and offer them jobs.

DoLifeRight: Do you have a regular schedule in your life? How does this work with outside commitments and responsibilities?

Sandra: When Kirby was young he had karate twice a week and we worked with and around that. We had a park day once a week, and it had been a babysitting co-op playgroup when the kids were toddlers, and it evolved into an unschooling group we kept up ourselves after other families' children went to school or moved out of town. Both the other unschooling families moved, but we picked up some new ones and kept that group going until Kirby was twelve years old.

Our schedules have always involved commitments to other people first (sports, park day, karate, ice skating, dance, theatre) and then things we wanted to do together (movies, meals out, visiting friends, exploring, taking the dog to run in wilder places). When Kirby turned fourteen he was offered a job, and that became a major work-around because he didn't drive for another three years, but it was an advantage to everyone because he worked in a gaming shop, and Marty got a good discount and lots of volunteer opportunities (setting up for tournaments and such in exchange for store credit). Many of their current friends came from the gaming shop days.

DoLifeRight: How important have support groups been for you? Do you have online ones, in person ones, or a mixture? Please list any you want to share.

Sandra: We had both. Conferences were fun, and we've visited families we met at conferences, and they've visited us. Sometimes the whole family goes, and sometimes just one or two of us. We've hosted single kids and just a parent, all in various combinations. We've driven several states in several directions to visit other unschoolers I only knew online.

I've been writing online and collecting other people's best writings for over a dozen years. I was doing it today. I'll do it tomorrow!

DoLifeRight: What resources do you use for your children's "educations"? Feel free to comment on the word "education".

Sandra: We don't "educate" our children. We help arrange so that they have so many learning opportunities they can't possibly take advantage of them all. We have friends with interesting jobs and hobbies. We invite them over, and we visit them. We have a house full of books, music, games, toys, movies, art materials, plants, food and dress-up clothes. We don't expect learning to happen in the house, nor in museums, but we know it happens everywhere. We don't expect learning to happen during daylight hours or on weekdays. We know it happens all the time. So we don't "use resources" except that we see every thing we discuss or see, smell, touch, hear or taste to be a resource. It's not a word we use, because it's all of life.

DoLifeRight: How did your friends and families react when you told them your children wouldn't be going to school? Have their opinions changed over the years?

Sandra: Some people overstate their cases and say "Our children will never go to school." We didn't. First of all, it's not something any parent can insure. But we didn't burn our bridges or commit to an unseen future. What we said was "Kirby's staying home this year." And then "Kirby's going to stay at home again." When people asked the inevitable questions, we said things like "It's working for now," or "If it stops working we'll try something else," or "If he stops having fun, he can go to school." Then we were careful to make sure he had lots of fun!

Because I was a teacher, and because of my hobbies, many of my friends were teachers (still). I had a special answer for teachers who asked "What if they get behind?" I'd say "Well we could put them in special ed, and they would get them all caught up in no time!" They would blanche and I would see everything they knew about special ed passing before their eyes. That shushed every single teacher who ever asked, and there were several. They knew I knew, and I knew they knew that special ed isn't really designed to get kids caught up and back into the mainstream.

DoLifeRight: What have been the benefits (unexpected and expected) to homeschooling?

Sandra: Speaking of unschooling, and not of homeschooling in general, I gave a talk on this topic in 2005, and the notes are here: http://sandradodd.com/unexpected

DoLifeRight: How does your family make money? Do you have a job? Full-time or part-time or something in between? Can you tell us about your choices and how you made these decisions?

Sandra: When Keith and I were first together, I was teaching and he was working minimum wage jobs while deciding whether he would go back to college. He had just finished a degree in computer science with a minor in theatre and we had been married a year when we discovered to our surprise that we were going to have a baby. That was good timing. He got a job as an engineer with Sperry Aerospace, which was bought by Honeywell, and he's worked there ever since. I know it's a sacrifice for him to work while I got to play with the kids and hang out with other families and write, but he's noble and a great husband and father and takes good care of us. And for my part, I've taken great care of the kids and the peace of the family. I'm not a great housekeeper, nor always an enthusiastic cook, but we figured out ways to be happy and things have worked out well.

We never have pressed our children to get jobs, but they've all had jobs. Kirby from the age of 14, and the job he got at 21 paid him to move to another state, and he was making more than Keith made when he was first an engineer. It might not lead to as much as Keith makes 22 years later, but we have no idea what Kirby will be doing in 22 years, so we're leaving a good situation alone!

Marty was offered a job making historical reenactors' leather boots and pouches, when he was 15. He worked full time in a grocery store when he was 17 (and a few months before and after). He saved money and traveled.

DoLifeRight: How have *you* personally grown since you started unschooling/homeschooling your children? How has your relationship with your spouse/partner grown?

Sandra: Keith and I have enjoyed our children and the success of our experiments and experiences has been a joint project at which we were very successful. The effect of sharing something difficult, like parenting in a way that's not universally acclaimed and supported, can be strengthening to a relationship. We had always worked at being courteous to each other. We always said please and thank you about any "pass the salt" or "could I have a Kleenex." It was easy, then, to model that for our children and for them to see the valuable effect of it.

I was interested in teaching and people and writing my whole life, and the intensive experience of learning so much about unschooling and parenting, and learning to use new resources to help other people have opportunities to learn wasn't "on the schedule." It evolved hour by hour over the years and has brought us all many great friends and memories.

DoLifeRight: Are you able to find time to have your own hobbies, interests, and friends? Beyond your children (of course), what are your interests?

Sandra: My children's interests affected mine, and ours affected theirs, and so there's not a great dividing line between my hobbies and interests and friends and theirs. They have friends of all ages, as do I. I have hobbies I've had all my life, some of which one or more of my kids have picked up and some of which are still just mine. As the children get older the parents have more time and space and energy for hobbies.

DoLifeRight: How do you respond to other people's questions about the following: completeness of education, socialization, college plans, etc.? Do you give different answers to different people? Why?

Sandra: If I didn't give different answers to different people, it would be recitation and not conversation. Depending what the person already knows and what and why he seems to be asking, I'll give him an answer I think will be satisfying and possibly lead to another question. I do the same when I talk with my husband or my children or my everyday friends.

DoLifeRight: Any regrets? We want to hear the good and the bad! This is the best way to make informed decisions.

Sandra: I wish I had spent more time just sitting and watching what they were doing. I wish I had taken photographs of Kirby's "Ninja Turtle Sculptures" (scenarios). I wish I were the kind of person who could drive for six or eight or ten hours straight, but I get sleepy. I wish I had found another driver (single adult, or teen) to go on trips with us. I wish we had gone more places when the kids were little, but compared to my own childhood they had been LOTS of places. It's still a regret, though, because we had a car and the time. When the kids were old enough to drive, they'd get jobs. At the moment Holly's 17 and can drive and she and I could go ANYwhere! But she has two jobs. And she's about to house-sit/dog sit for two different families, and got a website maintenance job just this afternoon. So for a while here she will have five jobs! She can't drive me around the country.

I regret not having had the focus and patience to watch the Pokemon cartoons and learn more about Pokemon. I had learned all about Ninja Turtles and Power Rangers, and I didn't have it in me to do Pokemon. I wish I could have a do-over. I wish I were a girlie-enough mom to have played Barbies with Holly.

DoLifeRight: Any last thoughts or advice for DoLifeRight's readers?

Sandra: Cynicism and pessimism are poison and will destroy families and learning. Happiness and joy will create more happiness and joy, and families and learning and the individuals within the families will be better off!

A lifetime worth of thoughts and advice are collected and linked here (Holly's lifetime, and Marty's, and Kirby's, and mine too, come to think of it): SandraDodd.com/unschooling

Not quite an interview, but a fun set of questions, also in May 2009. Other unschoolers mentioned or quoted in this book have participated in that project too.

The blog owner and organizer is Debbie H., the project is called *Homeschooling Family Interviews*, and her blog is homeschoolingisfreedom.blogspot.org

Always Learning: Sandra Dodd's Interview

Anyone who does an online search to learn more about the educational philosophy called unschooling will probably run into the name of Sandra Dodd at some point. Sandra has been out on the front lines for a long time now helping people understand that learning happens quite naturally, if we only relax and let it happen.

Sandra has a website about her life in general, another link inside this website about unschooling in particular, and a blog. She also runs an email list and is generally all over the internet sharing her thoughts about unschooling.

Let's see how she answers my 4 questions about homeschooling freedom and fun...

The Dodd children in 1998 (playing Zoombinis).

1. How long have you been homeschooling (or if finished, how long did you homeschool)?

Over 18 years, and attachment parenting for four years before that.

2. One of the main benefits of homeschooling is the freedom and flexibility it allows. Can you give us a few examples of how this freedom and flexibility benefitted you (your family)?

When we were sharing one computer, we would work shifts on it. Kirby would stay up late, I would get up early, the younger kids could use it during the daytime. We didn't time "turns," but would let whoever was using it use it until he was done, but Kirby knew he could have it to himself when Holly and Marty fell asleep, and I knew if I got up at 6:00 in the morning I could have e-mail and message board for an hour or two before anyone got up. Eventually Kirby got his own computer. After a while Marty got one, and then Holly. Our habit of showing people the good stuff remains, though, and of sharing photo files.

We could have company, or visit other people, on weekdays as well as weekends, and that opened up the schedule tremendously. Because there weren't three or four hour times when we couldn't get to food, the kids didn't need to be hungry, or wait and wait for a school cafeteria lunch or an after school snack. By the time they were old enough to have their own jobs, they were easily able to remember to eat before they went in, and wait for a break for more food. They didn't need to "train" for it.

Because I was able to be home with them, they didn't have to wait hours to consider whether to talk to me about something or to just share with school friends, as I usually did when I was a kid. Other kids don't always make the sagest of advisors.

We could watch movies together at leisure, and pause and come back to them, or watch the good parts over and over. Some families are trying to squeeze a movie in between "dinnertime" and "bedtime" and wouldn't even think of watching one in the morning or during lunch!

3. Another benefit of homeschooling is the fun factor. Can you give us a few examples of some especially fun times you had as a result of homeschooling?

Meeting other unschoolers has always been fun. Our children knew other unschoolers in town, but to meet a whole family with children who also were happy and not school-bound was always a joy.

I think everyday things were made more fun by unschooling, because when we went to a play or to dinner or a picnic or to visit grandparents, the preparation and the drive and the discussion after were sweet and peaceful and supportive. We weren't argumentative and blaming as so many families around us were. It was very rare for someone to get too cranky to talk to others in the car, even on cross-country trips. We sang along with the radio and CDs a lot, too. Surely the most rulebound of families might have had similar fun, but ours wasn't occasional, it was the predominant mood.

When someone was very sick or had minor surgery, it helped that school wasn't a factor (nor "schoolwork"), but that the new injury or disease or recovery became an opportunity for learning, compassion and aid.

The Dodd family in 2008.

4. We all have funny experiences while homeschooling. Can you share one of yours with us?

Once Marty was eight or nine, he woke up hungry and whiney. I said I had a hard time understanding him when he was whining, and could he say it another way. He stood at attention and in a movie-marine voice said "MOTHER, I require Food NOW!" I couldn't stop laughing.

Kirby was 14 and had an 8th grade girlfriend who invited him to her middle school graduation. Marty and I were delivering him there, and we were parked right outside the front of the school. No one else was around at all. Kirby was reaching into the back seat of the car, where Marty was, for his jacket. The school bell rang—one of those big domed wall bells. I wasn't surprised at all, but both Marty and Kirby jumped in fear and Kirby jumped back and said "What was THAT!?" Kirby was 14 and Marty was 12 and they had never heard a school bell before.

In a comment I left there later about that bell incident:

> They were both sharply startled, and Kirby kind of leaped back out of the car in case the noise was coming from inside the car or something. It was the total "I don't know which way to run" physical reaction. When I was a kid, and when I was a teacher, I heard bells like that over a dozen times a day. In my life at that point I must have heard a school bell (180x14x17...) Yikes! over 40,000 times. I'll trade in days I was absent for years there were three lunch periods. And when I was in elementary school we shared the campus with 7th-9th grades and they had lots of bells we could hear.

About the Author

Autobiographically speaking, I was born Sandra Lynn Adams in 1953 in Augusta, Georgia, as my dad, Kirby Lynn Adams, was working in Aiken, South Carolina at the time. The family moved back to Texas where all the grandparents were, and before long to Española, in Northern New Mexico.

Keith Dodd and I met in 1977, married in 1984, and have had three children, all of whom were unschooled:

Kendall Kirby Dodd	July 29, 1986
Martin Alexander Dodd	January 14, 1989
Holly Lynn Dodd	November 2, 1991

Keith has a degree in computer science with a minor in theatre. That's what comes of taking twelve years to get a degree, and changing programs every year or two. He's an engineer and a musician and a part-time Viking re-enactor.

I have an English degree with minors in Psychology and Anthropology and took the requisite classes to be certified to teach secondary education. I was employed as an instructor of English for six years at Española Jr. High. When I tried to escape, I was offered a sabbatical (at the age of 27), and turned it down. They gave me a leave of absence. I relented. I'm still absent. I like to think of it as having retired from teaching early.

I have since had several other jobs involving helping people learn something or other, and herding words onto paper for various purposes.

I've been helping other people unschool and understand unschooling since Kirby was little.

I've spoken at nearly 40 homeschooling or unschooling conferences as I'm touching this keyboard, but it will have been over 40 by sometime in 2010. Dozens. Scores. Many.

Every day I write about unschooling, somewhere, answering questions online. Thank you for reading!

SandraDodd.com/bio

Made in the USA
San Bernardino, CA
29 August 2014